The Vitality of India

The Vitality of India

A Regional Perspective

Gopal Krishan

RAWAT PUBLICATIONS

Jaipur • New Delhi • Bangalore • Guwahati • Kolkata

ISBN 978-81-316-0877-7

Published by
Prem Rawat for **Rawat Publications**
Satyam Apts, Sector 3, Jawahar Nagar, Jaipur 302 004 (India)
Phone: 0141 265 1748 / 7006 Fax: 0141 265 1748
E-mail: info@rawatbooks.com
Website: www.rawatbooks.com

New Delhi Office
4858/24, Ansari Road, Daryaganj, New Delhi 110 002
Phone: 011 2326 3290

Also at *Bangalore, Guwahati* and *Kolkata*

Typeset by Rawat Computers, Jaipur
Printed and bound in India

Contents

List of Maps

List of Tables

Preface

India is said to be a mystery to both pessimists and optimists. Some find much to criticize it. Issues of poverty, disease and ignorance, and many more are on their list. V.S. Naipaul did not hesitate to title his travelogue about his journey through India as *An Area of Darkness*. Meanwhile, some find it as a land of wonders and without limits, as Mark Twain affirmed in his book *Following the Equator*. Still others extol India for the energy, ingenuity and adaptability of its people but are inclined to describe the country as functioning anarchy, as John Galbraith observed in his 1958 article published in *Foreign Affairs*. By nature and habit, I tend to be on the side of optimists, and find something amazing about India. The country has survived centuries of onslaught in political, economic, social and environmental realms but has come out kicking and alive. Which are the sources of her ability to sustain? What is it that keeps her going? Where does her vitality lie?

Such ideas brewed in my mind for long. These got a stimulus when an opportunity emerged for me to edit a book, *The Vitality of India*. This was an outcome of a weeklong deliberations from 23 to 28 June 2004 at an International Conference organized by the Centre of Research in Rural and Industrial Development at three venues, including the Indian Institute of Advanced Studies, Shimla; India International Centre, New Delhi; and its own campus at Chandigarh. Over 50 eminent delegates participated. There were extensive discourses on the philosophic parameters, historical roots, socio-cultural dimensions and security aspects of India's vitality. The experience of the conference led me to a realization that the vitality of India cannot be comprehended without taking into account the vitality of its different regions. A whole derives preeminence from the quality of its parts. This discernment called for a manifestation in practice.

The possibility emerged when the idea was supported by the Indian Council of Social Science Research, New Delhi, by way of awarding me the

National Fellowship for the years 2013–16. An inner urge to conflate vitality with geography as a regionally varying and characterizing element proved to be a final command. The intention was to look at the vitality of India as a tapestry woven by the functional synergy of its various regions.

Conventionally a region is defined as an area which is physiognomic or homogeneous in form, such as Rajasthan desert; or physiological or functionally integrated, such as the National Capital Region. I opted to define a region as a spatial unit which has acquired a distinct personality over time, wherein the inhabitants have a sense of belonging to it, and for which an administrative and political endorsement exists as well. Tamil Nadu or Gujarat or Sikkim can serve as an illustration. Accordingly I felt justified in treating regions of India coincident with various states and union territories. This is how the country functions at the sub-national level in the spirit of cooperative as well as competitive federalism.

Harnessing the states and union territories as the building block of analysis, an effort was made to research representative aspects of vitality as embedded in their evolved configuration. The specificity of their location, internal spatial organization and external linkages was deemed as constituting the basic analytical framework. Added to this was an awareness that historical antecedents provide the background, the prevailing conditions define the ground realities and technological advancements indicate the scenario of emerging foreground. All this has also to be a part of reckoning.

Polity has been moving in favour of states. The issue of ethnic identity was resolved to a great extent years ago through reorganization of states on linguistic or ethnic or historical basis. Meanwhile, the items like land, agriculture, health, local bodies and law and order, among 61 entries, were listed as subjects under the purview of the state governments in the Schedule VII of the Constitution of India. This bestowed upon them considerable autonomy in management of public affairs. The issues of harnessing new economic opportunities as also of conserving natural resources have now come into prominence. The way these are taken care of by different states will influence their vitality, and thereby of the country as a whole.

Today, the Indian states are vibrant with a fresh regional consciousness. Regional identity and regional vitality are becoming synonym for each other. Competition among various states is on high swing. Meanwhile, their dependence on each other, especially as sources of inputs and venues of market, and upon the national government, particularly for financial and technical support, is on the rise. Interstate cooperation demands that states be ideological friends and economic partners. This will serve the cause of their own vitality as also of the country as a whole.

The book is selective of the themes which I considered as most pertinent to vitality of India today. It is structured into eight essays. The first essay takes a snapshot of the vitality of India. Where is located the foundation of India's vitality? How has it got structured over time? What is its present manifestation? Answers to such questions required a wide sweep of literature in history, social sciences and humanities at large.

A discussion on the concept of regional vitality was deemed as not only obligatory but also essential, and this defines the scope of the second essay. What has been the scenario of the politico-regional configuration of India through history? How did the contours of the present system of states and union territories take shape in the country? In which manner have the Indian states acquired vitality in their political and economic landscape? These questions gain strength when contextualized globally in terms of the rise and fall of empires and formation of nations in the world history. This necessitated a purposeful perusal of the treatises on the life history of world civilizations and empires. The process of identity affirmation and state formation in India also needs to be traced. Of special interest in this case were the regional histories and tourism brochures of different states which project their past and attractions at present in each case.

The quality of governance is deemed as a key factor in determining the vitality of any political territory, the Indian states in the present case. With this realization, the third essay was devoted to a theoretical and empirical analysis of this theme. Which criteria and indicators are most representative of the quality of governance? How do various states of India measure on this parameter? Which factors are supportive of good governance? While dealing with such questions, the available conceptual and analytical studies on this subject were rendered a perusal.

Economic dynamism is considered as a concomitant process of good governance. The fourth essay provides a discourse on this theme by way of analyzing the regional variations in performance of Indian economy. How do various states of India differ in their income level, growth behaviour, and economic potential? What is the relative contribution of different states to India's economic vitality? Which are the states with outstanding performance and which are the laggard ones? Answers to such questions called for an intensive treatment of statewise data culled from a variety of sources, such as the Central Statistical Organization, National Sample Survey, Organisation, Centre for Monitoring Indian Economy and Census of India, among others.

The rise of middle class in association with recent rapid economic growth forms the subject matter of the fifth essay. What is the story of origin, evolution and spread of the middle class in modern India? How do different states compare in terms of the share of middle class in their demographics? Can pro-middle class policies prove a more effective route to eradication of persistent poverty in India? In view of the non-availability of requisite data on the middle class by states in India, an attempt was made to fill the gap by harnessing a number of surrogate indicators.

Following an understanding of the spatial patterning of India's population on class lines, the sixth essay turns to the reality of religious, linguistic and regional pluralism of India. To what extent has the country been successful in managing its cultural diversity? Whether cultural homogeneity or else cultural heterogeneity is more critical to a region's vitality? How does this scenario differ by states in India? A statistical analysis of relevant data from the Census of India and other sources was carried out to arrive at authentic responses.

The people of India celebrate diversity not only within the country but also at the global level, and that forms the narrative of the seventh essay. In which way does the Indian diaspora display the scatter of the country's diversity across the world? Which regions of India have demonstrated their vitality by virtue of being prominent source areas of diaspora? How have the economy, society and polity of these regions back home been impacted? A perusal of a variety of regional emigration literature, in addition to search for relevant data, became essential to gain insight into this dimension.

The eighth essay identifies the representation of India and its various regions in the *National Geographic* to discern how the vitality of India has been projected in this magazine acclaimed for the largest readership in the world. This involved an analytical reading of all the articles pertinent to India published in this magazine during 1947–2015. It turned out as an exercise in qualitative research.

True enough, the formulations of this book may not align with the skepticism of several intellectuals in India who are inclined to question 'Where is the vitality of India'? They may highlight its failings of all variety. This is a matter of opinion. The present book carries an urge to be an inhabitant of a different territory. It takes the vitality of India as an established fact by virtue of its sustained integrity, vibrant democracy, economic dynamism and rise of the middle class, in particular. The idea here is to have a view of India's vitality as an outcome of the collective vitality of its constituent states and union territories.

Any research venture of this kind cannot do without the support of healing hearts and holding hands. This is the reason why acknowledgement is rarely in singular; most often it is plural. To some you look for initiation and inspiration, to others for debate and ideas, and from few others one seeks quality logistics and an affectionate ambience.

To Professor Anu Kapur, at the Delhi School of Economics, University of Delhi, goes my abiding gratitude. Of immense value were her work and incisive suggestions on the draft manuscript. The style and substance of this book is not without her stamp.

As if by instinct, I shared the idea of this book with my friend, late Professor G.K. Chadha, former Vice-Chancellor of Jawaharlal Nehru University and then on President of the South Asian University. He strongly favoured this theme for research and observed that while enough work had been done on regional disparities, there was a need to look at other side of the picture in terms of vitality of different regions of India. This reassuring endorsement from Chadha Sahib carried a special meaning for me. Indeed to have such a person of academic excellence, administrative acumen and professional commitment as my lifelong friend was a rare blessing.

Right in the beginning of my assignment, I had an extended discussion with my teacher and mentor, late Professor G.S. Gosal on the topic of my interest. His response was very encouraging. His word inspired me with a lasting impact. To him are reserved my most venerable thanks.

During the course of my work, I had highly valuable interaction through correspondence or personal meetings with Professor David G. Dickason of the Western Michigan University, Kalamazoo, United States, Dr. Kulwant Singh, Advisor UN-HABITAT, Professor H. Ramachandran of the Institute for Study of Industrial Development, New Delhi, Dr C.K. Mathew of the Public Affairs Centre, Bengaluru, and Professor Sudeepta Adhikari of Patna University on issues relating to my research assignment. The ideas they shared on the geographic concept of regional vitality, economic transformation, quality of governance and evolving regional order in India respectively, served as valuable inputs for my work. I thank them individually and collectively.

Back home, equally rewarding were my occasional discussions with colleagues in the department at Panjab University. In particular my word of gratitude goes to Professors Surya Kant, Krishna Mohan, Ravinder Kaur, Smita Bhutani and Dr Simrit Kahlon. Most endearing was their questioning on my conceptual, methodological and inferential formulations. An additional special gratitude is reserved for Professor Surya Kant who was a regular help in access to latest literature. In plenty are my heartfelt thanks to him. Meanwhile Ms Reena Choudhary, Senior Research Fellow, was always a ready help in computer printing of my writings.

Professor Nina Singh of the M.D. University, Rohtak, was kind in taking up the responsibility of reading the entire manuscript with an eye for detail and mistakes. Combining calibre with care, she accomplished this assignment with exceptional dedication. It is rare to receive the support she rendered and I am hugely thankful to her. In no small measure, my gratitude goes also to Professor Mehar Singh Gill, former Chairman, Department of Geography, Punjabi University, Patiala, for going through the manuscript most meticulously and offering highly useful suggestions.

To Mr Mohan Singh, Senior Scientific Officer in the department, I express my gratitude for designing and bringing out the final maps on software suitable for printing. Highly admirable are his professional care and technical skill. The maps prepared by him formed the basis of analysis in the text. A mature cartographic advice from my former colleague, Mr Mehar Singh, was helpful in refining the disposition of several maps. This is gratefully acknowledged.

Dr Pawan Kumar Sharma of the Centre for Research in Rural and Industrial Development, Chandigarh, contributed the best in printing and formatting the entire manuscript. I am wordless in thanking him adequately. Not to miss, I am thankful to Dr Neela Thapar, now working in the United States of America, for her collaboration with me on two research papers in

1990s. Some parts of these papers have been used in an extensively updated form in my present work.

To the Indian Council of Social Science Research, New Delhi, most specifically its Chairman Professor Sukhadeo Thorat, I shall remain ever in abiding gratitude for the award of National Fellowship. May I profusely acknowledge the great help rendered by this institution to the cause of my research. In plenty are my thanks for all this.

At the family level, I received all too loving support from my spouse Kanti, son-in-law Amit, daughter Manishika, son Gaurav and daughter-in-law Kelli. They created most favourable ecology for my work. My grandchildren, Sahiba, Aryan, Maurya and Noor gave endearing love which kept things in constant flow. In ways more than many, they all instilled the necessary vitality in me to bring my assignment to a finish.

March, 2017 **Gopal Krishan**

1

The Vitality of India

Abstract nouns distinguish themselves by their power to synthesize a concept but these always signify more than what a human mind can comprehend. This is as much true of the idea of vitality of a nation-state. One way out is to construct a well-founded definition for the purpose.

Vitality essentially represents holistic strength and energy of a system. It may be embedded, manifest or potential. In the case of a nation-state it stands for nourishing of and enhancing its identity and eminence. The efficacy to harness vigour as also the capacity to rejuvenate itself and reinvent on a continuing basis are crucial to this vitality. An audacity to give a quality response to any challenge, including political crisis, economic breakdown or sudden disaster, and an ability to bounce back and revive also delineate the parameters of vitality. The capacity to influence and impact upon others also falls in its domain.

Going beyond the semantics of the concept, we may translate the idea of nation-state in geographic phraseology. A nation-state owes reason of its existence to authority and capability in keeping different parts of the country together, ensuring a balanced regional development, and promoting interconnectivity among various regions on a win-win basis. This is possible through a spatial structure of decentralized governance, management of ecology on interregional basis, and adoption of a policy of specialization at microlevel and self-sufficiency at macrolevel. The manifestation of vitality on external front is subject to an impregnable order of security to combat any territorial aggression, a strategy to emerge as a nodal agency for peace and development, and an urge to evolve as a model for other countries. At the final go, it is imperative for any nation-state to appraise itself of the way people perceive the vitality in different parts of the country. The vitality of a nation-state, after all, is a blend of its cultural resource, societal vibrancy and universal pride.

The criticality of understanding the vitality of different countries was realized at the international level by Luxembourg Institute for European and International Studies. They took an initiative in evaluating the vitality of some select nation-states and brought out conference-based books on the *Vitality of Britain (1997), Japan (1997), Netherlands (1999), China (2004)* and *Russia (2004)*. The Centre for Research in Rural and Industrial Development (CRRID), Chandigarh, was the first to project this theme in India by publishing a book on the *Vitality of India* (Krishan, 2004). Meanwhile, scores of books on India, such as *Reimagining India,* edited by McKinsey and Company (2013); *Implosion: India's Tryst with Reality* by Elliott (2014), *Rebooting: Realising a Billion Aspirants* by Nilkani and Shah (2015), and *An Economist in the Real World: The Art of Policy Making in India* by Basu (2016), to name a few, have started flowing in the academic channels since the adoption of the new economic policy. A hilarious view of India is offered by the book *A Strange Kind of Paradise* by Miller (2014). Such exercises expounded not only on the vivacity of India but also laid bare its vulnerabilities.

One cannot ignore the fact that the idea of vitality of a nation was expounded much earlier. Nehru (1946: pp. 55–56) in his book, *The Discovery of India,* offers his perspective of vitality of certain countries. In the case of the United States, he found this in its innovation propensity and youth, free from encumbrances of the past; in Russia in its reincarnation in the form of a new kind of a political regime; and in China in combining its current struggle with enduring past. He found the vitality scenario of India as comparable to that of China. He underlines that the country has an exclusive quality of a legend and a dream, and yet very real and present and pervasive. It is a case of suppressed energy and unharnessed potential.

Integrated India

A striking dimension of India's vitality is the fact that it has stayed integrated since its emergence as an independent entity in 1947 (Krishan, 2000). That India has endured as a unified country is one of the politico-geographical miracles of the twentieth century (Blij and Muller, 1994: p. 194). The country is a success story in resolving any secessionist tendency. A simple but pertinent question crops up here: How could India manage to stay integrated? Why did it not go the Soviet way? How did it escape the fate of Yugoslavia? How did it encounter any centrifugal political tendency?

A corollary to such questions is also raised: What led many to believe that India is fragile enough to ultimately suffer dismemberment? Strachey (1888) had observed long ago that the first thing to learn, according to the European ideas, is that there never was an India possessing any sort of unity – physical, political, social or religious. Churchill in a speech in 1931 had described India as a mere geographical term, comparable to equator, which is not supposed to make a union of all those countries through which it passes. India can be deemed as an unnatural entity and any search for its unity is misconceived (*Encyclopaedia Britannica,* 2009: p. xii). Several other western scholars expressed their assessment on similar lines. The manifest reality falsified all such pronouncements.

The highly fragmented political map of India posed the most serious problem of integration at the time of Independence in 1947. It was laid with the boundaries of nine full or part British provinces (East Punjab, United Provinces, Bihar, West Bengal, Assam, Central Provinces and Berar, Orissa, Madras and Bombay), along with five centrally administered areas (Delhi, Ajmer-Marwara, Panth Piploda, Coorg, and Andaman and Nicobar Islands), and 556 princely states. The prophets of doom, especially the British press, had predicted that the ship of India's freedom would founder on the rock of princely states (Menon, 1956: p. 91). Some of the princes had argued that if the Indian subcontinent could be partitioned into India and Pakistan, why it could not have a third segment of 'stateistan' comprising the princely states (Phadnis, 1968: p. 203).

Reacting to the turmoil caused by the issue of linguistic reorganization of Indian states in 1956, Toynbee (1958) raised a dismal question: Will India succeed in sustaining this experiment without bringing on itself the tragic fate of Balkan states? The tumultuous conflicts, with which this event was attended, in practically all parts of the country, were the basis of his deep concern. Harrison (1960), envisaging dangerous time ahead, also opined that the country would not survive as one political entity. When the Soviet Union disintegrated in 1991, many western scholars wondered if India could evade a similar collapse. Such an apprehension was fuelled by the militant uprisings in Jammu & Kashmir, Punjab, Assam and Nagaland.

Divisive Streaks

The sheer vastness of the area and complexity of demographics of India, marked by diversity of ethnicity, disparity in development level, variety of regional historical experiences and divergence in political aspirations, are seen as a threat to the unity of the country. Keeping things together is a daunting task. Interstate issues pertaining to sharing of river waters, devolution of financial resources from the centre and rival territorial claims have cropped up from time to time.

Meanwhile, the British colonial policy of 'divide and rule' had made the people more conscious of their differences than of similarities. The political map of provinces, centrally administered areas and princely states carried enormous boundary oddities to contend with. There were territorial peculiarities in both physical form and population composition. Some scattered remnants of the Portuguese and French colonies also existed on the Indian soil. All these were also to be appropriately absorbed as an integral part of the country.

The question of religious differentiation was the first to manifest its sensitivity. Partition of the Indian subcontinent in 1947 was primarily on religious lines: All Religion India and Muslim Pakistan. Despite its predominance of Hindu population, India opted to be a secular nation-state and Pakistan a theocratic one. Today 96 per cent of Pakistan's population is Muslim. Meanwhile, the Hindus in India make 80 per cent of the country's population, and are in majority in most areas. Among 29 states of the country, however, three (Nagaland, Mizoram and Meghalaya) are Christian majority, one (Jammu & Kashmir) Muslim majority, and one (Punjab) Sikh majority. By reason of their location on the periphery, most of them displayed a centrifugal tendency, at one time or the other.

It is through a large number of languages and dialects that India communicates with itself. A linguistic survey of the British India in early decades of the last century had counted 179 languages and 544 dialects as being spoken in different parts of the subcontinent (Grierson, 1902–29). The first post-Independence Census of India in 1951 recorded 720 mother tongues, claimed by at least 100,000 persons in each case. The 2001 Census of India makes a mention of 122 languages, including 22 listed in the Eighth Schedule of the Constitution of India. The scheduled and non-scheduled languages are an amalgam of 234 mother tongues, each spoken by at least 10,000 persons. Hindi, the first ranking, is the language of only 41.1 per cent of India's population. Impact of the linguistic variety, as a divisive force, became manifest at the time of reorganization of the states in 1956. Linguistic chauvinism prevailed and the spirit of Indianness was perceived as lost. Later in 1963, the strong reaction in the non-Hindi states to the passage of the Official Languages Act to install Hindi as the national language for the purposes of the Union laid bare the sensitivity of the language issue. The Act had to be amended in 1967 in favour of English as an official language in addition to Hindi. A stern message had been conveyed that any attempt at imposing one language over the entire populace, for the sake of promoting unity, would just be counter-productive.

Caste loyalties and their politicization are also viewed as a worrisome schism generating phenomenon. In several cases, people cast their vote on caste lines at the time of elections. A socio-political categorization of castes/tribes renders a threefold division in terms of general castes, scheduled castes/tribes, and backward classes. The report of the Mandal Commission, submitted in 1980, estimated their comparative share in total population at about 25 per cent, 23 per cent and 52 per cent respectively (Government of India, 1980). Implementation of recommendations of the Report in 1990 in respect of reservation for backward classes in public sector jobs and admission to professional and educational institutions was described by many as a step toward sharpening the caste-based division of the society. The proponents of reservation claimed that it was an effective way of ensuring social justice.

Associated with the question of religion, language and caste/tribe was the issue of aggressive regionalism. It took the form of 'sons of the soil' doctrine at places. This was an attempt to bar the outside-the-state migrants from government jobs and institutional benefits and to reserve these only for the domicile of the state. Regional demands reached secessionist limits at times. This has been true equally of the Hindu Manipur, or Christian Nagaland, or Muslim Kashmir, or Sikh Punjab. Nor was there an absence of demands for carving out smaller states out of unilingual ones; may it be Uttarakhand, Telangana or Vidarbha. Such regional sentiment transcended the contours on the development map of India. The relatively prosperous Punjab or backward Jharkhand both displayed a tendency of similar kind at a time. Regionalism does have virtues, even for nation building, but in virulent form it tends to be disintegrative.

The unfriendly among our neighbours saw any divisive situation as an opportunity to destabilize India. They were ever keen to lend support to or even cause insurgency. Our sensitive border regions were more vulnerable to this effect. India continues to suffer on this count.

Finally, the disintegration of the Soviet Union sent a dubious message to a few who would have been happy at redrawing of India's border in a manner that they are outside of it. Meanwhile, under the spell of globalization, some intellectuals had started viewing an adherence to the ideology of nation-state as political fundamentalism. The very rationale of having sustainable nation-states, such as India, came under question.

While the huge subcontinental dimensions of India, its apparent faultlines on religious, linguistic and regional basis, and devious designs of its hostile neighbours rendered vulnerability to the unity of India, yet the country was endowed with a variety of integrative forces which enabled it to withstand all these challenges and manifest its vitality.

Unifying Mechanisms

India has endured. It has stayed integrated. Part of this was the legacy of the past; part adoption of appropriate strategies. We may recapitulate these. For convenience of understanding, the ensuing discussion takes a view of the pre-Independence heritage and post-Independence policy ethos.

India, more so in a historic sense, had been a well-defined physical entity. Its overall configuration was such that it inculcated a natural feeling among people of being an inhabitant of a geographic container. Although diversity got built within because of external arrivals or internal separations, yet the people perceived themselves as 'having been put together by nature' to live like an extended family. Such a sentiment was endorsed by the outer world too. The diverse communities of this realm were seen as forming one entity, which they always defined as India. Throughout historical times, the travellers, who reached North India by land or South India by sea, had the satisfaction of having arrived in India (Rajivlochan and Rajivlochan, 1992: p. 96). It is fascinating to realize that the Indian Ocean is the only one to get its name after that of a country.

Again going by the physical backdrop, the entire realm is marked by a remarkable similarity in the rhythm of life and range of practices, significantly linked with the climatic regime of the monsoons. This is said with particular reference to rural India whose economy and society remained conditioned by the behaviour of these rain-bearing winds. There is a lot common in the great tradition of Indian culture and practices of agriculture in response to the play of this natural phenomenon.

In terms of human scenario, India is acclaimed for maturation of a civilization which honours diversity and values unity. Hinduism functioned as a liberal and all-embracing religion. Islam spread spatially and so did Christianity for centuries. A tradition of shared values evolved and persisted. A hierarchy of the religious places and the tradition of pilgrimages, cutting across regions, had a unifying effect.

The caste system was a unique solution to the problems of a plural society. As an interdependent societal order based on division of labour, it held together, if not welded, diverse kinds of people for millennia (Spate and Learmonth, 1967: p. 166). It rendered stability to a highly plural society. As a part of the caste system, the priestly class of Brahmins was ubiquitous and had an almost equitable distribution, accounting for around five per cent of total population in most regions (Bellman, 2007). They played an important role in the diffusion of life principles and rituals, which happen to be fairly common in different parts of the country. Notably, despite all linguistic variety, personal names of Indians display a remarkable similarity all over India. Many of these have their root in Sanskrit. The primarily non-Brahmanic *Bhakti* movements (religious and social reform drives during the medieval period) originating in different parts of India were eventually pan-India in character. These reinforced the idea of equality and unity among various religious and caste affiliations.

The massive size of India notwithstanding, most of its inner physical features, such as hills and rivers, are more like boundary fences rather than total barriers. These are high and wide enough to ensure distinctiveness of various regions and also low and crossable enough to allow regular mutual interaction. Resultantly, the diverse regions, while maintaining their identity, were conscious of their essential cultural unity (Dikshit, 1975: p. 121). Equally complementary were the different ecological zones in India which fostered symbiosis and exchange (Keay, 2010: p. xxii). These were interconnected through river regimes.

Regionalism has not been historically a strong force in India. Nothing like regional nationalities or nations had emerged on the subcontinent (Khilnani, 2004: p. 156). Empire building at the macro-level and the clan/tribal organization at the local level were the usual territorial arrangements. No region consistently grew inordinately powerful or established its vast colonies abroad, as did the United Kingdom, France, Spain, Portugal, and the Netherlands in Europe. Had the developments in India been on the same lines as in Europe, its several regions could have emerged as separate countries in their own right.

Some crucial role of the British rule in strengthening inter-linkage between different parts of India and rendering unity in several ways cannot be denied. A pan-India administration they organized, a professional army on apolitical lines they raised and a network of railways they laid brought people of diverse regional background into an active interface with each other. It is noteworthy that military stood as a deterrent to regional fragmentation, separatism and secession, and at the same time, India's diversity acted as a deterrent to any army designs on political power (Cohen, 1971: p. 196). The entire Indian subcontinent was sewed together by stitching of railway tracks. The physical fabric of the country was also re-engineered through strategic scatter of cantonments and setting up of hill stations. A policy of free migration across British provinces and princely states resulted in an inter-mixing of all variety of people. English as the lingua franca made various linguistic areas intelligible to each other. The effect was best seen in capital cities, plantation areas, mining towns, industrial centres, and newly reclaimed agricultural lands. Hence it will not be appropriate to equate 'all colonialism is bad' with 'colonialism is all bad' (Robb, 2007: p. 10).

The British had kept most of the provinces as multi-lingual, and the territorial jurisdiction of princely states, with whatever linguistic variety within, was not much disturbed. A significant heterogeneity prevailed in each case. The British province of Madras was a conglomerate of four major language areas of Tamil, Telugu, Malyalam and Kannada. The case of the princely state of Hyderabad was on similar lines. This postponed the maturation of aggressive language-based regionalism beyond the date line of independence. By that time the new nation-state had equipped itself with sufficient capability to meet and resolve many a conflict situation.

More than railways, army or English language, it was the national movement, against the British, which welded different parts of India together. There was a common goal to be achieved by the people who otherwise were so diverse. The impact is felt till date. The spirit of nationalism today, in various parts of India, is largely proportional to their historical involvement in the national movement. If the North-East India had been roped in more actively in this struggle, several hot spots of insurgency here could have been pre-empted from emergence.

Taking an account of developments since Independence, it is learnt that the national policy right since then has been geared towards unity and integrity of the country. To begin with, the Constitution of India duly acknowledged the federal nature of Indian polity but found a unitary bias as necessary in its formulation. It emphasizes the indestructible character of the union, and the nation-state has the necessary strength to deal with any secessionist movement. There were sensitive moments of centre-state conflicts, including demand for secession in a few cases. These were overcome even through the amendment of the Constitution. The 16th Constitutional Amendment, passed in 1963, made it mandatory for anyone seeking election to the Parliament or the state assembly to swear faith and allegiance to the

Constitution of India and to uphold the sovereignty and integrity of the country. This proved an effective measure. The Dravida Munnetra Kazhagam of Madras state, in particular, amended its constitution soon after and gave up the demand for secession (Chandra et al., 1999).

In addition to a political design of federalism, secularism as a social policy was adopted to deal with the question of ethnicity. An economic policy of planned development was simultaneously put in practice to stimulate growth, reduce regional disparities and involve people in the process of national construction. The education policy was geared towards reinforcing all these processes, thereby inculcating a spirit of nationalism.

Fortunately, India did not opt for a division of the country into five sub-national units: north, east, south, west and centre, at the time of recasting its administrative map. There were some well-meaning votaries of such an arrangement in early years of Independence. They believed that such a macro-scale five-fold division of the country would ensure an integrated utilization of resources for faster development and would also strengthen a sense of solidarity. In all likelihood, a formation of this kind would have been counter-productive. Some of the zones could have grown as highly viable, aspiring and demanding of the status of separate countries.

The spatial framework of 29 states and 7 union territories, as it evolved over time, ensured their dependence upon each other, especially when development became a cherished goal (Map 1.1). There was a realization on the part of the constituent parts of the country that they were better off as a component of the union rather than as independent entities. This situation got a further fillip from the protectionist economic policy that independent India followed for decades. Various states looked to each other rather than to other countries for sharing their surplus or meeting their deficits. Economic federalism matured along with political federalism.

To India's good fortune, India's development contours did not follow ethnic lines (Mitra, 1967). A unipolar-periphery structure did not take shape. There is no single primate city but multiple ones with their own regional domains. The geographical heartland has rather been economically weak and periphery comparatively strong. There was less of reason for the periphery to harbour any feeling of neglect, exploitation or alienation.

India's political economy, which envisaged a collaborative participation of the state and market, required an extensive field for its operations. This could be said with particular reference to the processes of industrialization and urbanization. The elite, political, administrative or intellectual, also saw their interests served better in a wider national space. Virtues of the economy of scale were duly acknowledged. All this favoured India as an extensive playing field. An effective integrative role was played by the film industry, the media and ever densifying transport and communication network. Adoption of English as a pan-India associate official language was no less significant.

Map 1.1

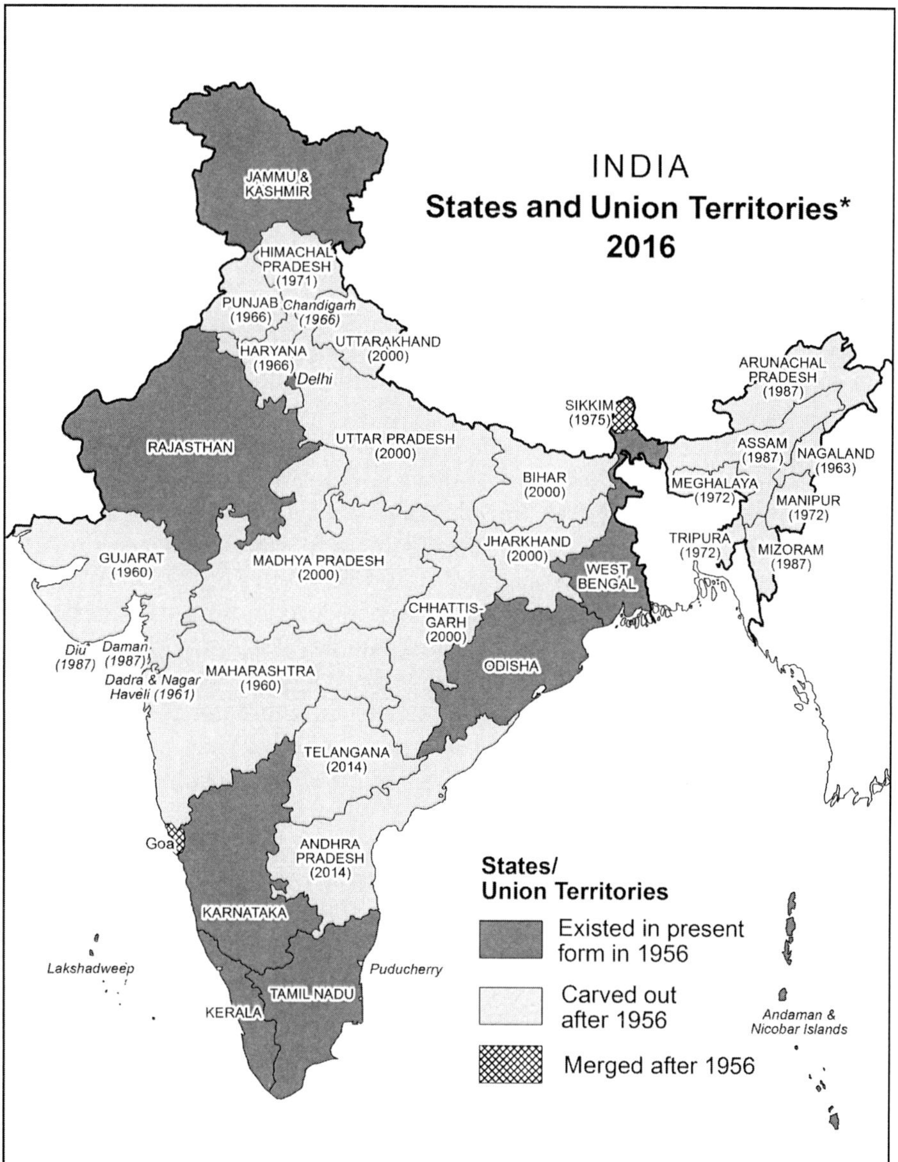

* Year of formation of a state/union territory after 1956 is mentioned in parenthesis.

To ensure regional vitality, the reform of administrative map of India on considerations of ethnic identity, historical background and development needs has been a continuous process and today the country is organised into 29 states and 7 union territories.

Several western scholars do contend that historically India has never been a nation-state prior to its formation in 1947. This is true that the country could not define itself as a nation-state in the European sense of such an entity. A greater truth is that India has ever been a civilizational state. It acquired the nature of a nation when the national movement took birth in the latter half of the nineteenth century, and since 1947 it is a nation-state with a vibrant democracy.

Civilizational Unity and Beyond

The most critical factor underlying the unity in diversity of India can be identified as the cultural heritage of the country. Living with diversity has been its destiny. Beyond and behind this diversity is a spiritual reality, called unity (Luce, 2006: p. 2). Such substantiality confirms that the country could transform the state-craft into social-craft. It evolved as a society of societies (Wilson, 2016: p. 11). India could demonstrate greater cultural stamina than any other part of the world, with the possible exception of China (Wolpert, 2005: p. 2).

An interesting paradox may be pointed out here. The structural division of the Indian society on ethnic lines is popularly perceived as a destabilizing factor. It needs to be realized that these structural divisions have promoted some or the other kind of spatial unity. Scheduled castes or backward classes or agricultural castes, anywhere, find themselves as more united than ever before across states or regions. The rising middle class, notwithstanding its internal differences in religion, region or caste, is also surfacing as a homogenizing factor in the Indian society. It accounted for only 5 per cent of the total population at the time of Independence; it was almost 20 per cent at the turn of the twenty-first century (Das, 2000). Now its share is estimated at nearly one-third of the total population.

The singular credit for sustaining as integrated India goes to its democratic polity. The nation-state has withstood the onslaught of difficult situations of widespread discontent, violent protest and even insurgency. Indian democracy has convincingly demonstrated its strength and virtue in reconciling conflicting interests and fusing diverse perspectives. The idea of nation-building has taken firm roots. The Indian system, instead of breaking apart, is coming to reflect the country's diversity in an increasing regionalization of politics (Walsh, 2011: pp. 333–34). The vitality of India is manifest in its capacity to keep on constantly constructing a democratic space (Krishan ed., 2004).

The idea of India at its best is represented in the rupee note (Guha, 2009: pp. 41–42). On all the denomination notes, the amount is written in 17 languages with their respective scripts. This is an authentic tribute to India's diversity. India could instinctively anticipate the essentials of the European Union as a multi-lingual state.

What does the future hold for the unity of India? Will it remain integrated in years to come? What is the likely outcome of the insurgent situations at times? It all depends upon the efficacy in management of federal polity. Also, one cannot remain indifferent to certain voices of concern. A time has come when we must be conscious of what unites us and take care of what divides us. Indian democracy intelligently responded to any divisive challenge and ensured unity. The discourse on India's disunity went rather too far in certain quarters. Invariably the wisdom and will of the people challenged all this and kept the country unified.

The experience of virtually all the developing countries has been that of staying together despite internal divisions and associated serious difficulties. The constitutional might of a nation-state, like that of India, is not to be underestimated. India's integrity is assured and it is not going to disintegrate through any secessionist movement (Robinson, 1989). One could add that the unity of the country is guaranteed at least till the time its democracy is sustained.

Will a shift to the presidential form of government strengthen the process of its nation-building? One cannot say for certain whether such a change over would invigorate India's unity or prove counterproductive. The issue calls for an extensive debate. Any change of this kind will also call for a reform in the mode of election to the office of the President. To incorporate the element of diversity, it would be imperative to make it mandatory for the candidate to get some specified minimum percentage of votes from every state and union territory. The moot point, however, remains for deliberation.

An exploration of India confirms that 'it is a country without limits'. May it be the bounty of physical and human resources, or the system of its ancient sacred places, or the emergence of modern tech-locations, it defies a precise description. No wonder it has acquired several prefixes, such as Timeless India, Incredible India, Shining India and Emerging India. Not to be missed is also Vulnerable India. An appreciation of parameters of its vitality-vulnerability syndrome calls for a discussion on such select aspects of this country.

Resourceful India

The vitality of India is embedded in the variety, quantity and quality of its physical and human resource base. Thanks to its strategic location in the middle of South Asia, the country constituted the main component of a relatively prosperous subcontinental entity for centuries. It combined the virtues of a continental as well as maritime location. The land connectivity defined its relations with the Central Asia and West Asia in particular and the sea connectivity linked it to the South-East Asia, Middle East and Africa. For centuries together, it distinguished itself as a relatively flourishing segment of the earth. In the beginning of the eighteenth century, the country's Gross Domestic Product was almost one-fourth of the world total (Robinson, 2014: p. 11). The wealth, moderate climate, level topography, and easy accessibility made it a frequent target of invasions from the West. North India remained a more active theatre of Indian history for centuries.

The beginning of the maritime age since the fifteenth century redefined the locational parameters of India. This brought South India into greater prominence because of its maritime disposition vis-à-vis the Arabian Sea, Bay of Bengal and the Indian Ocean. The British marked their colonial entry into India through the coastal belt and gradually brought its large part under their direct control. Even today the locational vitality of India is affirmed by its maritime bearings as a viable sea power in the Indian Ocean.

The *Land Resource Atlas of India,* brought out in 1996 by the National Atlas and Thematic Mapping Organization, Kolkata, is a veritable source of information on natural resources of the country. Most integrative is the map depicting the 'status of land resources' (Map 1.2). A synoptic view of the land resource status as it differs from one part of India to another is made available. The seven criteria employed for the purpose include physiography, climate, agricultural land capability, irrigation, forest cover, mineral wealth, and predominant settlement and wasteland cover. About 40 per cent of the land area of the country was assessed as very good or good, 36 per cent as of moderate quality and the remaining 24 per cent as poor to fair. The best of lands are located in northern plain, valleys and deltaic tracts of the peninsular rivers, large parts of the western coastal belt, Mysore and Tamil Nadu plateaus and Kashmir valley. The lands of moderate quality adjoin the best ones and are characteristically more typical of the North-East, Central India, North-Eastern peninsula, and Andaman and Nicobar Islands. By contrast, predominance of the land of poor quality is noted in the higher Himalayas, Rajasthan desert, and rain shadow zone of Western Ghats. Nature has endowed most of India with a rich resource base.

The numerical strength of India's population was recorded as 1.21 billion at the 2011 Census. An enriching dimension of India's population is the diversity of communities on the basis of religion, language, caste/sect and tribal affiliations. A *Survey of the People of India,* conducted under the aegis of the Anthropological Survey of India, counted as many as 4,693 communities of all varieties (Singh, 1992: p. 209).

About 80 per cent of India's population is Hindu by religion. Despite an overwhelming majority of the Hindus, India did not declare itself as a theocratic one. It opted for the status of a secular nation-state. India has more Muslims than in the entire Middle East, more Christians than in Australia, and more Buddhists than in Tibet (Guha, 2009). Nine among every ten Sikhs in the world live in India.

The linguistic diversity of India is just as astonishing. There is no national language. Hindi and English are the two official languages. There are 22 scheduled or regional languages. The states are empowered to adopt any language, even other than the two official and 22 scheduled languages, as their state language. Mizo, for instance, is the official language of Mizoram. This language does not find a place among the scheduled languages.

Map 1.2

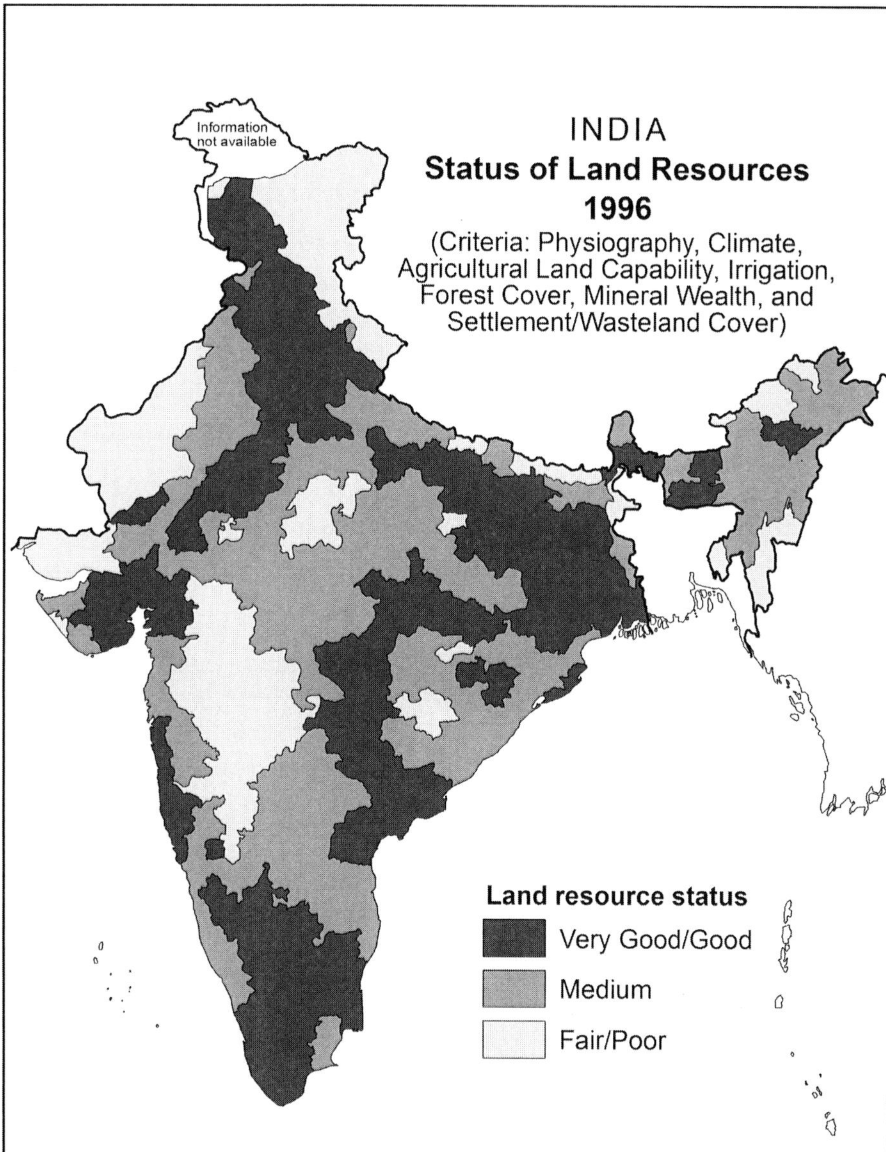

Nature has gifted most parts of India with a variety of physical resources.

Source: Land Resource Atlas of India, National Atlas and Thematic Mapping Organisation, Kolkata, 1996.

Women constitute nearly half of the India's demographics but the spread of their economic and social space has been relatively much narrower. Many of them speak the language of silence while undergoing subordination and submission at the family and societal levels. Some of them may be aborted even before their cry-at-birth. To live in scarcity and frugality is the model they personify. Things are changing now. There is a growing appreciation of the fact that it is the women who imbibe the tradition and convey the message that family is at the heart of cultural stability and peace. They are being given greater recognition. *The Report of the Annual Status of Higher Education in India: 2015* informs that over one-half of the students in medical colleges are women and their proportion is nearly one-third in engineering colleges. Women account for almost one-fifth of the employees in public sector. At least one-third of the elected members of the village *panchayats* and *nagar palikas* today are women under the provisions of the 73rd and 74th Amendments of the Constitution. All these proportions are on the rise. The day is not far when one-third of the seats in the Indian Parliament may be reserved for them.

In no less measure the vitality of India is contingent upon youthfulness of population. Almost two-thirds of its population belongs to the economically active age group of 15–64 years. Nearly the same proportion forms the voters' constituency of 18-plus age group. The so-called demographic dividend or economic growth potential is massive, around 800 million people. It is modernizing under the impact of education, technology and global change, and is expected to contribute *additionally* 2 per cent annually to the per capita GDP (Aiyar and Mody, 2011: p. 4). The dividend may turn into disaster if the requisite job opportunities are not created for this section of population. Equally important is to ensure its quality education, vocational training and proper health.

The virtues of human resource of India lie in being diverse, youthful and technology-oriented. It's becoming gender sensitive as well over time. Physical resources are also in plenty. An integral product of the two, maturing and ripening over time, are its geographical indications goods, such as pashmina shawls, Darjeeling tea and Kannauj perfume. These are the goods made only in India, and make India, India (Kapur, 2016: p. 182). Geography has been benign to India and perhaps that made its history belligerent more often than not.

Sacred India

A critical ingredient of the vitality of India is a wide scatter of its sacred places belonging to different faiths, their existence in close proximity in several locales and the long established practice of pilgrimage among all faiths. The landscape of India is ever vibrant with such places attracting multitude of followers and devotees from far and wide. Such fervour is at its peak at the time of some fair or festival. The fact is that every religious place has a history and, conversely, every story in the vast storehouse of myth and legend has its place (Eck, 2012: p. 5).

If a map of sacred places were prepared, these would show a heavy concentration in all the deltaic tracts, namely of the Ganga, Mahanadi, Godavari-Krishna and Kaveri, which are marked by predominance of Hindu temples. Historic capital cities such as Srinagar, Delhi, Agra, Hyderabad and Mysore, which in many cases have the Hindu and Muslim places of pilgrimage in close proximity to each other, would also stand out for their density of sacred places. The Middle Ganga plain is hallowed by the presence of Hindu and Buddhist places of pilgrimage in a large number. The river courses and mountain ridges anywhere are the ones where Hindu places of pilgrimage predominate. Source sites of rivers in the Western Ghats and their vicinity are distinguished by the spread of Hindu pilgrimage places and Buddhist caves. The Konkan belt presents a composite picture of religious places of Hindus, Christians and Muslims.

Pan-India is the spread of places of Hindu pilgrimage. These are scattered all over from Amarnath cave in Jammu & Kashmir in the north to Rameswaram in Tamil Nadu in the south and from Somnath in Gujarat in the west to Imphal in the east. Badrinath, Puri, Rameshwaram and Dwarka positioned on the four corners of the country, enjoy the prestigious status of *dhams* (abodes of the divine). Tirupati is the most revered temple in South India. Haridwar, Allahabad and Varanasi are eminent places of pilgrimage located along the Ganga. Pushkar in proximity of Ajmer has the only temple dedicated to Brahma, the lord of genesis of the universe. One can observe the spatial spread and interconnectivity of all these places contributing to the cultural unity of India. These find an association with different natural features, such as rivers, mountains and forests.

The life's dream and devotional obligation of every Muslim is to go for Hajj or pilgrimage to Mecca in Saudi Arabia. This is outside India but venerable to every Muslim. Within India, the pilgrimage among Muslims was popularized by the Sufi saints. The *dargah* or shrine of Moinuddin Chishti of Ajmer (d. 1235), of Qutubddin Bakhtiyar Kaki on the outskirts of Delhi (d. 1235) and of Nizammudin Auliya in Delhi (d. 1325) carry special fascination for the Muslims as places of pilgrimage. The *dargah* of Sayyid Salar Masud Ghazi in Bahraich, located between Lucknow and Faizabad, is another place which attracts thousands of Muslims.

While shrines of saints are special for the Muslims, for Sikhs it is a place dedicated to their Gurus. Several of these are located close to a water body or along a river. Amritsar is famous for its Golden Temple, associated with the fourth Guru, Ramdas. Sultanpur Lodhi was an abode for years of the first Guru, Nanak. Sis Ganj in Old Delhi has its affiliation with the ninth Guru, Tegh Bhadur. Hemkunt Sahib, Anandpur Sahib, Patna Sahib and Nanded owe their prominence to the tenth Guru, Gobind Singh. Pilgrimage places of the Sikhs celebrate the life events and achievements of their gurus and are meant to reinforce tenets of Sikhism.

Christians seek proximity to God at their places of pilgrimage. This may be for the purpose of penance or confession or for seeking physical, mental or spiritual healing. Among them, Basilicas of Jesus, Church of St. Cajetan and Church of St. Francis of Assisi, all in Goa, deserve a special mention. Santa Cruz Basilica of Cochin and Cathedral Church of St. Thomas in Mumbai hold an equal importance. All these basilicas and churches were raised by the Portuguese. By comparison, the Christ Church of Shimla and Cathedral of the Sacred Heart in Delhi are the creation of the British. The sacred places of the Christians in India find an association with the names of different Roman Catholic saints and apostles.

Virtually all the pilgrimage sites of the Buddhists are concentrated in the Middle Ganga plain. Notable among these are Bodh Gaya, where Buddha attained enlightenment; Sarnath, where he delivered his first sermon; Sravasti, which played host to Buddha during his frequent visits; and Kushinagar, where he acquired *nirvana* (liberation). All these places are marked by the presence of stupas (domes), relics of monasteries and temples. The 29 Ajanta Caves, located inside the fold of Western Ghats, carry wall paintings and sculptures representing Buddha, who otherwise had not visited this area. Evidently, all the Buddhist places of pilgrimage find an association only with the life history of Buddha.

Jain places of pilgrimage are also linked to the lives of their saints. The merit in visiting them is seen as a lesson in endurance and austerity. An additional consideration is to gain knowledge about Jainism. Above all, it is an act of paying reverence to noble souls. Such places display a bipolar concentration: one in the Middle Ganga Plain, where Jainism had its origin, and two in Rajasthan and Gujarat, in Western India, where it experienced maximum spread. Mount Parsvanatha or Sametsikhara and Pawanpuri, both in Bihar, fall in the first category, and Mount Abu, Ranakpur and Jaisalmer in Rajasthan and Girnar, Satrunjaya and Tarange in Gujarat belong to the second category. Besides, Shravana Belagola, about 100 km from Mysore in South India, is another place of Jain pilgrimage. All the Jain places of pilgrimage are characterized by the presence of magnificent temples dedicated to Jain *Tirthankaras* or saints.

The story of pilgrimage places in India is imbued with sanctity and devotion in a variety of ways. Places of the Hindu pilgrimage find an association with natural features like sacred rivers, mountain ridges and deep forests; those of the Muslims are often *makbaras* or shrines, and the ones of the Sikhs find an association with the lives and philosophy of their gurus. The Christian places of pilgrimage are concentrated in those few areas where the Portuguese ruled. Roman Catholic saints are their main focus. Buddhist places of pilgrimage are heavily concentrated in the Middle Ganga Plain and all are linked to the life of only Buddha. Likewise, the places of Jain pilgrimage find an association with the birth of Jainism in Middle Ganga plain and its spread in Western India.

As per the 2011 Census, India has 3,013,140 places of worship, including temples, mosques, churches, gurudwaras and others. About one per cent of census houses in the country are places of worship and there is one place of worship per square kilometre of area. These are proportionately more in rural India (2,419,700 or 80.6%) than in urban India (593,440 or 19.4%). The frequency of such places is high in the Ganga Plain, in coastal areas of sustained commercial activity area, and in the Western Himalayas. The scatter of places of worship is more dispersed than that of population distribution because several of them are located in remote and sparsely inhabited areas.

Democratic India

Democracy is the only political system that vests power with people or their representatives. It is an instrument of social justice through government as much as capitalism is for economic efficiency through market. The developed countries have tried to combine the virtues of both which otherwise may not be strictly compatible with each other. India opted for democracy guided primarily by the tenet of social justice.

India is the most populous and stable democracy in the developing world today. Its democratic institutions are remarkably functional not only at the national and state levels but also at the local *panchayat* (rural) and *nagar-palika* (urban) levels. The electoral system of the country has earned wide acclaim for its well-structured spatial organization, regularity and fairness. India is carved into 543 parliamentary constituencies and 4,120 assembly constituencies of the states and union territories. At the local level, it is noted for an orderly functioning of around quarter-million village panchayats and over 4,000 urban local bodies. Notwithstanding all and many kinds of inequalities, one fact stands clear that there is equality in per capita voting power of the people. Not only this. The regional or state parties are emerging as a critical factor in body politics of the country. Democracy at the grassroots level is gaining strength, steadily though slowly.

There was an initial apprehension that India could not sustain itself for long as a democracy because of illiteracy of its masses coupled with diversity of people. The actual experience has been to the contrary. The country could not do without democracy. Soon after Independence, it bestowed an equal voting power to every individual, irrespective of his or her educational economic or social status. This provided a viable mechanism for resolution of conflicting interests of all variety of people. Diversity defined the necessity of democracy. Federal democracy ensured an effective outlet to country's any regional tendency (Luce, 2006: pp. 337–38). Illiteracy was no barrier to political empowerment. Indeed, India's vibrant vitality is located in its dynamic democracy.

In one of his popular writings, Das (2000) observes that while historically democracy followed capitalism in almost every country, India presents a

Map 1.3

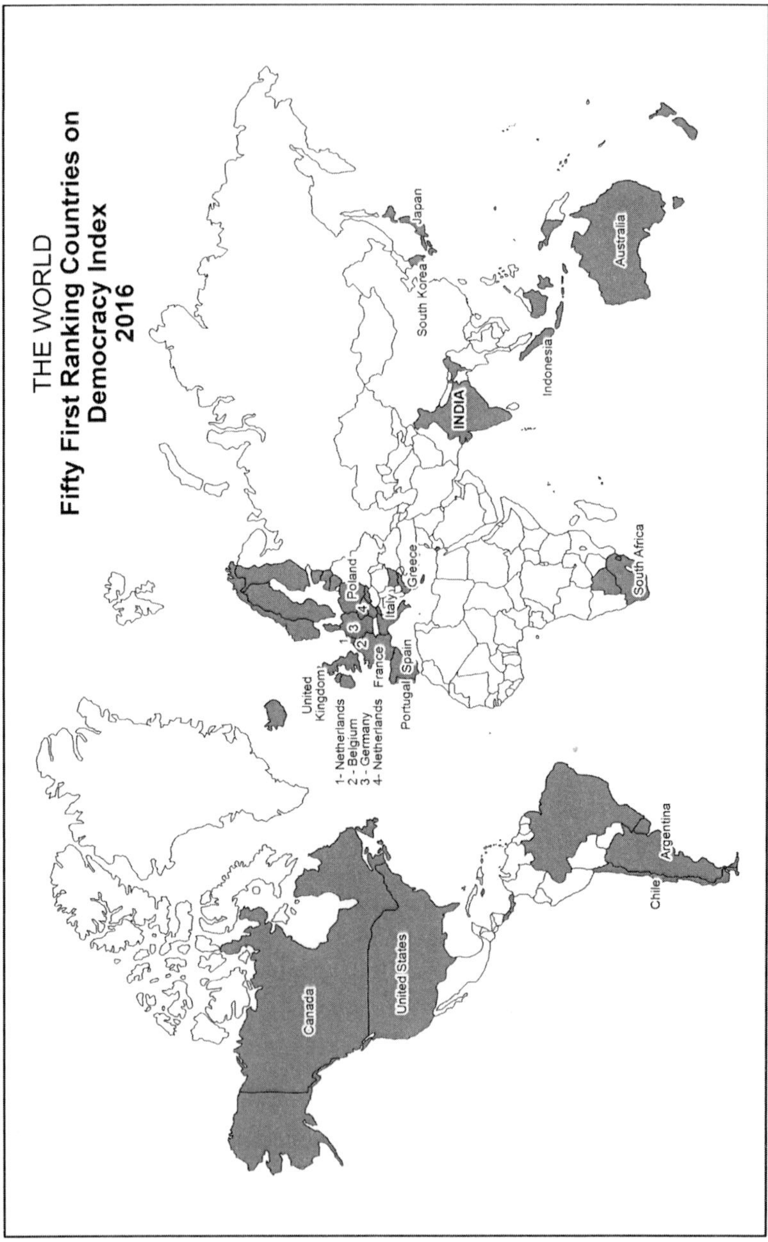

*On democracy index, India ranks among the top in developing world. It is strong on electoral process and management of pluralism.

Source: Economic Intelligence Unit. Countries with a population of at least 10 million are named.

unique case where capitalism followed democracy. The same was the case of the rise of middle class. It succeeded rather than preceded democracy. Meanwhile, social transformation had to wait for democracy to mature. All this resulted in a discourse among three sets of political forces: the conservative one of caste, religion and rural; the radical one of socialism; and contemporary one of market, globalization and urban. The political process has to negotiate with these three interest groups which are in constant conflict with each other in a democratic framework.

Historically, the vitality of any imperial power was subject to the valour of its armed forces. This was contingent upon the size, organizational skill and professionalism of its combatant forces. The International Institute for Strategic Studies, London, placed the numerical strength of defence forces in India at 1.3 million in 2014 as compared with 2.3 million in China and 1.5 million in the United States. The highly disciplined Indian defence forces are said to be one of the best in the world. Most creditable is its unflinching loyalty to the political system.

What is the synergy between bureaucracy and political authority in India? Do they play their defined roles or tend to work at cross purposes or connive in their mutual interest leading to indifference to the welfare of the people? To what extent the system is free of corruption? The public sector employs nearly 18 million people of different hierarchical status at the national, state and local levels. Despite its well-known inadequacies, the bureaucracy has ensured a regular functioning of the system. It has been a primary factor in enlargement of the middle class section of the society. It is also valued as an ingredient of India's uniformity and unity.

A word of caution is necessary here. While the electoral process in the country has been working towards an ever better mode, the democratic temperament among the populace is taking time to build itself. The Economic Intelligence Unit placed India at 32nd rank on democracy index in 2016 among different countries of the world (Map 1.3). For the purpose of analysis they had harnessed five indicators of electoral process and pluralism, functioning of the government, political participation, civil liberties and political culture. India was adjudged among the top in the developing world on the parameters of electoral process and inclusiveness of diversity.

Tech India

The biorhythm of vitality is certainly set by the sinews of science and technology. It is critical to not only manufacturing sector but also to primary, service and space sectors. For that reason India embarked upon a concerted effort for advancement of science and technology right since it became independent in 1947. Today it is one of the 31 major countries that are main contributors to the scientific and technological progress of the world at large. It has acquired a global name in the field of information technology, is reckoned as an important nuclear power and has made commendable strides in space research. All these achievements are outcome of several institutional measures like establishing Indian Institutes of Technology, setting up scientific laboratories, promoting defence research and development, initiating space programmes and giving a fillip to information technology and biotechnology in particular. Today, India is a home to one of the world's most progressive tech-entrepreneurs.

On Global Innovation Index 2015, India was on the top among the South Asian countries. A wider canvas of seven key indicators, including institutions, human capital and research, infrastructure, market sophistication, business enterprise, knowledge and technology outputs, and creative processes were put in service. At the global level, however, it ranked 81 among 141 countries, for which data was analysed.

How science and philosophy, representing rationality and spirituality, were harmonized in Indian thought process? Why philosophy, compatible with the Indian psyche, was defined as ancient, subjective and other-worldly, and science as modern, objective and pragmatic? How the worldview and life goals of the people got defined on the way? What has been the impact of such psycho-cultural mores on the nation's vitality?

Today the basic task is to revitalize the ethical and moral codes of conduct through integration of science and philosophy. Both material development and spiritual growth have to shake hands with each other. An organic relationship between the two has to be ensured. The nation-state can play a big role here especially through inculcation of desired human values and creation of a milieu in which such values can flourish. The recent adoption of 2015 as the year of *Yoga* by the United Nations was an acknowledgement of the spiritual vitality of India.

Vulnerable India

Vitality has ever to resolve the issue of vulnerability. The hard fact is that India is destined to meet and manage a variety of formidable situations. First of all, it has to bear with a number of issues vis-a-vis most of its neighbours. Pakistan is a constant thorn in the neck on Kashmir issue. China frequently raises question on several sectors of the international border. Bangladesh is a source of massive illegal immigration. Sri Lanka creates uneasy conditions related to its Tamil citizens who have affinity with India. Nepal, though friendly, is at times used as a sanctuary by criminals from India. Likewise Myanmar serves as an easy access to militants from states like Nagaland and Manipur. Bhutan is a dependable ally. The vitality of India remains ever on test in dealing appropriately with the geography of its immediate surroundings.

The second source of India's vulnerability is rooted within the country in the form of occasional disruptive movements and terrorist activities. A serious problem persists in the form of a Naxalite belt or red corridor in the north-eastern tribal zone of peninsular India from Andhra Pradesh to West Bengal. The situation in Jammu & Kashmir is also marked by frequent encounters between the militants and defence forces. The possibility of occurrence of a terrorist attack in any part of India can also be not ruled out. A lot of vitality of the country gets expended in managing this dimension of vulnerability.

The third major kind of vulnerability finds its association with the hazards ascribed to natural phenomena, such as earthquakes, floods and cyclones. Indeed, India's disasterscape is scripted by a multitude of hazards of this kind (Kapur, 2010). A distinct spatial variation is observed in all this. While snowfall disrupts life in Western Himalayas during the winter, heat wave has a sweep over the Northern Plains during summer. Hailstorm, lightning and thunderstorm strike most of western half of India; the cyclones are frequent visitors to the eastern coastal plain. Floods are typical of not only the river-laid Northern Plain and coastal regions but also occur in the Thar Desert. Drought in varying degrees is common to most parts of India, barring the North-East region. The Himalayas and adjoining parts of the Northern Plain are prone to earthquakes, in particular. The variety, frequency and intensity of disasters related to natural processes is the highest in the north-western and north-eastern regions as also in the Ganga plain and eastern coastal belt. While in the North-Western region it is snow; in the North-Eastern region it is earthquake. In the Northern Plain, it is flood and in the coastal region it is cyclone. Such events seep into vitality by way of causing destruction and damage to life, property and daily rhythm of life of the people. The flash floods in Uttarakhand in 2013; the Tsunami in Andaman and Nicobar Islands, Tamil Nadu and Kerala in 2004; Bhuj earthquake in 2001 in Gujarat and super cyclone in 1999 of Odisha are still fresh in the memory for the worst of calamity these wrecked in different parts of India.

Most critical is the fourth parameter of human-induced vulnerability related to untreated water, unattended sanitation and unconnected remoteness. The 2011 Census of India data on housing and amenities reveals that hardly 32 per cent of the households in India get treated water through a tap. This percentage is as low as three in Bihar. The situation is only slightly less worrisome in major states like Uttar Pradesh and Madhya Pradesh. Things are of course better in Southern and Western India as well as in all the union territories. Defecation in the open is an all India phenomenon in varying degree. Almost half the households in India are made to go by this practice. The frequency of such households is very high in Central and North India; comparatively low in North-West India, and the lowest in Kerala-Goa belt, all the union territories and parts of the North-East. Evidently a majority of India's population is vulnerable to diseases related to untreated water and poor sanitation. This disease-prone vulnerability gets further aggravated by lack of connectivity of several settlements with places offering health services. Almost one-third of roads in India remain unsurfaced. The situation is very bad in states like Assam, Bihar, Odisha and West Bengal where more than half of the roads are *kutcha* or unmetalled.

No less vulnerable is the population finding a shelter in the slums of Indian cities. These are the people who live in dwellings which are unfit for habitation by reasons of dilapidation, overcrowding, irregular lay out and faulty design of structures which tend to lack proper ventilation, light or sanitation. As per the 2011 Census of India, 21.5 per cent of population in 52 metropolitan cities of India are slum dwellers. They make a total of 25.1 million, a figure which exceeds the population of several countries in the world. More than 40 per cent of Mumbai's population is resident of slum. None of the metropolitan cities in India is free from slums.

Vulnerability of India is indeed a multi-source reality. Involved here are the elements of external threats, internal strife, natural hazards, disease ecology and poverty syndrome. Despite the lofty aspirations enunciated by India's founders and embodied in the country's Constitution, India remains a less-than-peaceful society (Guha, 2011: p. 62). About the defective development of India equally wary are Dreze and Sen (2013). They observe a contradiction of economic growth lacking human development in the country.

The multi-dimensional vitality of India is also a reality. Not only have its people displayed a remarkable resilience in addressing a calamity but also the government has been responding promptly to any eventuality of the kind, such as an earthquake, a cyclone or even a tsunami. Now the emphasis is upon reducing risk and enhancing resilience vis-à-vis geographical, environment, chemical, nuclear or fire related disasters among other things (National Disaster Management Authority, 2016). The vitality-vulnerability syndrome of the country is a blend of several co-functioning positive-negative tendencies. The tilt is in favour of optimism. All this has a regional dimension too which calls for a detailed analysis. This task takes us to successive chapters to follow.

References

Aiyar, S. and A. Mody. 2011. *The Demographic Dividend: Evidence from Indian States.* New York: IMF Working Paper 11/38.

Basu, Kaushik. 2016. *An Economist in the Real World: The Art of Policy Making in India.* New Delhi: Viking India.

Bellman, Eric. 2007. Reversal of Fortune Isolates India's Brahmins. *The Wall Street Journal*. 29 December.

Blij, Harm J. de and Peter O. Muller. 1994. *Geography: Realms, Regions and Concepts.* New York: John Wiley.

Chandra, Bipin, Mridula Mukherjee and Aditya Mukherjee. 1999. *India After Independence.* New Delhi: Penguin.

Cohen, Stephen P. 1971. *The Indian Army.* Oxford: Oxford University Press.

Das, Gurcharan. 2000. *India Unbound.* New Delhi: Penguin.

Dikshit, R.D. 1975. *The Political Geography of Federalism.* Delhi: Macmillan.

Dreze, Jean and Amartya Sen. 2013. *An Uncertain Glory: India and its Contradictions*. Princeton: Princeton University Press.

Eck, Diana L. 2012. *India: A Sacred Geography*. New York: Harmony Books.

Elliott, John. 2014. *Implosion: India's Tryst with Reality*. New Delhi: Harper Collins India.

Encyclopaedia Britannica. 2009. *Encyclopaedia of India*. New Delhi.

Government of India. 1980. *Report of the Backward Classes Commission*. New Delhi.

Grierson, A. 1902–29. *Linguistic Survey of India, Vols. I–XI*. Calcutta: Government Printing Office.

Guha, Ramachandra. 2009. Two Indias. *National Interest*. No. 102, pp. 31–42.

——. 2011. All Gandhi's Children. *National Interest*. No. 111, pp. 55–63.

Harrison, Selig S. 1960. *India: The Most Dangerous Decades*. Princeton: Princeton University Press.

Kapur, Anu. 2010. *Vulnerable India*. New Delhi: Sage Publications.

——. 2016. *Made Only in India: Goods with Geographical Indications*. London: Routledge.

Keay, John. 2010. *India: A History: From the Earliest Civilizations to the Boom of Twenty-First Century*. New York: Groove Press.

Khilnani, Sunil. 2004. *The Idea of India*. New Delhi: Penguin.

Krishan, Gopal. 2000. How India Stayed Integrated. *Annals of the National Association of Geographers, India*. Vol. 20, No. 2, pp. 3–9.

Krishan, Gopal (ed.). 2004. *Vitality of India*. Chandigarh: Centre for Research in Rural and Industrial Development.

Luce, Edward. 2006. *In Spite of the Gods: The Strange Rise of Modern India*. London: Little Brown Book Group.

McKinsey and Company. 2013. *Reimagining India*. New York: Simon and Schuster.

Menon, V.P. 1956. *The Story of the Integration of the Indian States*. Bombay: Orient Longman.

Miller, Sam. 2014. *A Strange Kind of Paradise: India Through Foreign Eyes*. New Delhi: Penguin India.

Mitra, Ashok. 1967. *Levels of Regional Development in India*. New Delhi: Indian Statistical Institute.

National Disaster Management Authority. 2016. *National Disaster Management Plan*. New Delhi: Government of India.

Nehru, Jawaharlal. 1946. *The Discovery of India*. Calcutta: Signet Press.

Nilkani, Nandan and Viral Shah. 2015. *Rebooting India: Realising a Billion Aspirations*. New Delhi: Penguin.

Phadnis, Urmila. 1968. *Towards the Integration of Indian States: 1919–1947*. Bombay: Asia Publishing House.

Rajivlochan, Meeta and M. Rajivlochan. 1992. Changing Conception of India as a Nation in Modern Times. *Social Sciences Research Journal* (New Series), pp. 95–105.

Robb, Peter. 2007. *Empire, Identity and India: Liberalism, Modernity and the Nation*. Oxford: Oxford University Press.

Robinson, Andrew. 2014. *India: A Short History*. New York: Thames and Hudson.

Robinson, Francis (ed.). 1989. *The Cambridge Encyclopedia of India, Pakistan, Bangladesh, Sri Lanka, Nepal, Bhutan and Maldives*. Cambridge: Cambridge University Press.

Singh, K.S. 1992. *People of India: An Introduction*. Calcutta: Anthropological Survey of India.

——. 1998. *India's Communities*. Oxford: Oxford University Press.

Spate, O.H.K. and A.T.A. Learmonth. 1967. *India and Pakistan: Physical, Economic and Regional Geography*. Suffolk: Methuen.

Strachey, John. 1888. *India's Search for National Identity*. New York: Alfred A. Knopf.

Toynbee, Arnold J. 1958. *East and West*. Oxford: Oxford University Press.

Walsh, Judith E. 2011. *A Brief History of India*. New York: Facts on File.

Wilson, Jan. 2016. *India Conquered: British Raj and the Chaos of Empire*. London: Simon and Schuster.

Wolpert, Stanley A. 2005. *India*. Berkeley and Los Angeles: University of California Press.

2

Regional Vitality

The idea of India as one integrated entity is fascinating and essential. In reality, a variety of Indias adorn the country's map. Imperative it is to have a view of many Indias, each contributing to its diversity, identity and vitality. In which way do different parts of the mosaic shape the whole of the nation-state and also the other way round? What are their respective roles in structuring and strengthening the system at large? How is their own destiny marked by the up-and-down swings? Such questions seek authentic answers.

We may begin by defining the concept of regional vitality. Regional vitality is basically the inherent distinctiveness, productive capacity and sustained dynamism of various components, such as a state or province, of a nation-state and their specific contribution, in nature and quantum, to the making of the entirety. At times certain symbols are created to represent the vitality of a region or place. In ancient Greece, each village, city or state raised its own central hearth and sacred fire to represent its unity and vitality. A parish church distinguishes itself as a pivot of the basic administrative unit in England. Each of the 50 states in the United States of America today has its own flag in addition to the national flag, as a mark of its identity.

The geographic approach to the idea of region has been evolving over time. For long a region was seen as a homogenous segment of the earth-space. It was a spatial unit through which the variable character of the earth surface could be conveniently comprehended and explained. Illustrations include a desert, a coastal belt, or a hilly tract. Then followed a phase when the idea of the functional region came into prominence. Such a region was defined not on the basis of formal homogeneity but on the consideration of operational unity within. City region, comprising the urban component and rural surroundings, is one such case. The relevance of a functional region was soon picked up in regional planning. It was deemed as the most appropriate spatial unit for planning and development administration. This led to an enquiry into the relative level of development of different areas. The theme of regional development was the natural outcome. Within it the backward regions called for a greater care. This created the rationale of regional policy.

In today's context, subnational administrative areas like states/provinces, districts and subdistricts, have evolved as authentic regions of varying hierarchical order. These have precisely defined territorial limits, their legal status and obligatory functions are clearly spelt out, and they generally command psychological affinity of the people. Of all kinds of regions, administrative areas are most comprehensive, comprehensible and consequential spatial units for the purpose of any research.

In the contemporary scenario of increasing inter-connectedness and interdependence with rapid interregional transportation, universal internet connectivity and rising globalization, the disposition of any region is being subjected to two opposites. On the one hand, its boundaries are losing the conventional sheen; on the other hand, its core is gaining prominence as a mark of its identity rooted in history, culture and popular bonding. A tendency to discover and assert the distinctiveness and dynamism of each region is on the board. Such propensity inevitably gravitates one to the domain of vitality of the region. After all, it is the vitality that sustains a region.

Rise and Fall of Empires/Civilizations

In an effort to understand the regional vitality of India, the first essential step is to explore the writings on the theme at the global level. Such studies are in the nature of rise and fall of empires and civilizations. These engage in mining the factors which were instrumental in evolution of a part of the world or a region into an empire and the factors which ultimately led to its collapse. The locational parameters of a region are not stable. At one time it may have been the core of an empire but, subsequently, it might have been relegated to the status of a periphery of some other empire. Certainly empires have not been immortal in history. Such an idea could also be applied in some manner to different regions within a nation-state.

Though the world today is divided into 193 nation-states, these were essentially parts of some or the other empires in history. There have been more than 150 empires over time in human history (*National Geographic*, 2013). The empire-building was, on the one hand, narrative in war, death and subjugation; on the other hand, it has been an engine of humanity's progress through interaction among people belonging to different climes and cultures. Every empire was characterized by diversity of people. The imperial highways and seaways were the channels of their interaction and also of diffusion of products, skill and ideas.

The empires emerged, waxed and waned in succession to each other. Kennedy (1989) traces the rise and fall of the Spanish, French and British empires and sounded that the American empire would be the next to fall in line. He underlined that it was the factor of economic productivity that allowed any world power to exercise and sustain its global hegemony. The decline began when an empire went for an overreach which it could not manage, withhold and command. Things started falling apart when the imperial power faced fierce internal disruptions and failed to keep things together.

Similar is the story of evolution and devolution of cultures and civilizations. Spengler (1918) identified eight cultures in history, namely, the Babylonian, Egyptian, Chinese, Indian, Greco-Roman, Arabian, Aztec or Mexican and the West. He believed that each culture had a life span of about one 1,000 years and every culture culminated in a civilization. The pattern of life at the civilizational stage of culture turned to be depletive of economic resources and proved as the root cause of its fall. He underlined that now is the winter time of the western civilization. Evidently his ideas represent cultural determinism in explaining the course of history.

In his 12 volume treatise, Toynbee (1934 to 1961) describes the origin, development and decay of 19 civilizations in world history. He also makes a mention of four abortive civilizations (Far Western Christian, Far Eastern Christian, Scandinavian and Syriac), which did not bloom to full form and five arrested civilizations (Polynesian, Eskimo, Nomadic, Ottoman and Spartan), which had little chance to flourish. He highlights the role of environmental geography in influencing the course of history. His argument was that history followed different courses for diverse people not because of biological differences but by reason of their specific ecological conditions. The degradation of environment led to decline of a civilization. He propounded the thesis of 'challenge and response' to explain a high level of development in some resource deficit regions. Japan is a ready illustration. He added a word of caution. An excessive challenge can cause crash of a civilization and a little challenge can lead to stagnation. A golden mean will only work.

A critique of the environmental impairment or imbalance between population and natural resource base as the factor underlying collapse of societies was offered also by Diamond (2005). He enlists five point framework of possible downfall – ecological degradation, climate change, hostile neighbours, loss of support from friendly trade partners and failure to respond adequately to the environmental problems in overall terms. Ecocides have been a fact of history. The role of military defeat or economic distress can also be not ruled out. There is a need here to distinguish between an immediate cause of devastation by an external enemy and that of a long-term process of internal gradual damage to environment.

The societies who had acquired supremacy in military power, technology, wealth and political assertion could build empires. They worked for unequal integration of diverse populations under their subjugation, by way of favouring some and being indifferent to others. Free trade economy and promotion of interface among different cultures were other hallmarks of their policy. That is how they raised and sustained their empires. The collapse took form when the subject communities started viewing their colonizers as exploiters and destroyers of their natural resource base. Eventually the breakdown of the empire was an outcome of its incapacity to avert the impending ecological damage.

An interesting question is raised by Tainter (1988): How could once flourishing civilizations now be in a ravaged condition? Did the people damage their environment, or some inner civil conflict led to anarchy, or a foreign invader put their cities to plunder, death and fire? Or was there some other mysterious dynamics of their rise and fall? He provides an equally stimulating explanation. His basic postulate is that any civilization, for that matter any empire, evolves into a complex entity at a stage. It requires ever increasing doses of management and investment for its sustenance. Gradually the marginal returns to investment in dealing with management of complexity start diminishing with a concurrent rise in cost. To meet such a situation, a still heavier dose of investment becomes necessary. When possibly this cannot be done, the complex system starts foundering and ultimately it collapses. The cause is, thus, economic in nature.

The life cycle of Roman, Chinese, Spanish, Ottoman, Japanese and British empires was traced by Hubbard and Kane (2013). They attribute their fall to financial downturn and rise of self-seeking interest groups. They depart from the historians who explain the decline of these empires in terms of external factors like military defeat. The causation lies in some internal developments, such as expansion of inflexible bureaucracy by Roman Empire, priority to unproductive careers like soldiering and priesthood by imperial Spain, acceptance of an exploitative oligarchy by Ottoman empire, and distancing from the colonized subjects by the British empire. They emphasize that such tendencies impaired the social base and economic system of these empires and led to their fall.

A credence to the factors of administrative style, historical experience and protestant work ethics in explaining wealth and poverty of nations was offered by Landes (1998). The rule of law and respect for property rights are of paramount importance. Degree to which a society is open to change, new technology and gender equality are no less important. This is the way Europe, rather the entire West, forged ahead after the discovery of America in 1492. Geographical, intellectual and cultural curiosity gave Europe a momentum as a whole but within it the British Empire made a mark while the Spanish empire was noted for a different experience. The two differed in the quality of their colonial administration. The former tried to be neutral to the religion and traditions of their colonial subjects while the latter worked to impose the superiority of the Christian faith. In any situation negative effects flowed from blind adherence to religion, internal suppressions and ethnic cleansings, even in the best of cases.

The fate of nations or empires is linked to institutional factors, thus assert Acemoglu and Robinson (2012). Inclusive economic and political institutions in the nature of genuine democracy lead to prosperity and growth while extractive institutions in the form of feudalism or dictatorship or things of similar genre cause their failure. There is enough historical evidence to demonstrate that extractive situations breed economic misery and political instability. They added that any theory of geography, culture or economic policy is inadequate in explaining a shift from extractive to inclusive institutions. Such a change is always associated with emergence of a critical juncture or an event serving as a turning point. This happened in England in 1688, France in 1789, Japan in 1868, Russia in 1917 and China in 1978. A tilt toward inclusive political and economic institutions is visible in all such cases. Such a juncture may ultimately fail if it does not pave a way for inclusive institutions, as it happened in the case of former Soviet Union.

Such a view is reinforced by Ferguson (2013). He believes that to understand the complex dynamics of convergence and divergence parameters of the world today, we have to delve into the history of institutions. While culture defines the value system of a society, institutions determine the quality of its functioning. The four institutions of overriding importance today include a representative government, a free market, the rule of law and order and civil society. Underlying any economic stagnation and geopolitical decline is the role of degeneration of institutions. The breakdown of empires in history was essentially linked to failure of their institutional framework.

The story of rise and fall of empires and civilizations has, thus, been subjected to ecological, economic, cultural and institutional determinisms. Empires glittered on the basis of military prowess and economic power. These suffered an eclipse on becoming complex and unaffordable due to an over-reach. Every empire or great power was destined to go into oblivion. The trigger was provided by an invasion and defeat, or some nature-linked disaster and devastation, or a critical juncture in terms of an event of a destabilizing nature, enough to destroy a system already rendered fragile. The overall context in each case was so complex that it defies a singular explanation or a unified generalization.

How did nation-states emerge out of empires, kingdoms, principalities and the like? Most scholars connect the evolution of nation-state with emergence of modern state system distinguished by clearly defined sovereignty and centralized government. Such states evolved on the basis of ethno-nationalism, particularly in Europe (Muller, 2008: p. 31). Ethnically, homogeneous societies are marked by greater internal solidarity, emotional affinity and administrative convenience.

The ground reality is that a large number of nation-states are multi-ethnic. A historical analysis of 145 countries in the world, out of which 139 became nation-states during 1816 to 2001, was conducted by Wimmer and Feinstein (2010). Many of them were a colonial construct. Modernization was not a virtue of most of such nation-states which took birth after World War II. These took form when a power shift allowed the nationalists to overthrow or absorb the established regime. The event was a product of the outrage against the existing situation. Regional aspirations and forces held the sway.

In overall terms, political regions based on ethnicity or colonial cartography, or accidents of history provided the spatial framework for formation of nation-states.

The Indian Scenario

What has been the India story about the play of the regions in history? Is it possible to discern an order underlying its changing political landscape and associated regional configurations over time? Does it conform to spatial details of ecological setting or socio-cultural arrangements or accidents in history? Above all, where were located the vital cores and their feeble peripheries?

A perusal of relevant literature is certainly of help. Schwartzberg (1978: p. 254) observes that 63 dynasties/states had the status of major powers in the history of Indian subcontinent since 560 BC. Five of them had a pan-India character. Included here are the Mauryas and Guptas during the ancient period; the Mughals and Marathas during the medieval period and the British during the modern period. The Magadha in the east; Sakas (Gandhar) in the north-west; and Satavahanas and Vakatakas in the northern part of the Deccan were the other four supra-regional powers at different times during the ancient period. Three major faultlines on the political landscape of India through history were located in the foothills of the Himalayas in the north, the Narmada river in the middle and Kaveri river in the south (Map 2.1). In overall terms, these find a faint expression in the present spatial structure of the state system of India under the impact of developments during the colonial and post-Independence periods.

It is notable that seven of these nine powers were centred on the Northern Plains of India. Endowed with a vast productive physical resource base, this part of Indian subcontinent was more populous too. No supra-power emerged in South India or the north-western region or the north-eastern one. These regions were located on the periphery of the essentially triangular landmass of Indian subcontinent. Also notable is the fact that all clusters of these power centres arrange themselves in the form of T. The Indo-Gangetic plain forms the bar of this T and its stem extends southward from the Delhi-Agra region through Malwa and further through north-west Maharashtra to Mysore.

A regularity is, thus, observed in spatial distribution of historical power centres in India and their regional reach. This framework coincides with the evolving ecological conditions or geographical settings in the subcontinent. Locational and physiographical parameters defined opportunities on the one hand, and on the other hand, these also tested the capability of various powers to combat constraints imposed by them. Through the history of Indian subcontinent, the influence of physical environment seems to have been pervasive in shaping the politico-territorial arrangements. Spate and Learmonth (1965: pp. 177–78) also find their association with physiographic and agricultural regions.

Map 2.1

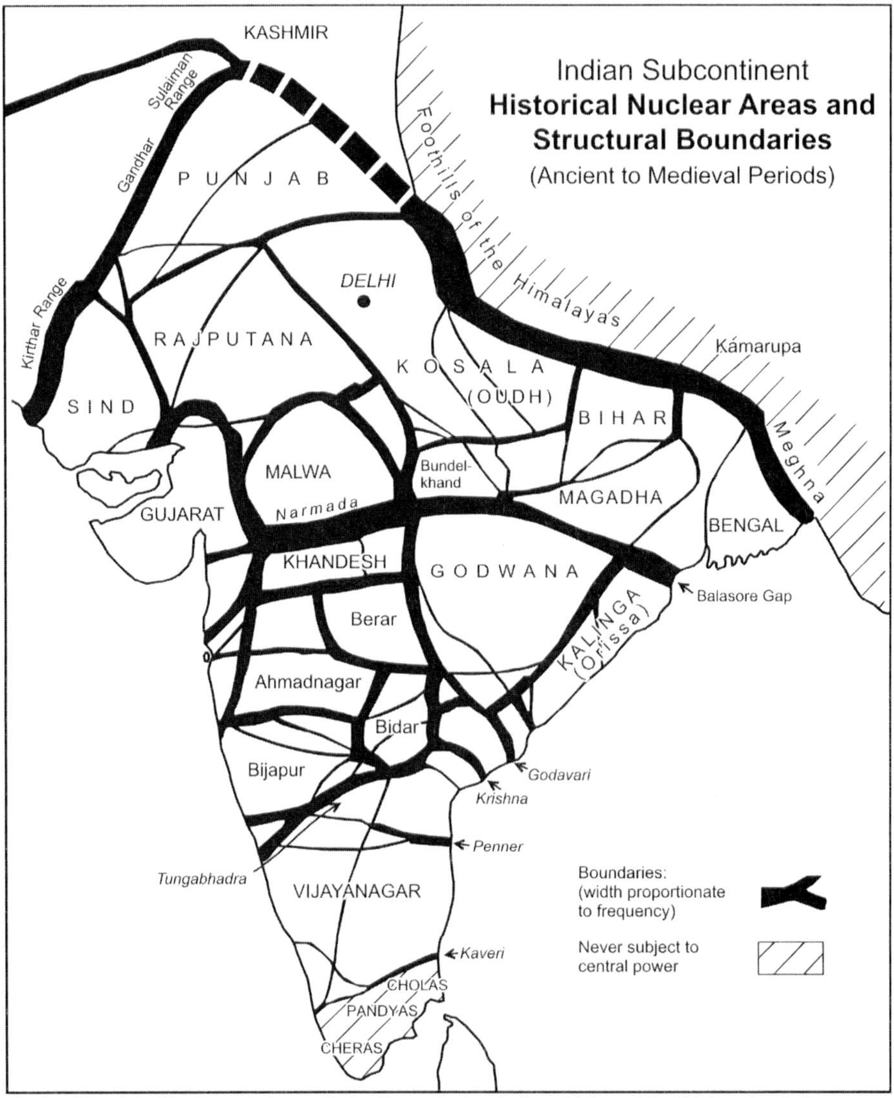

The foothills of the Himalayas in the north, the Narmada river in the middle and the Krishna river in the south have been the three major fault lines on the political landscape of ancient and medieval India. The spatial structure of states at present is not without some semblance with the historical areas.

Source: Adapted from, O.H.K. Spate and A.T.A. Learmonth, 1967. *India and Pakistan*, London: Methuen, p. 176

The underlying philosophy and associated methodology of organizing space for administration, for that matter the designing of politico-regional framework, differed over successive periods of Indian history (Kant, 1988: p. 235). Broadly speaking, this pattern was consistent with clan or tribal territories during the ancient period. Considerations of military control and revenue collection became paramount in medieval times. The colonial phase was marked by concerns related to ensuring strict control, maintaining law and order and raising revenue. In the post-independence era the issue of meeting regional aspirations came into prominence. The successive phases did not destroy the existing spatial arrangements at local level but in most cases modified them to their own requirements. One could notice the persistence for centuries of boundaries of administrative units like districts. A pertinent question arises here. Did administrative areas align themselves with cultural areas or cultures incubated themselves within the administrative areas? This may have been a two-way process.

Interlinked was the creation of cultural and political space in India (Deshpande, 1992: pp. 1–4). The role of clan territories, historical change, and resultant reorganization of political space was basic to formation of cultural landscape of India during the ancient period. The macro- and micro-level cultural regions took form during the twelfth century when regional kingdoms emerged in a big way. These were instrumental in promoting regional languages, cultures and architecture. Subsequently, during the medieval and British periods, the politico-administrative organization of space emerged as the defining factor of the cultural regions of India. The most vital development since Independence has been reorganization of states on linguistic, tribal, ethnic and historical lines. This was an effort to conform administrative space to cultural space at meso-level.

On somewhat different lines, Ahmad (1999: p. 72) also tries to trace the process of region formation in India. Basing his ideas on the findings of eminent archaeologists, historians and geographers, such as F.J. Richards, Arnold Toynbee and O.H.K. Spate, he elaborates that the inflow of people to the Indian subcontinent throughout history was in the form of cultural groups who opted to settle in ecological settings similar to those of their original homes. This led to conformity between socio-cultural diversity and physico-geographical variety. The evolved socio-cultural landscape was in the form of a mosaic wherein each segment was characterized by a distinct language. No wonder the linguistic map of India finds a fair correspondence with ecological conditions of different parts of the country.

The internal political boundaries of India both at the macro- and meso-scales were contextual in response to lay of the land and accidents of history and were redrawn from time to time. The process continues even at present. All this bears a similarity with the gradual evolution of nation-states at the global level which was driven by circumstantial political factors at regional and local levels (Wimmer and Feinstein, 2010: p. 764). If one tries to dig the basic structure of political landscape of India, it is found situated in an assertion of diversity operating within a framework of an over-riding civilizational unity. There were no fixed boundaries of or barriers to different empires or kingdoms as these existed at any time.

The fact remains that the geographers initially tried to comprehend the regional scheme of India in a physiographic framework. Methodology marked a change over time. Before Independence, the geographic distinctiveness of any region was viewed in terms of its topography, religious composition and the administrative regime of the British or of the princes. After Independence, the regional identity founded itself on the ideas of ethnicity, historical background and indigenous culture. Regional sentiment got a sharp edge and was valued as a path to political autonomy, especially for projecting identity and promoting economic interest. In their functional form, regions acquired the disposition of states and union territories, alongwith their internal administrative subdivisions. Not to be missed is the persistence of traditional socio-cultural regions within each (Map 2.2).

The Emerged Pattern

One notable feature of Indian states today is that none of them was in the nature of a sovereign state at the time of independence in 1947. These were as a whole or part of the British provinces, princely states or Portuguese or French colonies (Map 2.3). Sikkim had the status of a protectorate of India till 1975 when it became one of its states of India. The new nation-state had to reform its internal territorial arrangement for administration, more than once. Two primary considerations were involved in this process: to ensure integrity of the nation-state and to honour the regional aspirations. The issue of administrative cost and management were treated as a part of the game or were simply given incidental consideration.

At the first go, the internal administrative map of the country was recast to consolidate the patchwork of political territories inherited at the time of Independence. A system of 28 states of Part A, B, C and D categories was designed on the eve of commencement of the Constitution of India in 1950 (Map 2.4). Part A states were the former governor's provinces of British India; Part B states were the earlier big princely states or group of princely states; Part C states were the erstwhile chief commissioner's provinces of princely states; and Part D category had only Andaman and Nicobar Isles. In 1956, the 14 states and six union territories defined the new administrative map of India on linguistic basis (Map 2.5). Soon it became essential to tailor new states on the basis of historical legacy or tribal/ethnic considerations. Thereafter ensued a phase in which segmentation of linguistically homogeneous states like Bihar, Uttar Pradesh, Madhya Pradesh and Andhra Pradesh was carried out. Such carving out of the new states out of the existing ones was, thus, a reality of both Hindi and non-Hindi areas. The freshly formed states drew their rationale from the neglect they had suffered in development. The exploitation of their natural resources without proportionate benefit to them was an additional powerful argument. A previous existence as a separate political entity or distinct historical status strengthened their

Map 2.2

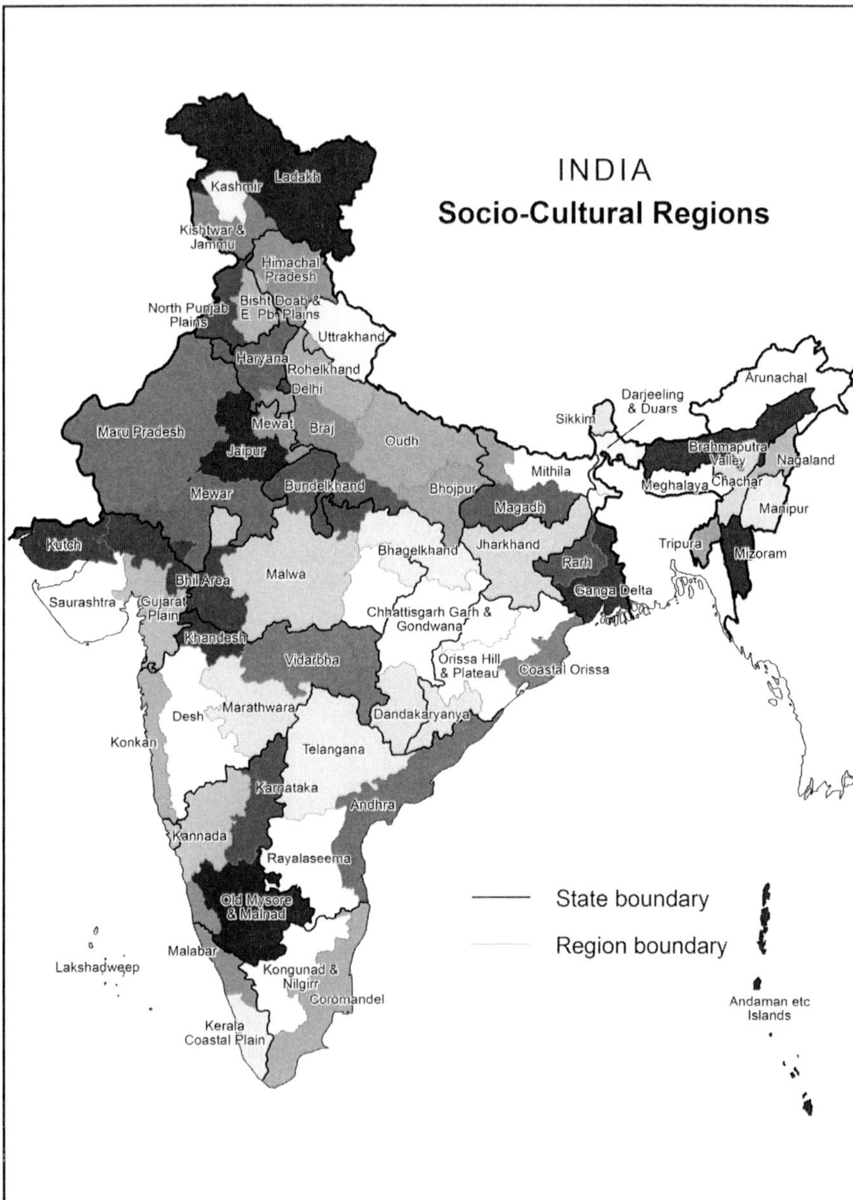

The traditional regions of India, when fitted into the framework of present boundaries of states and union territories, unfold the diversity of India in greater detail.

Source: Commerce Research Bureau of India, 1975.

Map 2.3

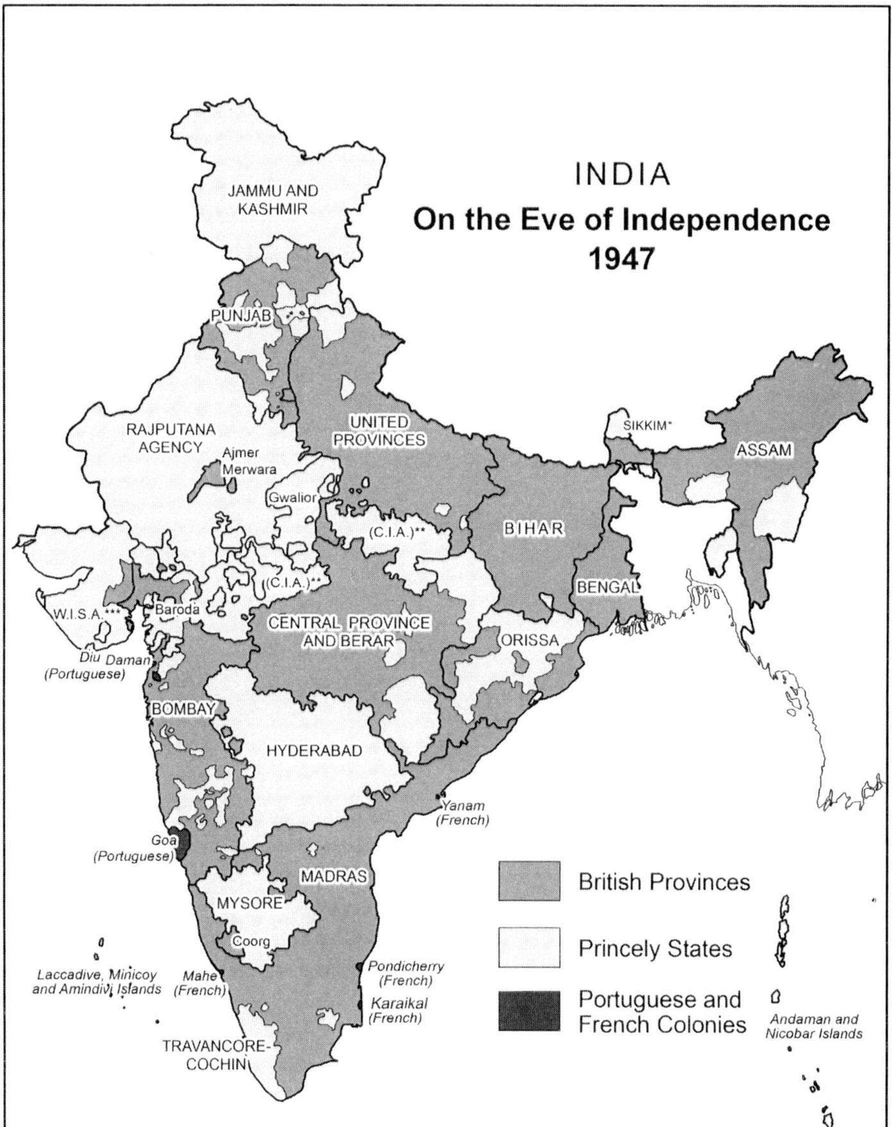

* Sikkim became a part of India in 1975
** CIA is Central India Agency
*** WISA is Western India States Agency

The pre-independence map of India was laid with boundaries of nine full or part British provinces, 556 princely states, five centrally administered areas, and some scattered Portuguese and French colonies.

Map 2.4

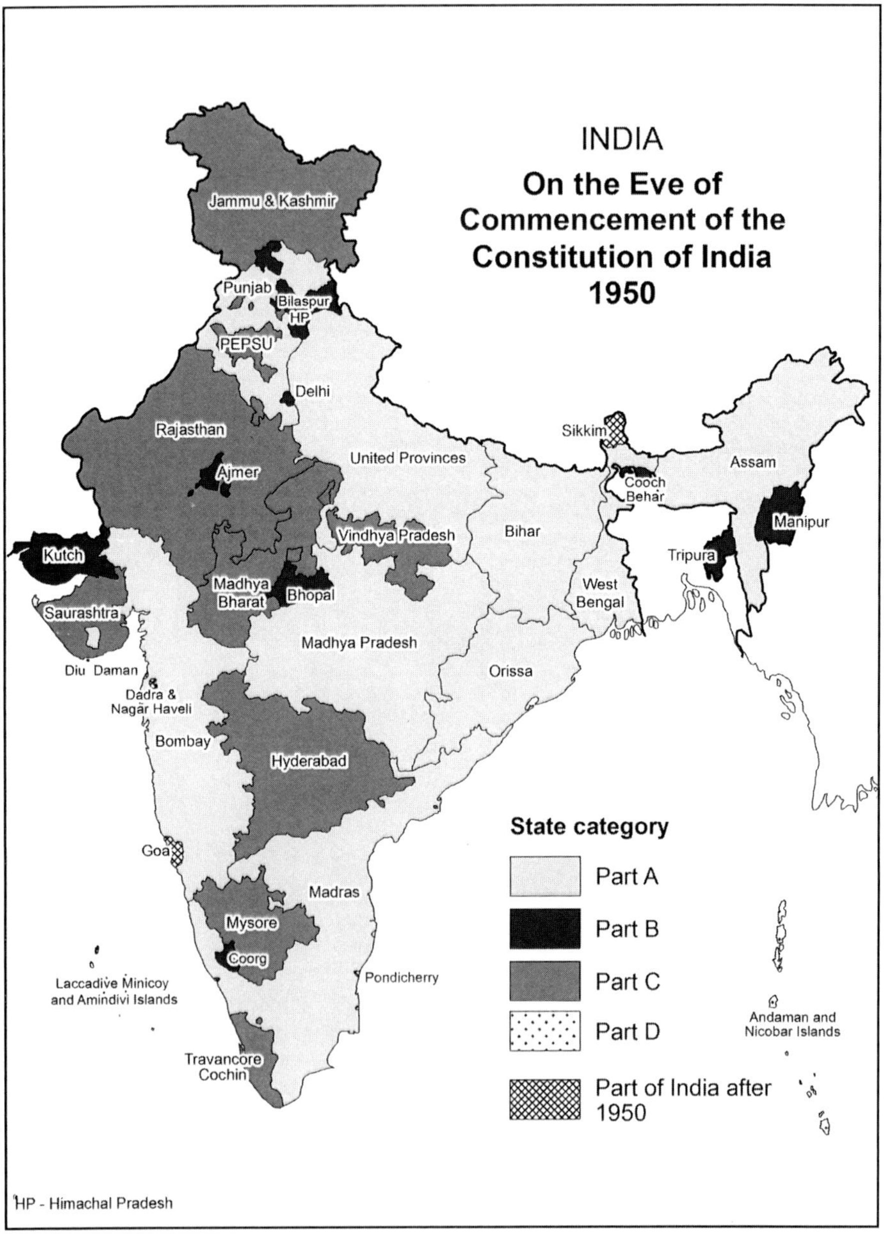

The administrative map of India was recast into 28 states grouped into four categories of hierarchial order after independence.

Map 2.5

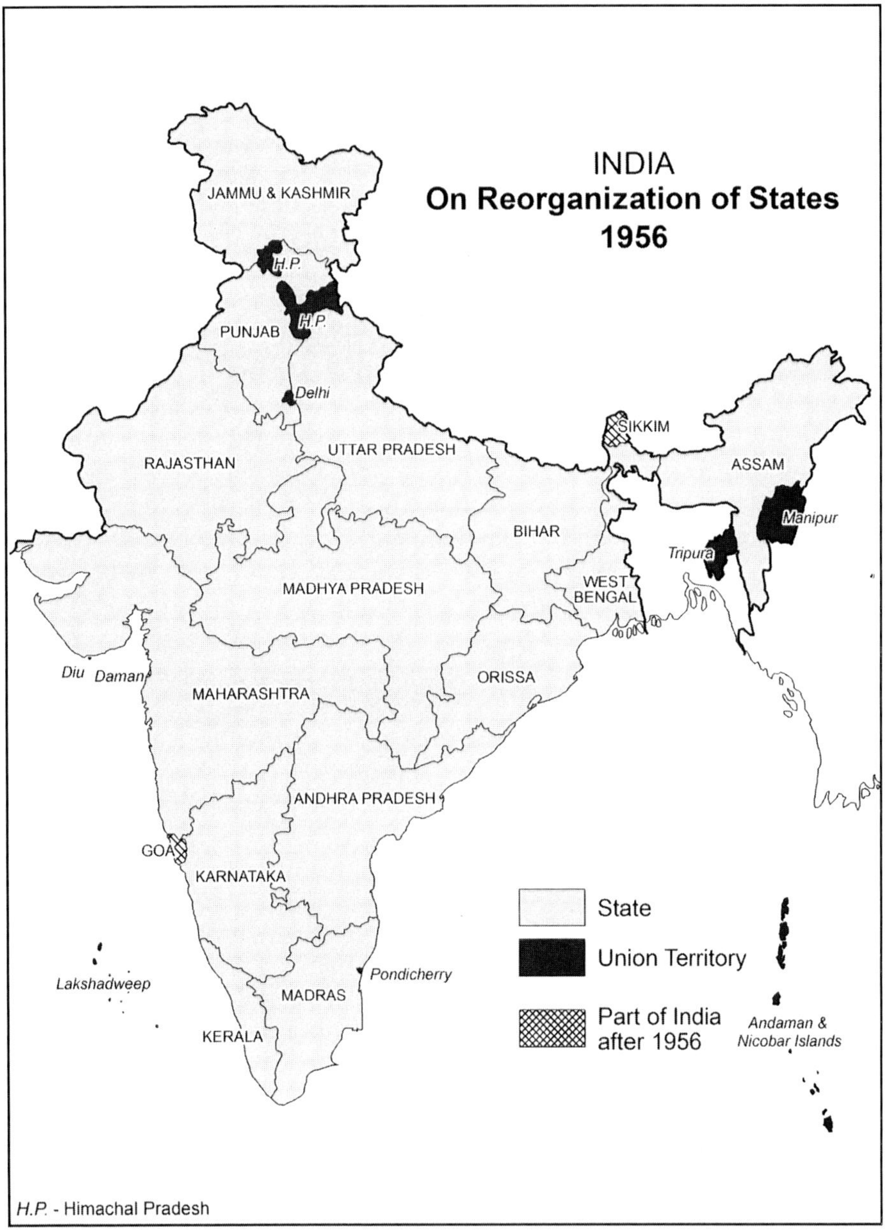

The administrative map of India was reorganized into 14 states and 6 union territories in 1956, primarily on linguistic lines.

case further. A rationalization process of the country's internal political map has been a regular feature since Independence and today India has 29 states and seven union territories.

What kind of a geographical hand one can discern underlying this process? Borrowing a term from quantitative geography, one can visualize the play of cluster analysis as operative on the internal political map of India. This rendered states more homogeneous within and simultaneously more distinct from each other in terms of ecology, sociology and history. Uttar Pradesh got bereft of its hilly and mountainous segment in the north-west for formation of Uttaranchal, later renamed as Uttarakhand. Punjab lost its Haryana part to become linguistically homogeneous within. Tribal territories of Nagaland, Meghalaya and Mizoram were taken out of Assam to emerge as ethnic states in their own right. Telangana got separated from Andhra Pradesh on the pretext of its different political history.

Essentially the formation of states involved linguistic, tribal/ethnic and historical considerations. The effort was to resolve issues relating to sharing of identity, power and resources. Official prerogatives and economic dividends were always in sight. With the territorial remoteness of distant peripheries having been reduced, incidence of inward looking sharpened among states. A fresh kind of development synergy materialized. This got manifest in a rise in interstate disparities and a reduction in intra-state imbalance. Paradoxically some of the states, such as Jharkhand, Chhattisgarh and Uttarakhand, which took birth on the pretext of backwardness, neglect and exploitation, were actually higher on several parameters of development than their parent states.

Khilnani (2004: p. 194) rightly sums up the picture by observing that in India the regional contest is over cultural recognition and economic opportunities. These goals could be achieved only through ownership of the state. The demand for formation of new states is unabated. One may come across further change in the internal political map of India in own life time.

Such a reality is facilitated by the Article 3(i) of the Constitution of India. While in the case of United States of America, the boundaries of individual states are sacrosanct, in India the situation is otherwise. Article IV (Section 3) of the Constitution of the United States of America states that new states may be admitted by the Congress into the Union, but no new state shall be formed or erected within the jurisdiction of any other state, nor any state to be formed by the junction of two or more states, or parts of states, without the consent of the legislature of the states concerned as well as of the Congress. In India, the territorial integrity of the nation-state is supreme but the boundaries of the states can be tampered with for formation of new states through simple majority of those present in the Parliament on the day of reckoning. An extreme hypothetical proposition is posed thus: In a joint House of 783 members (543 Lok Sabha members and 240 Rajya Sabha members) in the Parliament, where quorum is 10 per cent of the total or 78 members, 40 members present could work out an entirely recast territorial framework of states in India!

While reflecting on regionalism as operative in India, Adhikari (2011: pp. 258–61) identifies it as of three types. The first kind is supra-state in nature. This is the situation wherein one group of states vies with other group. This was the case when South Indian states and North Indian states came into conflict with each other on the adoption of Hindi as the sole official language in early 1960s. The former group was successful in thwarting this proposal. The second type is interstate regionalism. Several states have disputes over river waters, territory or other issues. The distribution of Kaveri waters has for long been a contentious situation between Karnataka and Tamil Nadu. Unresolved remains the situation of counter-claims of Punjab and Haryana over the territory of Chandigarh. Also, all the states do vie with each other on the criteria to be adopted for devolution of funds from the centre. With a tilt in favour of backward states, these are viewed as unfavourable by relatively developed states like Punjab. The third variety of regionalism is of intra-state kind in the form of subregionalism. This has been termed as regions within regions (Kumar, 2012), illustrated by a demand of Vidarbha in Maharashtra, Gorkhaland in West Bengal and Kalinga in Odisha. Several of such demands find their roots in pre-Independence political map of India marked by vivid diversity within British provinces and aggressive sense of identity in the case of large princely states.

An insight into regionalization of polity and emerging assertiveness on the part of states since 1990s is the thrust of various papers in the book edited by Dua and Singh (2003). Such a tendency finds varied expressions. States in general would like the transfer of at least one-half of the financial resources available with the central government and greater autonomy in spending these on the development agenda as per their own priorities. The less developed states complain the transfer of their bank deposits to more developed states for investment. This is testified by the credit-deposit ratio of various states. Not even half of the bank deposits in states like Uttar Pradesh and Bihar gets invested within the state. There are states like Tripura which desire a free hand in trade with other countries, such as Bangladesh. A fresh classification of states is also offered: ethnic states, such as Punjab, South Indian states and the North-East states; ecologically distinctive states, such as Himachal Pradesh, Uttarakhand and Jharkhand; and composite-plural states, such as Rajasthan, Gujarat, Maharashtra and Karnataka, wherein distinct subregions coalesce. In right earnest, Weiner (1968) had made a case for a comparative study of state politics in India. He underlined that the historical legacy, social structure and political economy of different states was not the same. A varying impact of all this on the functioning of their democracy and vitality is worthy of investigation.

How has globalization impacted upon the state system of India? Have states become less dependent upon each other? Are they looking more to other countries as market of their products and as source of raw materials? It looks that globalization has led to further integration of inter-state market (Nayar, 2014). Facilitated by the new regime of liberalized economy, every state is trying hard to increase production in different spheres and the already entrenched interstate dependence for inputs and market has got a further fillip. The rapid expansion of middle class has meanwhile created an increased demand for all variety of goods. The pre-reform internal market integration, which was supported by the national policy of import substitution and export promotion, has no weakness due to an overall spurt in the country's economic activity. Exports also had limits in the face of competition from other countries in the world market. Globalization certainly extended the entry of Indian states into world market but simultaneously reinforced their dependence upon each other.

From Nation-State to State-Nation

The very idea of India is taking a significant turn. It is getting transformed from a construct of nation-state to that of a state-nation. A nation-state by definition is a spatial entity marked by diversity but simultaneously possessing commonality of culture and history. Sovereignty, political legitimacy to rule and recognition by the international community are basic to its existence. Essentially it is a mosaic of historical-ethnic-spatial units each of which enjoys the status of a state or province at the subnational level. Gradually the ethnic basis of these units becomes secondary and their political autonomy acquires a higher assertion. The idea of political eminence of states starts overpowering the sentiment of ethnicity which is taken as an established fact. This marks the transition of a nation-state to state-nation. Herein every state enjoys a considerable degree of flexibility in adaptation of governance to requirements of its own specific political economy, sociology and tradition. This is a phenomenon common to several federal nation-states, such as Canada, Malaysia and the United Kingdom. For countries like Myanmar, which are characterized by aggressive ethno-territorial loyalties, the idea of state-nation is more appropriate to adopt in place of aiming at a hurried consolidation as a nation-state.

There is an increasing recognition of the role of the state in shaping the destiny of India. Panagariya, Chakraborty and Govinda (2014) highlight that today state governments are primarily responsible for development of their states. They enjoy considerable powers in respect of the subjects on the state and concurrent lists enshrined in the Constitution of India. They are the ones to implement all the programmes and schemes formulated at the national level. The centre may have framed a uniform development agenda but the specific priorities, implementation style, and performance levels do differ by states. Hence a lot what happens at the ground level rests within the state governments. This is a healthy trend no doubt (Yadav and Palshikar, 2008). The emergence of states as real and imagined political regional entities should be a welcome development. This is to be done without weakening the larger national unity or suppressing subregional communities. True federalism lies in 'self rule plus shared rule' (Elazar, 1987: p. 14).

By implication, India is now on a different model of nationhood which believes in celebration of the salience of individual states. Several of these are equivalent of major countries of the world (Table 2.1). Population of Uttar Pradesh equals that of Brazil; Maharashtra is of same population size as Mexico; and Tamil Nadu is equivalent of Iran in demographics (Map 2.6). There is a shift from an earlier ideology which saw powerful states as a challenge to the integrity of the nation-state. No more now. Such a development bears a comparison with current situation in Europe where a push toward more powers to the centre is visible in several countries, such as France, Germany and Spain. The diversity of Europe had been sorted out through evolution of countries on politico-ethnic lines but immigration on a considerable scale has given rise to a new multi-ethnic situation to deal with. This has called for a rewriting of the style of governance. In India, by comparison, diversity is taken as a legacy of history and enjoys the constitutional support of democracy, secularism and sub-national autonomy. The rise of regional parties, rooted in ethnolinguistic ecology, is generating a milieu of decentred democracy (Bose, 2013). As a result, states are acquiring a higher degree of leverage and play a significant role in formation of the government at the central level. An urge to control the affairs of the state is a political design of every regional leader.

An outcome of this upsurge of healthy '*stateism*' is vivid on the political landscape of India. Different states are in competition with each other on development agenda. Some of them have acquired brand identities. That is how we talk about Gujarat model of development or of Kerala for that matter, Tamil Nadu or even of Bihar. Made in Maharashtra, Madhya Pradesh, Chhattisgarh, Gujarat and Punjab (Ludhiana) are already in news. Sikkim favours a totality of focus on organic products. Such states are becoming models of development, friendly governance and magnets of investment.

The spatial configuration of such a branding has been changing over time. Punjab was posited as a model of agricultural development for all other states at one time, not now. West Bengal enjoyed eminence as an industrially advanced state but no more. Bihar was known for an efficient administration in years after Independence but today is usually seen in another light. Meanwhile, there is a strong political voice in favour of 'Make in India'. Inferentially, it is a call for an India model concurrent with specific models of different states. An interesting chapter on branding architecture is turning pages in the country's production book. One is inclined to bear a searching question in mind. 'Is India going to be a branded house or a house of brands'. You can visualize and realize. Such a scenario is not seen as an existential threat to the country. It is in the destiny of India to evolve with a changing regional order from time to time.

Table 2.1 *Country Equivalents of States and Union Territories of India in Population, 2011*

Sr. No.	*States/UTs*	*Population in 2011 (in million)*	*Equivalent Country*	*Population in 2011 (in million)*
1	Uttar Pradesh	199.6	Brazil	203.4
2	Maharashtra	112.4	Mexico	113.7
3	Bihar	103.8	Philippines	101.8
4	West Bengal	91.4	Vietnam	90.5
5	Tamil Nadu	72.1	Iran	77.9
6	Madhya Pradesh	72.6	Turkey	78.8
7	Rajasthan	68.6	Thailand	66.7
8	Karnataka	61.1	United Kingdom	62.7
9	Gujarat	60.4	Italy	61.0
10	Andhra Pradesh	49.4	South Korea	48.8
11	Odisha	42.0	Argentina	41.8
12	Telangana	35.3	Algeria	35.0
13	Kerala	33.4	Canada	34.0
14	Jharkhand	33.0	Morocco	32.0
15	Assam	31.2	Nepal	29.4
16	Punjab	27.7	Malaysia	28.7
17	Chhattisgarh	25.5	Ghana	24.4
18	Haryana	25.4	Australia	21.8
19	Jammu & Kashmir	12.6	Greece	10.8
20	Uttarakhand	10.1	Hungary	10.0
21	Himachal Pradesh	6.9	Switzerland	7.6
22	Tripura	3.7	Moldova	4.3
23	Meghalaya	3.0	Armenia	3.0
24	Manipur	2.7	Mongolia	3.1
25	Nagaland	2.0	Macedonia	2.1
26	Goa	1.5	Mauritius	1.3
27	Arunachal Pradesh	1.4	Qatar	0.9
28	Mizoram	1.1	Estonia	1.3
29	Sikkim	0.6	Bhutan	0.7
	Union Territories			
1	Delhi	16.8	Netherlands	16.8
2	Puducherry	1.2	Bahrain	1.2
3	Chandigarh	1.1	Fiji Islands	0.9
4	Andaman and Nicobar Islands	0.4	Bahamas	0.3
5	Dadar and Nagar Haveli	0.3	Belize	0.3
6	Daman and Diu	0.2	Vinatu	0.2
7	Lakshadweep	0.06	Bermuda	0.08

Source: Census of India, 2011 and World Statistics, 2015.

Here it would be apt to reflect on differing ideas on appellation of the caption nation-state to India. Keeping in view the reality of this country, Oommen (2009) suggests that it would be more appropriate to call it as a

Map 2.6

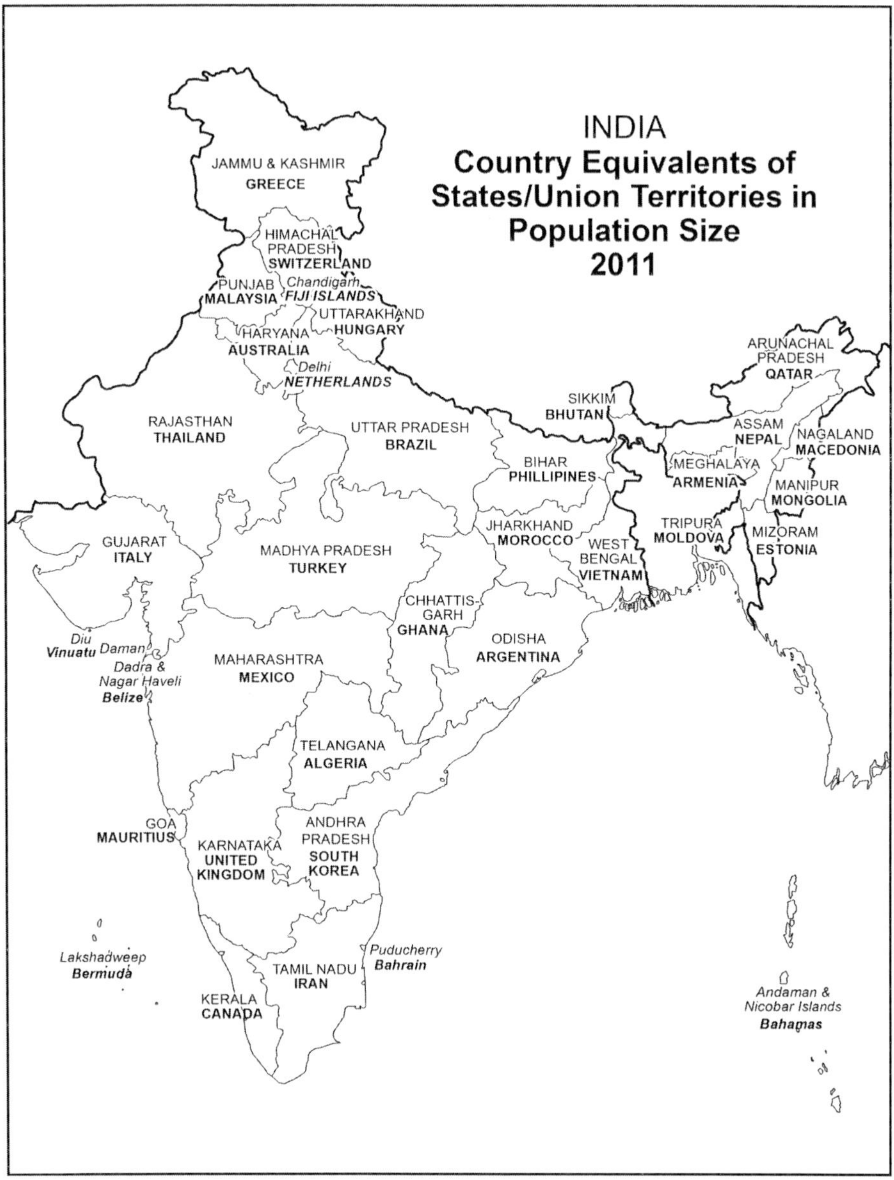

Population of several states of India approximately equals the population of a number of major countries in the world; Uttar Pradesh is Brazil, Gujarat is Italy, and Kerala, Canada.

Source: Census of India, 2011 and World population Statistics, 2015.

'multinational state'. The idea is to give recognition to the existence of several nationalities within the body structure of India. But then 'multinational' has a different connotation in the business world. There is an upper end control in its context and a spatial contiguity of the units under management is not an issue in the case of multinationals. India is not a fragmented entity. On somewhat similar lines, Tilly (1990: p. 43) had earlier suggested that it will be more apt to designate India as a national-state rather nation-state. He defines the national-state as the one which is 'relatively centralized, internally differentiated entity, in which the constituent units enjoy considerable autonomy'. This idea quite much aligns with the concept of nation-state. Then why not to hold on to a firmly established terminology. A more appropriate term would be the state-nation in the context of contemporary scenario.

One may raise an additional exacting question for consideration. Is India more than sum of its parts, as posed upon by Tharoor (2015)? Is there some methodology available to answer this question? What possibly it could be? One way would be to find out the proportion of people who assert that they are Indian first and in next order is their any other territorial allegiance. In no way this is meant to minimize their pride in the state to which they belong. It is geared to ascertain the pride in the contribution their state is making to the overall vitality of India.

Measures of Regional Vitality

With an overriding faith in eminence of nation-state, the vitality of its various regions is taken as a given fact. The assumption is that rules of the game for every part of the nation-state, as enshrined in the Constitution, are the same. Hence even a holistic spatial view of vitality will do. The substance and style of geography is let go in this process. One is left craving for a comprehensive treatment of the individual parts of the whole. This is for geographers to take it as a challenge and demonstrate their relevance by correcting such a perspective. A computation of the relative vitality status of various regions becomes necessary for the purpose. This raises, in its own turn, the question of selecting representative, meaningful and measurable criteria and indicators.

One powerful criterion to gauge the vitality of a region is the quality of governance. A peaceful law and order situation, stable policy regime, and dynamic functioning of every component of the system are the hallmarks of quality governance. In a liberal context like that of India, the share of private sector in total investment is a summary representative of all such conditions. The operational dynamics of the private sector investment is contingent upon the capacity of governance to create and ensure a milieu which is promotive of individual and collective effort.

Many would vote for economic dynamism as a conspicuous criterion of a region's vitality. This has a symbiotic relationship with the quality of governance. It aims at a regular rise in productivity to ensure continuing promotion of economic well-being. For that reason, the incremental capital-output ratio or the ratio between investment and growth emerges as its strong representative indicator. More output with less input is a measure of economic vitality.

Good governance and economic dynamism are expected to give rise to a desired quality of living space. This refers to the housing conditions and availability of amenities which promise healthy and happy living for the people at large. The percentage of households having the facility of a *pucca* house, treated water supply, desired sanitation arrangements and assured provision of electricity are viable indicators on this count.

The rise of the middle class, which is described as harbinger of change and transformational in nature, is a criterion of high value. This class of populace is the most vibrant ingredient of a system. The contribution they make as a human and economic resource of any society is universally acknowledged. The percentage of population belonging to the middle class is indeed a powerful indicator of a region's vitality.

Since in India every region is characterized by diversity of people belonging to different religious communities, linguistic groups and domicile background, the capacity to manage multi-cultural situations emerges as an imperative criterion of vitality. The extent to which the governance is capable of balancing the conflicting interests of different groups, the civil society is successful in mobilizing variety of people for a common cause, and individuals honour otherness and enjoy diversity is a test of a vitality of a region. This can be evaluated through the indicator of relationship between the indices of demographic heterogeneity and development level.

The vitality of a region is reflected in the degree of its interconnectivity with the wider global context. This interconnectivity is best established through international migration. The diaspora plays a critical role in building bridges across nations and ensures dividends to both the source and destination areas. They are the ones who took a challenge in raising new homes in other countries and at the same time retained their allegiance to homelands. Hence one is justified in adopting 'diaspora size' as one critical measure of a region's vitality. The associated indicator can be suggested as 'percentage of households with at least one member as emigrant'.

By any reckoning the above listing is illustrative. These are covered in detail in successive chapters of this book. One could conceive more of such significant criteria and related indicators. The criterion of technology input in the system deserves a special mention in this reckoning. Technology is emerging as essential, rather indispensable factor for efficient and just governance, cost-effective and quality production and comfortable and exciting living condition of the people. The incidence of e-governance, e-commerce and population making use of internet facility offers itself as a reliable indicator of this parameter. Likewise the vibrancy of the people's life journey and rhythm of daily life of people in India is significantly associated with mass energy of religious centres and places of worship. An analysis of vitality of regions will be incomplete without incorporation of the power of faith as a criterion. A ready indicator to this effect would be the size and spacing of the places of pilgrimage as also the frequency and density of the places of worship. While such parameters are worthy of consideration, these were left out for want of requisite data. It is important to reiterate that the selected criteria are powerful enough to realize the intended purpose.

Folk Songs as Vitality Melodies

At the deeper philosophic level, every piece of land on this earth is vital or else how our planet would be functioning as an integrated entity. For that matter, every part of India has its own virtues which only its inhabitants can tell you. You have to hear the folk songs with a purpose. On this ground the folk songs are a ready help. One discovers the vitality of every land captured in their words, rhythm and melody. Enjoy these expressions scrabbled from a Mizo folk song in English translation:

Mizoram is a land of
Clear blue skies and mist laden hills....
On its fragrant trees
You will find a song bird
To smoothen your nerves.
This is real celebration of life
In the lap of nature with which
Mizoram is abundantly blessed.

Here is another nugget from Ladakh:

On the height of Taru, my village,
A mighty glacier is being formed...
It will give birth to a turquoise lake
Where there is a genesis of bubbling dancing stream
Flowing impetuously, foaming and roaring
It will infuse life in the valley
Fields and pastures will become verdant.

....

Amidst snow ice and boulders
I will go to collect the herbs of divinity
The incense of herbs may reach heaven
Riding the horse of pluming smoke.

Hence, in any study of regional vitality, it is essential to capture the way the concerned people will define this concept. Every piece of land is sacred. Only its natives can confirm in which way they revel in its glory and revere its exceptionalism. Primary source of vitality is indigenous. It is essentially a cultural resource. It is a creative societal energy. All this is reserved for a separate special study.

References

Acemoglu, Daron and James A. Robinson. 2012. *Why Nations Fail: The Origins of Power, Prosperity and Poverty*. New York: Gown Business.

Adhikari, Sudeepta. 2011. *Political Geography of India*. Allahabad: Sharda Pustak Bhawan.

Ahmad, Aijazuddin. 1999. *Social Geography*. Jaipur: Rawat Publications.

Bose, Sumantra. 2013. *Transforming India: Challenges to World's Largest Democracy*. Harvard: Harvard University Press.

Deshpande, C.D. 1992. *India: A Regional Interpretation*. New Delhi: Northern Book Centre.

Diamond, Jared. 2005. *Collapse: How Societies Choose to Fail or Succeed*. New York: Penguin.

Dua, B.D. and M.P. Singh. 2003. *Indian Federalism in the New Millennium*. New Delhi: Manohar.

Elazar, Donald J. 1987. *Exploring Federalism*. Tuscaloosa: University of Alabama Press.

Ferguson, Niall. 2013. *The Great Degeneration: How the Institutions Decay and Economies Die*. New York: Penguin.

Hubbard, Glenn and Tim Kane. 2013. *Balance: The Economics of Great Powers from Ancient Rome to Modern America*. New York: Simon and Schuster.

Kant, Surya. 1988. *Administrative Geography of India*. Jaipur: Rawat Publications.

Kennedy, Paul M. 1989. *The Rise and Fall of Great Powers: Economic Change and Military Conflict from 1500 to 2000*. London: Vintage.

Khilnani, Sunil. 2004. *The Idea of India*. New Delhi: Penguin.

Kumar, Ashutosh. 2012. *Rethinking State Politics in India*. New Delhi: Routledge.

Landes, David. 1998. *The Wealth and Poverty of Nations*. New York: W.W. Norton.

Muller, Jerry Z. 2008. Us and Them: The Enduring Power of Ethnic Nationalism. *Foreign Affairs*. Vol. 87, No. 2, pp. 18–35.

National Geographic. 2013. *Concise History of the World*. Washington, D.C.

Nayar, Baldev Raj. 2014. *Globalisation and India's Economic Integration*. Washington, D.C.: Georgetown University Press.

Oommen, T.K. 2009. Development Policy and the Nature of Society: Understanding the Kerala Model. *Economic and Political Weekly*. Vol. 44, No. 13, March 28, pp. 25–31.

Panagariya, Arvind, Pinaki Chakraborty and M. Govinda. 2014. *State Level Reforms, Growth and Development in Indian States*. New Delhi: Oxford University Press.

Spengler, Oswald. 1918 and 1922. *The Decline of the West, Volumes I and II*. New York: Alfred A. Knopf.

Schwartzberg, Joseph E. 1978. *A Historical Atlas of India*. Chicago and London: University of Chicago Press.

Spate, O.H.K. and A.T.A. Learmonth. 1965. *India and Pakistan: A General and Regional Geography*. London: Methuen.

Tainter, Joseph A. 1988. *The Collapse of Complex Societies*. Cambridge: Cambridge University Press.

Tharoor, Shashi. 2015. *Indian Shastra: Reflections on the Nation in Our Time*. New Delhi: Aleph Book Company.

Tilly, Charles. 1990. *Coercion, Capital and European States, AD 999–1990*. Cambridge: Basil Blackwell.

Toynbee, Arnold J. 1934 to 1961. *A Study of History (12 Volumes)*. Oxford: Oxford University Press.

Weiner, Myron. 1968. *State Politics in India*. Princeton: Princeton University Press.

Wimmer, Andreas and Yuval Feinstein. 2010. The Rise of Nation-state Across the World. *American Sociological Review*. Vol. 745, No. 5, pp. 764–790.

Yadav, Yogendra and Suhas Palshikar. 2008. Ten Theses on State Politics in India. *Seminar*. No. 591, November, pp. 14–22.

3

Quality of Governance

The vitality of a region has a symbiotic relationship with the quality of its governance. Precisely governance refers to all variety of institutions and traditions by which authority is exercised (Kauffman et al., 2004: p. 3). This is operationalized through a well organized system, sagacious policies, appropriate decisions, effective implementation and visible impact. A professional bureaucracy, an efficient provision of public services and a dependable system of law and order are to be ensured for the purpose. Governance covers not only the three different wings of the government, that is executive, legislature and judiciary, but also includes the way private sector is managed, civil society is involved, households are made to participate and individuals are facilitated in playing their constructive roles.

Governance refers to the quality of public and private institutions, which in turn is related to 'how decisions get made and in whose interest' (Stiglitz, 2006: pp. 55–56). The foremost change in the mode of governance has been a transformation from centralized government to a plurality of self organizing, coexisting networks and partnerships that interact at diverse spatial scales (Hubbard et al., 2002: p. 202). By that token, governance is pertinent to not only national governments but also subnational units, local bodies, private/corporate sector and international organizations, among others. More often the concept is analysed for the governments at the national and subnational levels. Matters related to the process by which actors in governance are selected, law and order is maintained, efficient and equitable development is secured and public-private partnership is harnessed also fall in the domain of governance theme. The concept, thus, covers practically the entire scope of government and society (Indian Institute of Public Administration, 2012: p. 3).

Good governance has been adorned with elegant vocabulary in development literature. It is described as efficient, equitable, effective and inclusive. A plea for reinventing government on these lines was made by

Osborne and Gaebler (1992). The objective is to create an environment which enables individuals to raise the level of their well-being, upgrade their capability level and realize their potential. For this, good governance is to function in the mode of public management. It has to ensure rule of law, decentralization of the planning and implementation process, and effectiveness of the administrative cost involved. The most challenging task for any governance is to build a trust in the government.

The real test lies in translating all this in practice. In the field of planning, this finds a concrete expression in the *Twelfth Five Year Plan 2012–2017* document of the Planning Commission of India, now NITI Aayog or National Institution for Transforming India (2012: p. 286). It states that good governance is critical to translating plan outlays into significant outcomes on the ground. There has to be rational allocation of available resources, impactful implementation of development projects, and regular monitoring and evaluation of what was intended. This is expected to have desired effect on conservation of natural resources which are sovereign wealth. Guidelines on similar lines are to be laid out for other spheres of public life.

A thought provoking commentary on the relationship between the quality of governance and its various determinants is presented by La Porta et al. (1999). The observations they make are based on a regression analysis of data for 152 countries, mostly for 1990s. They affirm that the following factors are promotive of good governance: (i) an optimal size of the government; (ii) economic development; (iii) ethnic homogeneity; (iv) English legal roots as opposed to the French, German or Socialist; (v) Protestant cultural ethos vis-à-vis Catholic or Islamic; and (vi) location on northern latitudes. A cultural and locational bias of this formulation cannot be missed. They assert that in some situations good governance and development can be neutral to each other. Dictatorial regimes have proved more productive in certain cases, of course, for a limited period of time. Meanwhile, one cannot dispute their contention that political freedom plays a positive role, political polarization is divisive and ethnic strife is detrimental to good governance.

Functional Trajectory of Modern State

Micklethwait and Woolridge (2014) trace the evolutionary ecology of the modern state. They identify four revolutions in this context. The first revolution refers to the emergence of the nation-state wherein the territorial integrity and political sovereignty are the main concerns. The second revolution pertains to upgradation of a nation-state into a liberal one wherein issues of personal liberty and group rights come into prominence. The third revolution transforms a nation-state into a welfare state wherein government is responsible for providing and maintaining quality services to the people, especially in respect of education, health and social security. These revolutions in succession can be illustrated by the case of the United

Kingdom. Now a fourth revolution is in the offing. One of its manifestations is the Singapore and Chinese models of governance. Herein state directed capitalism and authoritarian modernization are the catchwords for raising a 21st century state. Such a line of thinking gives rise to a question. What should be the key directive principle for functioning of a nation-state; paradigm of efficiency or that of ideology? The current thinking favours the one that works best. Pragmatism triumphs over idealism.

A perusal of literature on the theory and practice of governance informs that efficacy of government is measured generally on its success in matters relating to macro-governance. In focus remains the steering capacity of those who run the administration. Size, structure and function of bureaucracy, framework of public finance and design of public policy are listed as major parameters of such an analysis.

A time has come when the thrust of studies on governance should shift from macro-governance to micro-governance. There is a need to move from the ashes of the traditional bureaucratic theories to a new *avatar* of interactive governance (Gupta, 2014: p. 28). This interactive dimension of governance is a scenario where bureaucracy and the people come into direct interface with each other. Reference is being made here to services which people require and are entitled to obtain from government institutions. Some illustrations include the imperative of getting, without hassle, certification of birth and death, registration of property and attestation of hailing from a reserved category and so on. All this pertains to what people expect from the government rather than what government proposes to do for them. The same idea of focusing upon the felt requirements of the people has been urged by Hilton (2016). He favours human in place of technical dimension of governance to prevail. This is how governance translates itself into vitality of a state.

Criteria and Indicators of Quality of Governance

Most of the studies aiming at international comparisons of governance quality are based on the criteria and indicators of macro-governance. The Sustainable Governance Indicators, formulated by the Organization of European Countries for Development (OECD), refer governance to two first-level indices: 'Status Index' and 'Management Index'. 'Status Index' covers the parameters of democracy, economy, employment, social affairs, security and resources. 'Management Index' has, under its umbrella, the items of steering capability, policy implementation and institutional accountability. Obviously several of these criteria refer to the desirable context of government rather than to performance text of the government.

Using such a theoretical framework, Bertelsmann Foundation has devised a Bertelsmann Transformation Index (BTI) to analyse the quality of democracy, market economy and political management in 129 developing and transition countries. Quality of democracy and reach of economy embody the 'Status Index' and political functioning covers the 'Management

Index'. The index is updated every two years. In 2016, Taiwan was at the top rank on this index, India 28th, China 84th, Pakistan 106th and Somalia 129th at the bottom.

A simple quantitative measure of good governance is provided by Huther and Shah (1998). They processed data for a sample of 80 countries. Central to the formulation of their idea is that good governance is obliged to align the provision of all variety of services to what people need and desire. The four criteria and related indicators include: (i) citizen participation (political freedom, political stability); (ii) government orientation (judicial expediency, bureaucratic efficiency, lack of corruption); (iii) social development (human development, egalitarian income distribution); and (iv) economic management (outward orientation, central bank independence, inverted debt to GDP ratio). On this reckoning, among 80 countries in the sample, Switzerland is at the top in good governance and Liberia at the bottom. The United States of America ranks 5th, India 54th, China 59th and Pakistan 66th. A detailed analysis suggests that, among several factors, a prudent decentralization is most promotive of high quality of governance.

In their study of 64 countries, which were at one time under colonial rule, Acemoglu et al. (2000) found that as much as three-quarters of the differences in their current state of affairs can be explained by the gap in the quality of their governing institutions inherited from their colonial masters. The colonial style of the British differed from that of the French, and of the French from that of Spanish or Dutch. While Britain is noted for largely pacific decolonization, other empires got fragmented by huge disorder. The colonial impact persisted. The post-colonial societies could not free themselves from the governance legacy of their colonial masters even after gaining Independence.

The World Bank, through Worldwide Governance Indicators (WGI) Project, has also been constructing aggregate and individual indicators of governance for 215 economies on annual basis since 1996. These are consistent with definition of governance as a set of institutions and modes of practices by which authority is exercised in a country. This has threefold operational ramification. First, the processes by which governments are selected, monitored and replaced; second the capacity of the government to effectively formulate and implement sound policies; and third, the respect of citizens for the state institutions that govern economic and social interaction among them. Six dimensions of governance are enumerated: (i) voice and accountability; (ii) political stability and absence of violence; (iii) government effectiveness; (iv) regulatory authority; (v) rule of law; and (vi) control of corruption. Needless to add that all these criteria are overwhelmed by the considerations of macro-governance. A fresh wave is discernible in favour of people-centric micro-governance. The nature and intensity of interaction between the people and government is what defines the quality of governance.

In that way, Gorden (2014: p. 218) believes that the key to assessment of performance of any government is by way of addressing the following four questions: How much is it accessible to the people? To what extent are its policies and activities easily understood by people? In which way are people encouraged to interact with the government? How much feedback does government try to tap from the people about the relevance of its programmes or projects? Such questions can be transformed as viable indicators of governance quality.

The most critical aspect of governance is cultivation of trust in the government. This is subject to the promotion of a democratic culture, regular reform of administrative functioning, and involvement of civil society and private sector in affairs of governance. A real challenge lies in answering the call of multi-ethnic situations. This requires seriousness on part of the government to honour its commitments made to different groups of people whose interests clash with each other. It is in the nature of good governance to constantly reinvent itself to meet the emerging needs of the changing composition of population.

The preceding discussion, representing the ideas of a number of scholars, can be harnessed to identify criteria and indicators of good governance on theoretical lines. Such exercises invariably face serious constraint of data availability on indicators as identified on conceptual lines. There is another approach to look for indicators which aligns with the popular perception of the quality of governance. A sustained pace and inclusiveness of development is to be accorded the first place (Kohli and Sood eds., 2010: p. 2). Decentralization of governance to grassroots level is no less critical. Next in line is the success rate of the government in implementation of its own welfare schemes. Status of the Right to Services Act is also a serviceable indicator since it ensures that government provides what people urgently need. Equally important here is to consider the extent to which the cost on administration and provision of public services aligns with financial viability and propriety.

The rate of investment by private sector is still another powerful indicator on this count. It effectively mirrors the status of the functional infrastructure available in a state, the situation of its law and order and credibility of the government in honouring the negotiated obligations. Private sector is allergic to administrative lethargy, unreliability and instability. Another criterion of great significance is the spread of e-governance, which among other things, facilitates the access of people to a variety of information, services and prescribed proformas made available through information technology. Technology combines service with speed. Singapore's e-portal provides access to 1,600 e-services of which 1,300 relate exclusively to transaction between the people and government. Such an arrangement ensures efficiency, economy and transparency in the whole system.

The quality of the governance is also a function of the geographic efficacy of the organization of space for administrative purposes. This refers to the optimality of administrative areas at different levels, such as states, districts and blocks in terms of their area, shape, population size and centrality of headquarters. Too large territories tend to become unmanageable and too small are rather expensive and non-viable.

The above listed indicators conform to the line of thinking of the common people. The way the government is assessed in facilitating their daily life gets captured. The focus is upon output rather than input of governance.

There is still another approach to the issue that tends to be more comprehensive by way of covering diverse dimensions of good governance. In addition to governance index, these include decentralization mode, policy effectiveness, ease of doing business and overall performance. This is what has been done in the present study while comparing the quality of governance of various states and union territories of India. Both inputs and outputs of macro-governance as well as of micro-governance have been taken into account. A purposeful use has been made of the data generated by already available studies on the theme.

Governance Index

In a recent study, aimed at comparing the major states of India on their governance performance, Mundle et al. (2012) computed the governance indices in each case for the years 2001 and 2011. This was a sequel to their previous study in 2012 on similar lines. They maintain that criteria for this purpose should be relevant to three pillars of a developmental state, namely the executive, the judiciary and the legislature. The executive pillar is further fabricated into four key parameters: (i) delivery of infrastructure services; (ii) delivery of social services; (iii) fiscal performance and (iv) maintenance of law and order. Delivery of legal services represents the judicial pillar while composition and functioning of the legislature stands for the legislative pillar. They add that all these parameters of governance are not independent of the development level of the area concerned.

Five criteria operationalized through 14 indicators adopted for analysis included infrastructure services delivery (road and power); social services delivery (rates of infant mortality, maternal mortality, life expectancy, literacy, gross enrollment and average years of schooling); fiscal performance (development expenditure and own tax revenue); justice, law and order (proportion of trials completed in less than three years and negative rate of violent crimes); and quality of legislature (elected members free from any serious pending charge and proportion of women elected members). A comparative picture was obtained for the years 2001 and 2011. Table 3.1 presents the picture of results as obtained.

It is learnt that Gujarat and four South Indian states of Tamil Nadu, Andhra Pradesh, Kerala and Karnataka stand out for their relatively high quality of governance in both 2001 and 2011. The same is true of Punjab. By contrast, the North Indian states of Uttar Pradesh, Bihar and Jharkhand and

East Indian states of Assam, West Bengal and Odisha were noted for poor governance and stagnation during 2001–2011. The behaviour of the other states varied. While Rajasthan, Madhya Pradesh, Chhattisgarh and Uttarakhand displayed an upgradation in this respect, Haryana, Maharashtra and Himachal Pradesh showed a tendency to the contrary. Considering only the governance scores of various states over time, most of them recorded an improvement. Among various criteria, provision of infrastructure and delivery of social services were the most expressive of the overall governance performance of various states.

Table 3.1 *India: Ranking of the Major States on Quality of Governance, 2001 and 2011*

States	*Governance index in 2001*	*Rank*	*State*	*Governance index in 2011*	*Rank*	*Remarks*
Gujarat	0.66	1	Gujarat	0.65	1	At relatively high level
Tamil Nadu	0.60	2	Tamil Nadu	0.61	2	At relatively high level
Punjab	0.60	3	Andhra Pradesh*	0.59	3	At relatively high level
Kerala	0.57	4	Kerala	0.59	4	At relatively high level
Haryana	0.55	5	Punjab	0.58	5	At relatively high level
Andhra Pradesh*	0.53	6	Karnataka	0.57	6	At relatively high level
Karnataka	0.51	7	Uttarakhand	0.56	7	Rise in the middle
Maharashtra	0.5	8	Chhattisgarh	0.54	8	Rise in the middle
Himachal Pradesh	0.5	9	Haryana	0.53	9	Fall in the middle
Chhattisgarh	0.48	10	Maharashtra	0.50	10	Fall in the middle
West Bengal	0.44	11	Himachal Pradesh	0.50	11	Fall in the middle
Assam	0.43	12	Rajasthan	0.50	12	Rise in the middle
Madhya Pradesh	0.38	13	Madhya Pradesh	0.49	13	Rise in the middle
Uttarakhand	0.36	14	Assam	0.35	14	Stagnant at low level
Odisha	0.35	15	West Bengal	0.34	15	Stagnant at low level
Rajasthan	0.34	16	Odisha	0.31	16	Stagnant at low level
Jharkhand	0.27	17	Jharkhand	0.3	17	Stagnant at low level
Uttar Pradesh	0.19	18	Bihar	0.29	18	Stagnant at low level
Bihar	0.16	19	Uttar Pradesh	0.29	19	Stagnant at low level

Source: Sudipto Mundle et al. 2012. Governance Performance of Indian States. *Economic and Political Weekly*. Vol. 51, No. 36, pp. 55–64.
* Includes Telangana.

Mathew et al. (2016) have recently prepared an elaborate report on the comparative governance quality of different states of India. They carried out a rigorous analysis of the data covering 10 themes, 25 focus subjects and 68 indicators for the purpose. The themes and focus subjects (listed in parentheses) included essential infrastructure (power, water, roads and communication, and housing); support to human development (education and health); social protection or welfare (public distribution system, social justice and empowerment, minority welfare and employment); children and women (woman and child care); crime, law and order (violent crimes, atrocities and policing); delivery of justice (pendency of cases and vacancies of presiding officers); environment (pollution and environmental violations, forest cover and renewable energy); transparency and accountability (transparency and public accountability); fiscal management (revenue surplus/deficit, fiscal surplus and deficit burden, and resource generation and development expenditure); and economic freedom (economic freedom).

Table 3.2 *India: Quality of Governance Index of Different States, 2016 (Along with their relatively strongest and weakest focus subjects)*

States	*Index*	*Rank*	*Strongest focus subject*	*Weakest focus subject*
Kerala	0.568	1	Elected local bodies	Fiscal management
Tamil Nadu	0.550	2	Law and order	Transparency
Karnataka	0.547	3	Elected local bodies	Law and order
Mizoram	0.543	4	Public distribution system	Fiscal management
Himachal Pradesh	0.539	5	Human Development	Fiscal management
Maharashtra	0.536	6	Economic freedom	Fiscal management
Gujarat	0.535	7	Economic freedom	Woman and child care
Punjab	0.533	8	Essential infrastructure	Justice
Sikkim	0.508	9	Human Development	Transparency
Goa	0.507	10	Essential infrastructure	Environment
West Bengal	0.505	11	Public distribution system	Human development
Manipur	0.500	12	Law and order	Economic freedom
Andhra Pradesh*	0.499	13	Public distribution system	Fiscal management
Jammu & Kashmir	0.488	14	Public distribution system	Transparency
Arunachal Pradesh	0.488	15	Environment	Transparency
Meghalaya	0.484	16	Justice	Economic freedom
Haryana	0.481	17	Essential infrastructure	Law and order
Uttarakhand	0.479	18	Justice	Environment
Rajasthan	0.473	19	Economic freedom	Woman and child care
Chhattisgarh	0.472	20	Elected local bodies	Environment
Uttar Pradesh	0.461	21	Fiscal management	Human development
Nagaland	0.459	22	Law and order	Transparency
Tripura	0.453	23	Justice	Economic freedom
Madhya Pradesh	0.452	24	Economic freedom	Human development
Assam	0.446	25	Elected local bodies	Essential infrastructure
Odisha	0.442	26	Woman and child care	Essential infrastructure
Jharkhand	0.389	27	Fiscal management	Justice
Bihar	0.370	28	Fiscal management	Human development

Source: C.K. Mathew et al. 2016. *Governance in the States of India: Report*. Bengaluru: Public Affairs Centre.
* Includes Telangana.

The index of governance quality ranged from the highest of 0.568 in the case of Kerala to the lowest of 0.370 in respect of Bihar (Table 3.2). There

Map 3.1

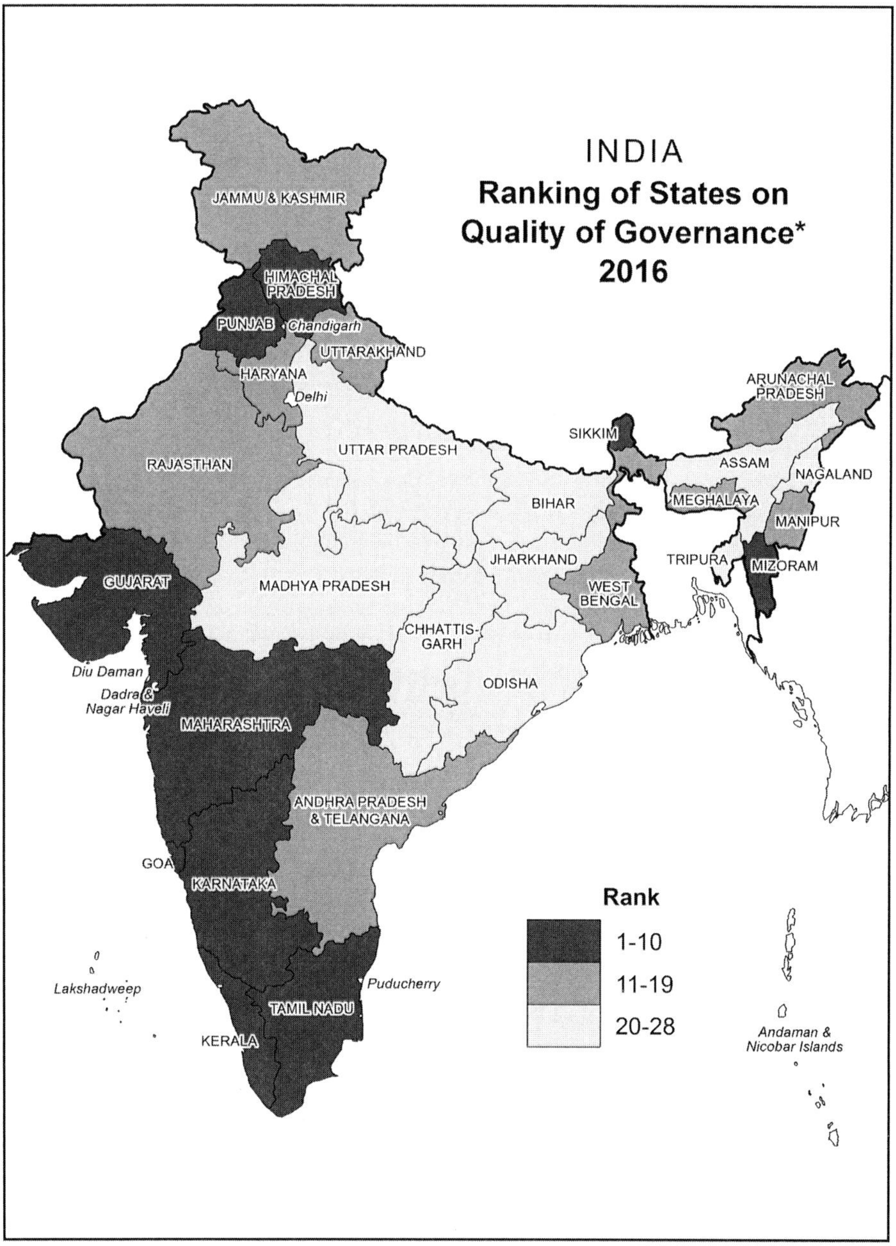

* The governance quality of different states finds a strong association with their performance in social sector, primarily health and education, apart from their income level.

Source: Governance in the States of India: Report. Public Affairs Centre, Bengaluru.

was a distinct regional pattern on this parameter. The South Indian states of Kerala, Tamil Nadu and Karnataka, the West Indian states of Maharashtra, Gujarat, and Goa, the North-East Indian states of Sikkim and Mizoram, and North-Western states of Punjab and Himachal Pradesh were noted for relatively higher quality of governance (Map 3.1). On the other hand, the northern and eastern states of Bihar, Jharkhand, Odisha and Assam, the middle belt states of Madhya Pradesh and Chhattisgarh, and North-Eastern, states of Nagaland and Tripura scored low on the governance quality. Uttar Pradesh and Rajasthan also fall in the same group. The remaining states found themselves located in the intermediate category.

The study also brings out the fact that the quality of governance is marked by a strong association with the performance in social sector, including education, health and poverty alleviation. This relationship is only of moderate degree with per capita income. The governance quality bears a weak link with the inequality in rural consumption expenditure. Notably the inequality of this kind is of a low order in several poor states.

If one carefully scans the indices of governance quality of different states and evaluates them against the conventional grading system of examination results in India, then none of the states could claim to fall in the first class with at least 60 per cent marks. Inevitable is the governance deficit in any case. At the same time, no state is a failure case as each of them has a score higher than 33 per cent. All the states have a well defined system of governance, notwithstanding considerable difference amongst them at the implementation level.

Charron (2010: pp. 177–94) tried to construct a comparative interstate run-through of corruption level in India. The study is based on a survey conducted in 2005 to capture the perception of and experience with corruption of a sample of 20,000 citizens sample from 19 major states and National Capital Territory of Delhi. Kerala recorded the lowest corruption index of 2.40 and Bihar the highest of 6.95. By that token, the two extremes exhibited a ratio of almost 1:3. On a wider spectrum, Himachal Pradesh and Gujarat, along with Kerala, were found as relatively the least corrupt and Bihar, Jammu & Kashmir and Madhya Pradesh as most corrupt. The prevalence of corruption was of lower order in states marked by relatively higher level of development and greater degree of decentralization of financial resources to elected local bodies like *panchayats* (rural) and *nagar palikas* (urban). Factors of inequality in income distribution, diversity of religious composition and exposure to media were found as rather weak in this respect.

Decentralization Index

One essential measure of good governance is the decentralization of powers from the higher hierarchical levels to the lower ones, or from the state to the local bodies. To this effect, the 73rd and 74th Amendments to the Constitution were enacted in 1992. The former amendment devolved specific powers to the *panchayats* in rural India and the latter to *nagarpalikas* in urban India. Such a revolutionary change was intended to empower local bodies in taking pertinent decisions, setting priorities and implementing plans at their level. About three million representatives are regularly elected to a quarter million local institutions all over the country under this dispensation (Government of India, 2013: p. 149).

The Ministry of Panchayati Raj, Government of India, regularly carries out an exercise to rank states and union territories on the parameters of devolution of funds, functions and functionaries from the state to local bodies. The latest picture available for the year 2012–13 is presented in Table 3.3. A wide difference in the performance of various states/union territories is observed on this count.

Table 3.3 *India: Ranking of States/Union Territories on Devolution of Powers Index, 2012–13**

States/Union Territories	*Ranking*
Maharashtra	1
Karnataka	2
Kerala	3
Rajasthan	4
Tamil Nadu	5
West Bengal	6
Madhya Pradesh	7
Chhattisgarh	8
Haryana	9
Gujarat	10
Odisha	11
Tripura	12
Uttarakhand	13
Sikkim	14
Uttar Pradesh	15
Assam	16
Himachal Pradesh	17
Goa	18
Punjab	19
Bihar	20
Jammu & Kashmir	21
Jharkhand	22
Manipur	23
Lakshadweep	24
Chandigarh	25
Arunachal Pradesh	26
Daman & Diu	27
Dadra & Nagar Haveli	28

Source: Ministry of Panchayati Raj, Government of India, New Delhi.

* Evidently the states of Andhra Pradesh, Meghalaya, Mizoram and Nagaland and the union territories of Andaman & Nicobar Islands, Delhi and Puducherry did not provide the requisite information in time to the Government of India.

Map 3.2

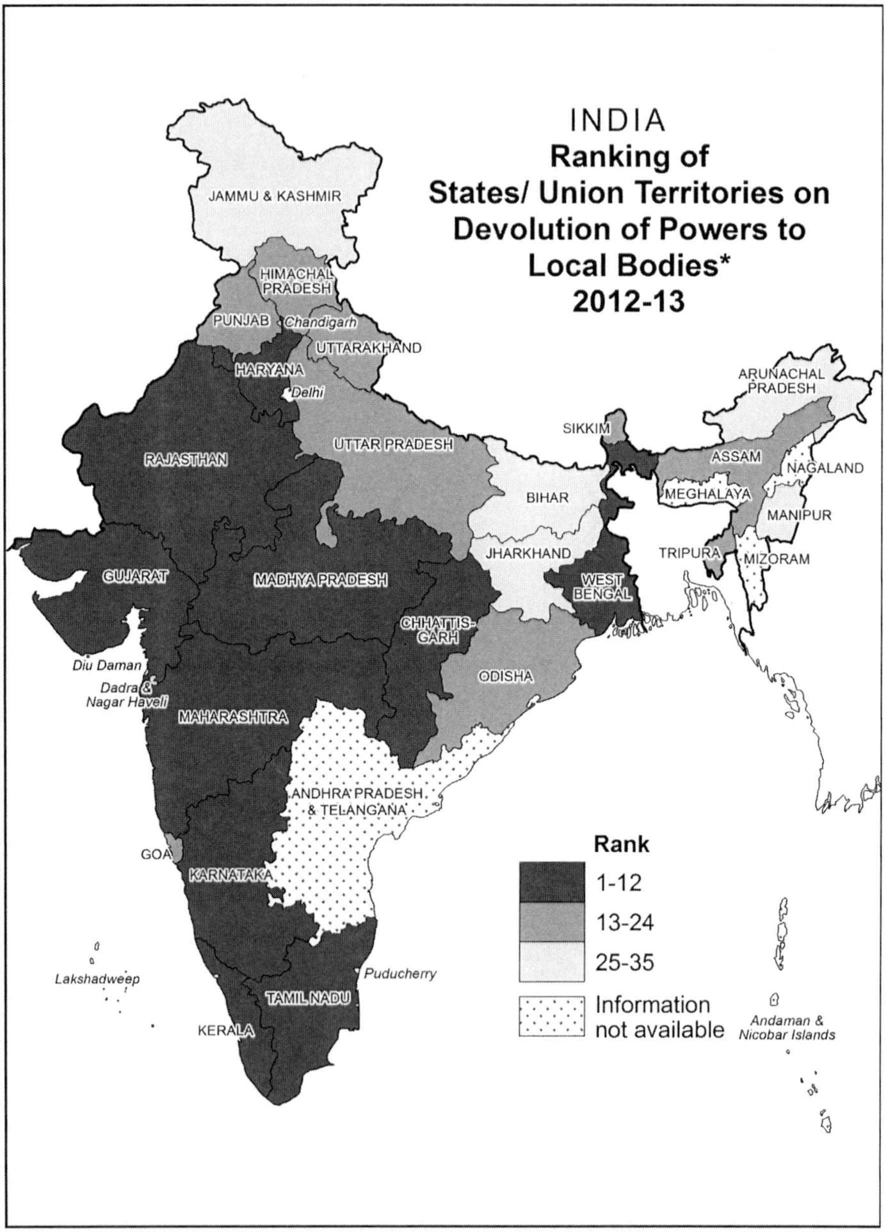

Some of the less developed states like Rajasthan and Madhya Pradesh are earnest in making their local bodies powerful while some developed states like Punjab and Goa are slow in this respect.

Source: Ministry of Panchyati Raj, Government of India, New Delhi

Some notable facts emerging from Table 3.3 are as follows. First, all the union territories are hesitant in devolving powers to the local elected bodies. Second, a number of less developed states, such as Rajasthan, Madhya Pradesh and Chhattisgarh, are showing a great enthusiasm in making their local bodies powerful. Third, some of the more developed states, on the other hand, like Goa, Punjab and Himachal Pradesh are shy in this respect. Fourth, the North-Eastern states have also a long way to go before their grassroot institutions become really functional. Fifth, the states with left orientation, namely Kerala, West Bengal and Tripura, score relatively high on strengthening local governance through decentralization of powers. Overall, the record of states in South and West India in devolving funds, functions and functionaries to the local bodies has been more creditable than that of the North Indian states (Map 3.2).

Policy Effectiveness Index

In his *India Policy Report*, Malhotra (2014) has worked out the policy effectiveness index of all the states and union territories of India. Effectiveness of a government policy is judged from the quality of its designing and implementation process and more so from its outcome in terms of human well-being. The index, in the present case, was arrived at by computing the geometric mean of indices of livelihood opportunity, social opportunity, rule of law and physical infrastructure development. Each index was further based on a number of indicators. All this could be deemed as a comprehensive exercise.

The ranking of various states and union territories in 2011 on the basis of policy effectiveness index is listed in Table 3.4.

Table 3.4 *India: Ranking of States/Union Territories on Policy Effectiveness Index, 2011*

States/Union Territories	*Index*	*Ranking*
Sikkim	0.566	1
Mizoram	0.493	2
Chandigarh	0.448	3
Goa	0.447	4
Lakshadweep	0.440	5
Punjab	0.400	6
Delhi	0.399	7
Meghalaya	0.383	8
Puducherry	0.372	9
Nagaland	0.371	10
Himachal Pradesh	0.359	11
Jammu & Kashmir	0.347	12
Arunachal Pradesh	0.345	13
Daman & Diu	0.338	14
Karnataka	0.337	15
Haryana	0.337	16

Cont'd...

Map 3.3

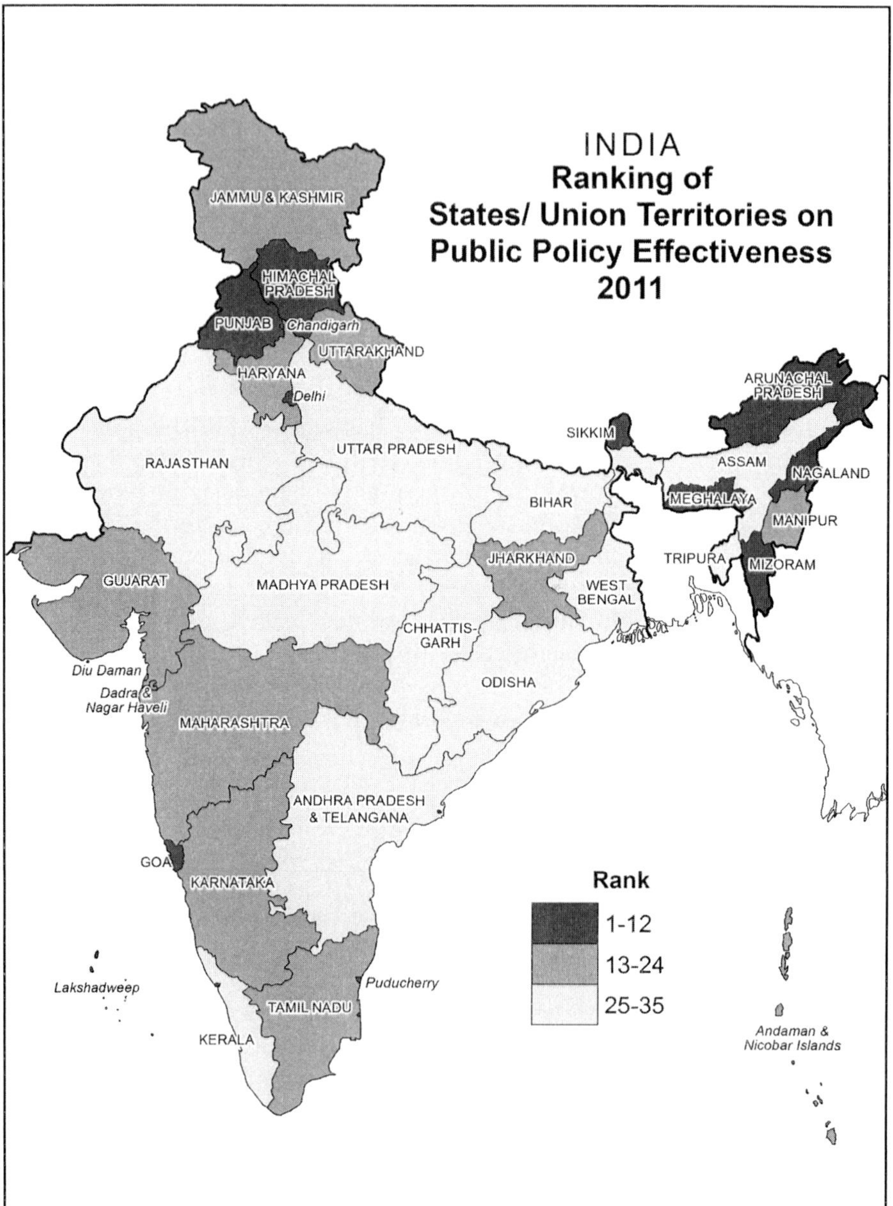

The union territories are noted for a higher degree of public policy effectiveness than the states.

Source: India Public Policy Report 2014, Oxford: New Delhi.

...Cont'd

Dadra & Nagar Haveli	0.331	17
Manipur	0.328	18
Andaman and Nicobar Isles	0.327	19
Maharashtra	0.314	20
Tamil Nadu	0.313	21
Uttarakhand	0.311	22
Jharkhand	0.310	23
Gujarat	0.305	24
Tripura	0.302	25
Rajasthan	0.281	26
Andhra Pradesh*	0.268	27
Uttar Pradesh	0.263	28
Kerala	0.256	29
West Bengal	0.251	30
Chhattisgarh	0.251	31
Assam	0.232	32
Madhya Pradesh	0.231	33
Bihar	0.223	34
Odisha	0.206	35

Source: Rajiv Malhotra. 2014. *India Public Policy Report*, New Delhi: Oxford University Press, p. 149.
* Includes Telangana.

Most of the states in North-East and North-West India are noted for a high impact of the government policies. The same could be said about the union territories. Meanwhile, the states in West and South India display only a modest impact on this count. The remaining states of India are low impact cases. A surprise inclusion in this category is that of Kerala (Map 3.3).

On the whole, this research effort does not permit much confidence. One wonders if Goa could be below Mizoram on policy effectiveness index or Nagaland could be higher than Himachal Pradesh on this count. This exercise places Manipur above Maharashtra and Uttarakhand above Gujarat. Kerala is seen as being at the same low level of state policy effectiveness as Uttar Pradesh. There seems to be some imperfection either in choice of indicators or adoption of the technique. This is said not to minimize the importance of policy effectiveness as one of the criteria of good governance.

Ease of Doing Business Index

A document, under the title *Assessment of State Implementation of Business Reforms in India,* was recently brought out by the World Bank (2015). The objective was to compare the different states and union territories in the country in terms of the favourable conditions they provide for investment in industry, services or infrastructure. Such a provision was deemed as linked to the administrative proficiency of a state/union territory. This could be referred to matters like efficiency with which a state/union territory responds to a proposal for investment, trust it can generate in its declared policies, necessary infrastructure it can provide and so on. All this makes the 'ease of doing business' a powerful indicator of governance quality. The ranking and composite score of various states and union territories, as worked out by the World Bank, are presented in the Table 3.5.

Table 3.5 *India: Ranking of States/Union Territories by Ease of Doing Business Index, 2015*

States/Union Territories	*Composite score*	*Ranking*
Gujarat	71.14	1
Andhra Pradesh*	70.12	2
Jharkhand	63.09	3
Chhattisgarh	62.45	4
Madhya Pradesh	62.00	5
Rajasthan	61.04	6
Odisha	52.12	7
Maharashtra	49.30	8
Karnataka	48.50	9
Uttar Pradesh	47.37	10
West Bengal	46.90	11
Tamil Nadu	44.58	12
Haryana	40.66	13
Delhi	37.35	14
Punjab	36.73	15
Himachal Pradesh	23.95	16
Kerala	22.87	17
Goa	21.74	18
Puducherry	17.72	19
Bihar	16.41	20
Assam	14.84	21
Uttarakhand	13.36	22
Chandigarh	10.04	23
Andaman and Nicobar Islands	9.73	24
Tripura	9.29	25
Sikkim	7.23	26
Mizoram	6.37	27
Jammu & Kashmir	5.93	28
Meghalaya	4.38	29
Nagaland	3.41	30
Arunachal Pradesh	1.23	31
Manipur	1.23	32
Dadra and Nagar Haveli	–	33
Daman and Diu	–	34
Lakshadweep	–	35

Source: World Bank, 2015. *Assessment of State Implementation of Business Reforms Report*, Washington, D.C.

For sake of comparability with data in other tables, the index of 42.45 for Telangana has been skipped over here.

– denotes data not processed.

* includes Telangana

Map 3.4

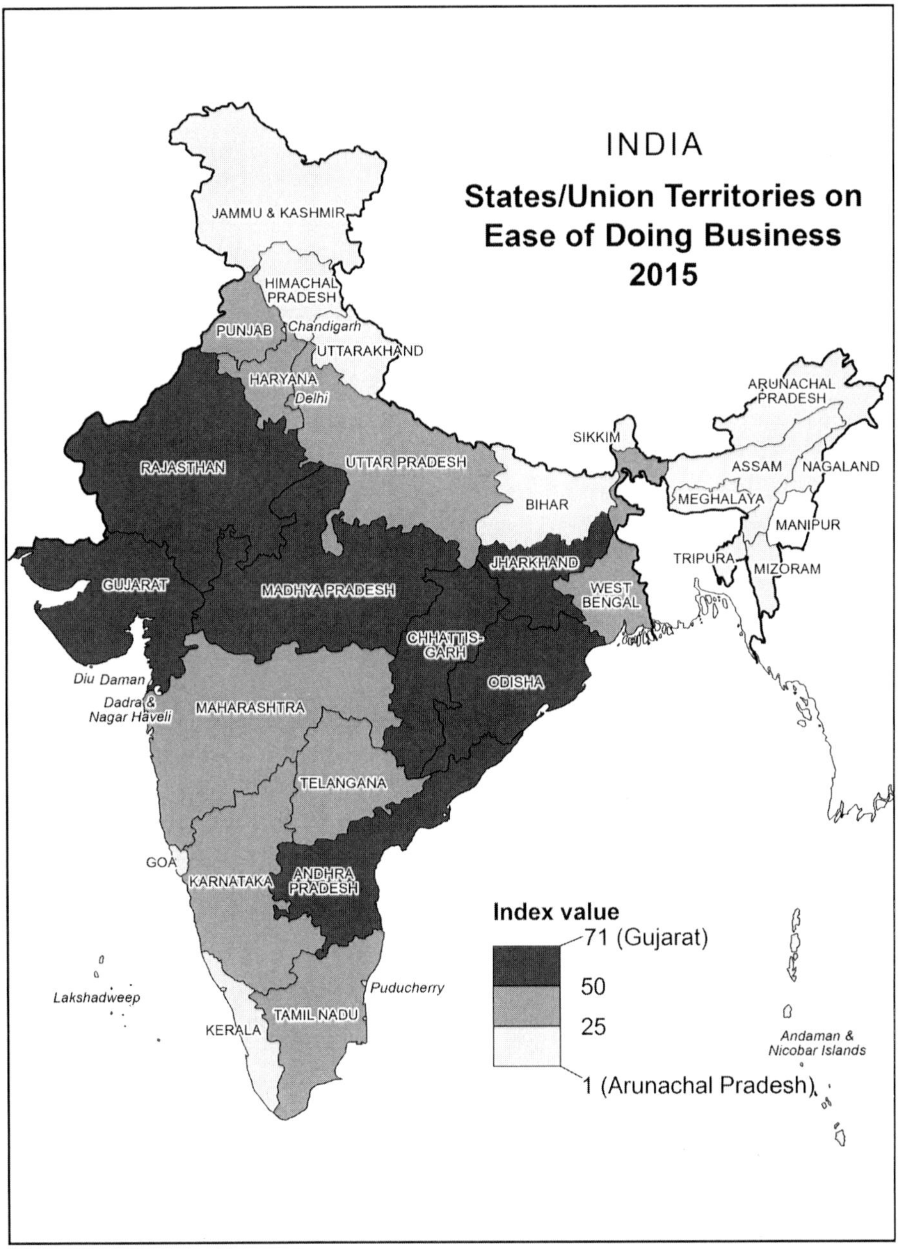

Many of the less developed states in the middle belt have emerged as prominent on this parameter.

Source: Assessment of State Implementation of Business Reforms Report 2015, World Bank, Washington D.C.

Gujarat has been rated as the best on the parameter of 'ease of doing business'. This conforms to the prevailing popular perception. The state welcomes, rather works for, attracting investment from any source, national or foreign. It is rated high on parameters of infrastructure, especially in respect of power, roads and e-connectivity. The law and order situation is also considered as congenial. Most expeditious is its response to any investment proposal.

Andhra Pradesh, in its reorganized form, is also working on similar lines. A variety of development activities, including the raising of the new state capital of Amravati, have created lucrative investment opportunities. The state is committed to following a favourable and stable investment policy.

Beyond these two already developed states, the picture changes in favour of previously less developed ones like Jharkhand, Chhattisgarh, Madhya Pradesh, Rajasthan and Odisha (Map 3.4). The political leadership here is keen to promote development at a fast pace. Availability of rich natural resources, like coal, iron ore, forest and land, provide a sound base for the purpose. An effective policy for attracting investment is being actively pursued by them.

The 'ease of doing business', though still at a high level, is noted as somewhat mellowed in vibrant states like Maharashtra, Karnataka and Tamil Nadu. They seem to have reached a stage where the cost of land, labour and energy are touching a new high. City life here has become difficult and expensive to a greater degree. New investment has to be massive if intended to make an impact.

Punjab is rather weak on the score of 'ease of doing business'. Land is the major constraint in its case. The price of land is exorbitant. Goa is suffering from a similar problem. A kind of saturation seems to have reached in its case. The three traditionally left-oriented states of Kerala, West Bengal and Tripura are also taking time to create an atmosphere conducive for the 'ease of doing business'.

The politically difficult states like Jammu & Kashmir, Assam and Nagaland are constrained in attracting investment from outside. In the case of states like Himachal Pradesh, Mizoram and Meghalaya, in addition to Nagaland and Jammu & Kashmir, restrictive land policies also emerge as a handicap to free inflow of investment. They need reforming and liberalizing of their land policies to make an easy entry for investment from outside.

Contrary to expectations, all the union territories are weak to modest on the 'ease of doing business' index. Most of them are highly urbanized, enjoy a relatively superior infrastructure and have robust administrative machinery. They have all the ingredients of emerging as powerful magnets for attracting investment. This has not happened to the desired degree. The main handicaps from which most of them suffer are exorbitant price of land, relatively small size of local market and high cost of living.

The 'ease of doing business', as an index of quality of governance, calls for a bit of elaboration. There is a distinct correspondence between the development level and the ease of doing business in the case of dynamic states like Gujarat, Maharashtra and Andhra Pradesh. Such an association between the two is rather weak in the case of union territories. Several states, such as Madhya Pradesh, Chhattisgarh, Odisha and Jharkhand, which were not high on governance, are emerging as rapid conveyor belts on the ease of doing business. This is explained by richness of their natural resources combined with an urge to attract investment by designing and implementing appropriate policies. On the other hand, the states of the North-East and hill states in the North-West region are not favourably placed in terms of ease of doing business, notwithstanding bounty of their natural resources. They continue to suffer from their locational, topographical, political and land policy constraints.

At its own level, the World Bank Report had grouped the Indian states/union territories into four categories, as presented in Table 3.6.

Table 3.6 *India: Categorization of States/Union Territories on Reform Measures for Ease of Doing Business, 2015*

	Category	*States*
1.	Leaders	None
2.	Aspiring leaders	Andhra Pradesh, Chhattisgarh, Gujarat, Jharkhand, Madhya Pradesh, Odisha and Rajasthan
3.	Acceleration required	Delhi, Haryana, Karnataka, Maharashtra, Punjab, Tamil Nadu, Telangana, Uttar Pradesh and West Bengal
4.	Jump start needed	All others

Source: World Bank, 2015. *Report on the Assessment of State Implementation of Business Reforms.* Washington, D.C.

This categorization was based on the implementation status of reform measures across eight areas. These included issues related to setting up a business, allotment of land and obtaining construction permit, complying with environmental procedures, complying with labour regulations, raising infrastructure related utilities, registering and complying with tax procedures, carrying out inspections and enforcing contracts. A 98-point reform framework was prepared for the purpose and shared with the states/union territories to obtain their inputs and feedbacks.

Performance Index

A comprehensive document under the title, *India's Economic Geography in 2025: States, Clusters and Cities,* has been brought out by Brar et al. (2014). Here an effort was made to capture the emerging investment scenario between 2012 to 2025, as reflective of the functioning of the various state governments. This has been done by way of projecting the spatial map of India's economic markets by factoring in the behaviour of the urbanization process and the pace of Gross Domestic Product. The three key dimensions to this effect are listed as infrastructure development (power, roads, water, ports and airports); structural advantages of geographic location and head start of higher productivity level already achieved and the stage of existing development level. A supportive role of the national and state governments was duly envisaged for the things to take shape. The entire exercise was meant to serve as a guide post to the policy makers and potential investors about the opportunities at the state, district and city levels. In the nature of a ready reckoner, the performance status of various states and union territories was worked out.

Based on their performance index, more specifically the per capita Gross Domestic Product, the study classifies the states/union territories of India into four groups (Table 3.7). Each state/union territory is described as performing but in varying degree. The very high and high performing states/union territories are marked by relatively superior levels of human development, urbanization and diversification of economy. These are noted for greater tax collection and better fiscal management. Most of them, in addition, are favoured by a long coast line and a high percentage of cultivated land. India's consumer class is concentrated in a large measure in such very high and high performing states.

Table 3.7 *India: Classification of States/Union Territories on Performance Index, 2014**

Level of performance index	*States/Union Territories*
Very high performing	1. Goa 2. Chandigarh 3. Delhi 4. Puducherry
High performing	5. Haryana 6. Maharashtra 7. Gujarat 8. Kerala 9. Himachal Pradesh 10. Tamil Nadu 11. Punjab 12. Uttarakhand
Performing	13. Karnataka 14. Andhra Pradesh** 15. West Bengal 16. Chhattisgarh 17. Rajasthan 18. Odisha 19. Jammu & Kashmir
Low performing	20. Assam 21. Arunachal Pradesh 22. Nagaland 23. Manipur 24. Mizoram 25. Tripura 26. Meghalaya 27. Sikkim 28. Madhya Pradesh 29. Jharkhand 30. Uttar Pradesh 31. Bihar

Source: J. Brar et al. 2014. *India's Economic Geography in 2025.* Mumbai: McKinsey and Company.

* Union territories of Andaman & Nicobar Islands, Dadra & Nagar Haveli, Daman & Diu and Lakshadweep not taken into account.

** Includes Telangana.

The performing states, by comparison, are noted for a concentration of aspirational class. These will catch up with the high performing ones in living standards by 2025. This would enlarge the demand for durable and luxury goods.

The low performing states would remain focused primarily on goods of basic daily needs. Several of these are located in the North-East, North and East India. The market potential in their case is likely to remain limited.

One wonders if one-time data as put in service by this study could provide a realistic picture of evolving scene of performance of different states even if these figures pertain to the final go. It hides the performance of those states which picked up speed of late and also glosses over the slowing down of performance of others who had attained a high level earlier. Hence only an analysis based on longitudinal data would have yielded a more reliable and meaningful picture.

Putting All Things Together

The foregoing discussion tried to capture the relative performance of the states and union territories of India on the quality of their governance. A number of parameters, such as provision of infrastructural facilities, delivery of social services, devolution of powers to local bodies, investment friendly policies, sound fiscal management and dynamic economic performance were taken into account for the purpose. Though there was considerable convergence of behaviour on various parameters in the case of certain states but instances of divergence were also quite many. One study placed Punjab on the top of governance quality, another puts it at a low rank on devolution of powers to local bodies, and still another assesses it weak on attracting investment. Kerala is high on decentralization of governance but lacking in public policy effectiveness. Goa is high in public policy effectiveness and performance of economy but weak on strengthening of local bodies. Hence, any attempt at a quantitative aggregation of scores of different states on various parameters of good governance will even out gross internal divergences within a state.

The best recourse in such a situation would be to synthesize things through a qualitative empirical assessment of the situation. This amounts to attempting an authentic summary evaluation. An additional input to such an exercise would be to trace the context of the governance of various states/union territories in terms of their size, administrative status, and degree of dependence on central government. Purposeful understanding is much more important than any quantitative measurement, as they say.

For the sake of a holistic grasp, the states and union territories of India can be grouped into seven categories. Considerations involved are the nature, ecology and quality of their governance. Details are provided in Table 3.8. The intention here is to highlight the regional dimension of governance vitality of India.

As it emerges, the states in contiguity display considerable degree of similarity in their relative degree of governance quality (Map 3.5). The states in West and South India are on a comparatively high score on this count. The states in the middle belt of India are noted for a significant improvement in their governance quality. The states in North India are by and large laggards.

The small sized ethnic states in the North-East India and the hill-states in the North-West India, though in race for putting their administrative culture in proper order, are proving rather expensive and their dependence on the central government for financial support is too heavy. Likewise, all the union territories, though administratively efficient, are a direct burden on the central government for financial and technical support. Ironically, these have been reluctant to a liberal devolution of powers to the local bodies, as the dominance of bureaucracy is more pervasive in their case.

Table 3.8 *India: Classification of States/Union Territories on Quality and Context of Governance, 2016*

Category	*Location*	*States/Union Territories*
States marked by comparatively better quality of governance	West and South India	1. Gujarat 2. Maharashtra 3. Goa 4. Tamil Nadu 5. Kerala 6. Andhra Pradesh 7. Karnataka
States marked by significant improvement in their governance	Central and East India	1. Rajasthan 2. Madhya Pradesh 3. Chhattisgarh 4. Odisha 5. Jharkhand
States in need of urgent improvement in their governance	North and North-East India	1. Uttar Pradesh 2. Bihar 3. West Bengal 4. Assam
States calling for rejuvenation of their governance quality	North-West India	1. Punjab 2. Haryana
Hill states in North-West India dependent upon the central government for regular financial support	Western Himalayas	1. Jammu & Kashmir 2. Himachal Pradesh 3. Uttarakhand
States in the North-East (excluding Assam) critically dependent upon the central government in overall terms	North-East Region	1. Arunachal Pradesh 2. Nagaland 3. Manipur 4. Mizoram 5. Tripura 6. Meghalaya 7. Sikkim
Union territories administered directly by the central government	Union Territories	1. Andaman and Nicobar Isles 2. Chandigarh 3. Dadra & Nagar Haveli 4. Daman & Diu 5. Delhi 6. Lakshadweep 7. Puducherry

Source: A synthesis attempted by the author.

A too large a population size of a state, such as in the case of Uttar Pradesh, Bihar and West Bengal, is a constraint to efficient administration, and too small, such as in the case of Sikkim, Mizoram or Meghalaya, makes the administration expensive. In any case, the impact of a state's population size on its governance quality is not consistent. Among the better administered ones are the large states like Maharashtra, medium states like Kerala, and small states like Goa. By and large, the coastal states excel over the mainland states on governance quality. These seem to have been exposed to external modernity influence to a greater degree.

Again it is difficult to make a distinction in terms of governance quality of states which have been under the administration of national parties and others which were administered by regional parties for a considerable span of time. On taking a wider view of things at all-India level, it is observed that states which have been consistently under the administration of national parties, such as Kerala, Gujarat and Haryana, are administratively better placed than those states which were under the care of regional parties for a long spell, such as Uttar Pradesh and Bihar. There are exceptions too. Gujarat and Tamil Nadu offer a ready comparison. Both have been rated as relatively high on quality of governance. The dominance of national parties in the case of the former and that of regional parties in the latter's case draws the line between the two.

Map 3.5

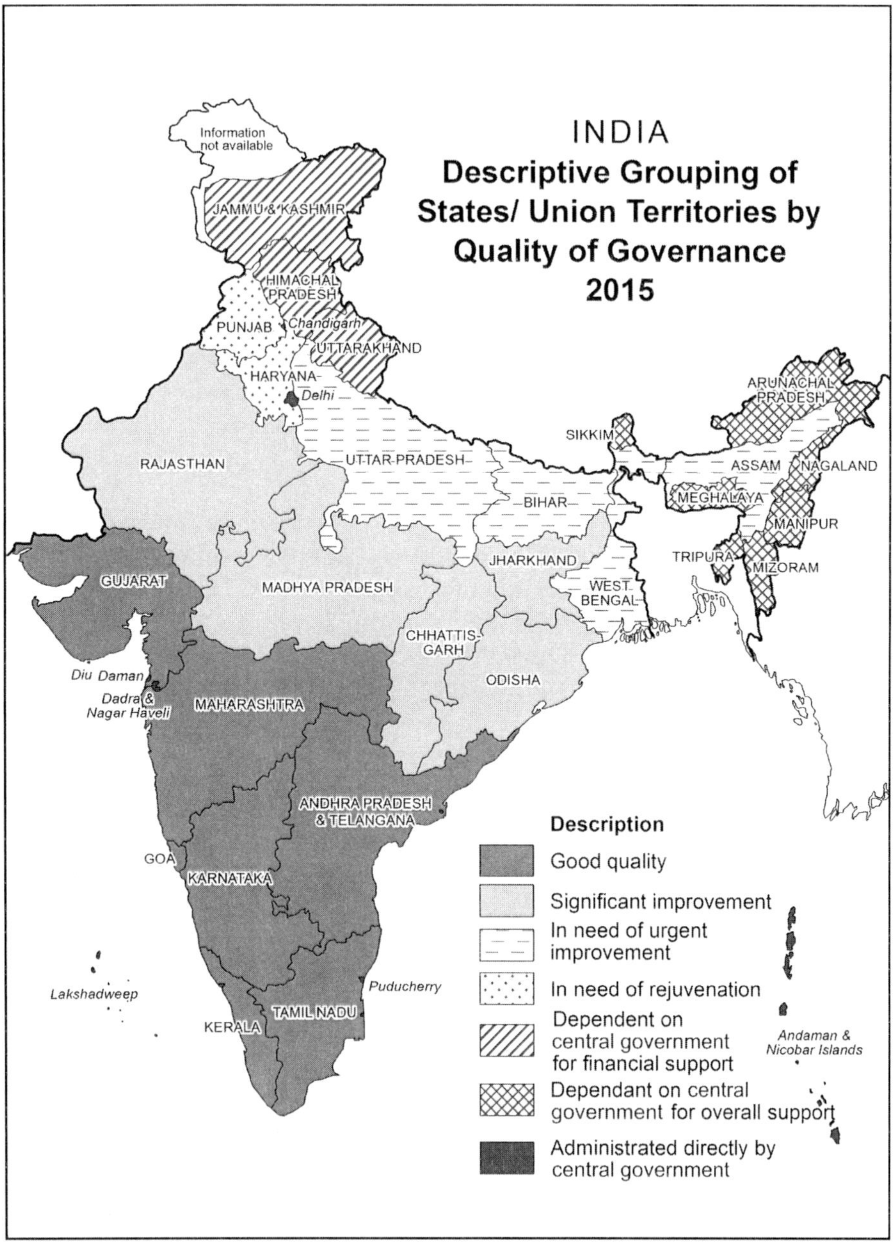

A south to north gradient is evident in the quality of governance of different states in India.

The Indian states may be significantly homogeneous on linguistic lines but they are marked by significant diversity in terms of their religious composition and in some cases with regard to general and tribal populations. A demographic diversity, such as in Uttar Pradesh, Assam and Jammu & Kashmir, is not without its implications for governance quality and a kind of homogeneity as in Tamil Nadu, is a favourable setting. Likewise, the states which are physically homogenous, such as Punjab and Haryana, are better governed than those which are physically diverse, such as Jammu & Kashmir.

The newly carved out states, such as Uttarakhand, Jharkhand and Chhattisgarh, are demonstrating a great enthusiasm in upgrading the quality of their governance. An acquisition of a distinct identity has imparted them a fresh pride and vigour. The richness of natural resources is proving a great asset for them. Most notable is the fact that any distinction between the governance quality of those states which were previously under the rule of the British and others which were under the princes is no longer visible. Among the better governed states, we have representatives of both. Tamil Nadu and Kerala, for example: The independent India created a level field for different states to nurture their administrative style.

The essay establishes the eminence of location as a factor in influencing the quality of governance of different Indian states. Neighbouring states tend to acquire lineaments of each other. A coastal location benefits more from the modern impulses emanating from the outside world. On the other hand, the remote periphery distant from the national capital feels more relaxed in respect of rules of the game.

References

Acemoglu, Deron, Simon Johnson and James A. Robinson. 2000. *The Colonial Origins of Comparative Development: An Empirical Investigation*. Washington, D.C.: National Bureau of Economic Research (Working Paper No. W7771).

Brar, J., Barnik Maitra and Anu Mudgavaskar. 2014. *India's Economic Geography in 2025: States, Clusters and Cities*. Mumbai: McKinsey and Company.

Charron, Nicholas. 2010. The Correlates of Corruption in India: Analysis from the Indian States. *Asian Journal of Political Science*. Vol. 18, pp. 177–194.

Gorden, Donald. 2014. *Transparent Government: What it Means and How You Can Make it Happen*. New York: Prometheus Books.

Government of India. 2012. *Twelfth Five Year Plan 2012–2017*. New Delhi: Planning Commission.

——. 2013. *Thirteenth Finance Commission 2010–2015, Volume 1: Report*. New Delhi: Ministry of Finance.

Gupta, R.N. 2014. *Governance Unbound: Public Services Players and Rules of the Game*. New Delhi: Aakar.

Hilton, Steve. 2016. *More Human: Designing a World Where People Come First*. New York: Public Affairs.

Hubbard, Phil, Rob Kitchin, Bredan Bartley and Duncan Fuller. 2002. *Thinking Geographically: Space Theory and Contemporary Human Geography*. London: Continuum.

Huther, Jeff and Anwar Shah. 1998. *Applying a Simple Measure of Good Governance to Debate on Fiscal Decentralisation.* Washington, D.C.: World Bank.

Indian Institute of Public Administration. 2012. *India Governance Report 2012.* New Delhi: IIPA.

Kauffman, Daniel, Aart Kraay and Massima Mastruzzi. 2004. Governance Matters. *World Bank Economic Review.* Vol. 18, pp. 253–287.

Kohli, Harinder Singh and Anil Sood (eds). 2010. *India 2039: An Affluent Society in One Generation.* New Delhi: Sage Publications.

La Porta, R., Florencio Lopoz-de-Silanes, Andrei Shleifer and Robert Vishny. 1999. The Quality of Government. *Journal of Law, Economics and Organisation.* Vol. 15, No. 1, pp. 222–279.

Malhotra, Rajeev. 2014. *India Public Policy Report 2014.* New Delhi: Oxford University Press.

Mathew, C.K., Athreya Mukunthan and Vivek Divekar. 2016. *Governance in the States of India: Report.* Bengaluru: Public Affairs Centre.

Mundle, Sudipto, Pinakai Chakraborty, Samik Chowdhury and Satadru Sikdar. 2012. The Quality of Governance: How Have Indian States Performed. *Economic and Political Weekly.* Vol. 47, No. 49, pp. 41–52.

Micklethwait, John and Adrian Woolridge. 2014. *The Fourth Revolution: The Global Race to Reinvent the State.* New York: Penguin.

Osborne, David and Ted Gaebler. 1992. *Reinventing Government.* Reading, Massachusetts: Addison-Wesley.

Stiglitz, Joseph. 2006. *Making Globalisation Work.* New York: W.W. Norton and Company.

World Bank. 2015. *Assessment of State Implementation of Business Reforms Report.* Washington, D.C.

4

Economic Dynamism

Economic dynamism and good governance have been affirmed as the two mutually reinforcing attributes of any political entity. A sustained economic dynamism can be ensured only through efficient and inclusive governance which in turn is always in need of requisite financial resources for its optimal functioning. The symbiosis between the two is an axiom.

How do we assess the dynamism of economy of a country or of its various states or subnational units? Which are the most representative criteria and indicators for this purpose? What has been the practice of economic geography in this regard? How do various parts of India compare on this parameter and differ in their contribution to vitality of India? Answers to such questions require a prior understanding of the substance of economic dynamism.

The Concept

The growth rate of economy, the shift of economy in favour of secondary and tertiary sectors from a primary one and a regular rise in real per capita income are the three basic measures of economic dynamism. Linked to these attributes of efficiency are the considerations of equity, as represented by the pattern of income and wealth distribution, alleviation of poverty and check over incidence of unemployment. Efficiency and equity in the system have to be accompanied by a productive job creation. Absence of any of the aforesaid parameters is a poor reflection on economic dynamism.

The scope of economic dynamism includes the policies and processes by which a nation improves the social and political well-being of its people (O' Sullivan and Sheffrin, 2003). This involves a constant effort at quality upgradation of the economic system. The state of any economic system is to be assessed through indicators like real Gross Domestic Product, money supply, consumer confidence, stock index, manufacturing status, current employment and retail trade sales. All these broadly cover the situations in respect of flow of income; production and consumption of goods and services and related cost involved and pace of investment, generation of employment and construction rate of new homes (Lefranc, 2015). In other words, the economic dynamism of any country or region is best reflected in the rate at which the prosperity of the people is rising, employment avenues are multiplying and diversifying and innovations are blazing in trail.

Some scholars believe that among the various indicators of economic dynamism, 'productivity rise' or 'increase in the rate of productivity' is most robust. This indicator can be referred to the behaviour of 'Incremental Capital-Output Ratio (ICOR)' or the ratio between the investment rate and growth rate. In mathematical formulation, it is a measure of inefficiency in utilization of capital wherein Capital is in numerator and Output in denominator. Higher the ICOR, lower the productivity. It lies in the neighbourhood of 3 in the world at large, meaning thereby that to get an output of one unit, an investment of three units is required. In India, the ICOR is around 4, indicating a relatively lower level of productivity (International Monetary Fund, 2014).

In their book, *Mis-Measuring Our Lives*, Stiglitz et al. (2010: pp. 1–22) observe that for better measurement of economic performance not only quantity but also quality of goods and services produced should be taken into account in compilation of Gross Domestic Product; the relative share of the private and public sectors be considered not only vis-à-vis expenditure but also in relation to their contribution to the economy; and any evaluation system should shift its emphasis from economic production to people's well-being. Greater prominence should be given to consumption distribution rather than per capita income. It is most essential to cover income, consumption and wealth, representing the material living standard in totality in any such exercise. The distinguishing point of any economy is consumption and possession of assets by everyone at large. Production and distribution are no doubt means to that end.

Which could be the geographical measures of economic dynamism? The state of regional disparity, nay regional equity, could be listed as the first indicator on this count. Divergence at a low level of development process and convergence at higher level is suggestive of economic dynamism (Williamson, 1965). Any persistent polarization is not conducive to rapid growth. A policy intervention is essential for effectuation of convergence (Davies and Hallet, 2002). The distributional pattern of urban places with spread effect on their surrounding areas can be rated as the second important indicator. A hierarchy of growth centres is essential for spatial diffusion of development. Leveraging urbanization can help in raising economic productivity and reducing incidence of poverty (Ellis and Roberts, 2015). The third in line would be the volume and value of flow of people, goods and messages along the transport and communication lines. Interregional connectivity generates systemic vibrancy and promotes interdependence. Rural road connectivity is crucial to commercialization of agriculture. Finally, an optimal organization of space, especially for administration, ensures efficiency and equity (Krishan, 1989: p. 257).

For sustaining and accelerating the economic growth trajectory, a due note is to be taken of the supporting factors. These include, in particular, the quantity and quality of infrastructure, investment rate of private, public and foreign sectors, and availability situation of technical and professional personnel. Also essential is to make an allowance for the relative cost of development as it differs from one region to another in line with topographical conditions, management culture and technological advancement. A few illustrations may be cited as construction cost of one kilometre of road, production cost of one unit of electricity and investment cost of generating one job, which are marked by wide variations even over different parts of the same country, depending especially on the nature of topography, already available infrastructure and quality of governance.

The nature of political institutions is a critical factor in influencing the economic dynamism of a country (Acemoglu and Robinson, 2012). One has to distinguish between inclusive institutions, which promote entrepreneurship and protect private property rights and extractive institutions which place power in the hands of the few who frame policies in their own interest and exploit the system. Inclusive institutions being democratic in nature are conducive to competition, innovation and profit generation. These tend to speed up development. On the other hand, extractive institutions soon run out of economic steam and cause misery at large. Democracy and prosperity are co-travellers in a marathon though.

Consistent with geographical approach, the purpose of this essay is to have a comparative view of economic dynamism of various states and union territories of India and to assess how they together shape the vitality of the country. Economic dynamism in the present case has been referred to net state domestic product, contribution of each state and union territory to augmentation of the national kitty, alleviation rate of poverty, level of the development and quality of living space. The net state domestic product, in simple words, is the gross domestic product minus depreciation. Depreciation is the deterioration in the capital goods, such as machinery, vehicles and built structures, over a given unit of time, for instance one year. The depreciation is to be replaced failing which the obsolescence caused would reduce the productivity of the capital goods. Net state domestic product is evidently a more authentic measure of economic well-being than the gross domestic product. If calculated in terms of per capita, the factor of differential population density and growth rate of various states and union territories gets neutralized. This is the way the ensuing discussion has been structured.

Net State Domestic Product

At the 2004–05 constant prices, the per capita net state domestic product (NSDP) of India works out as ₹ 11,711 in 1980–81. By 2011–12, this figure had risen to ₹ 41,255 rendering a multiple of 3.5 times (Map 4.1). This represented a compound annual growth rate of no less than 4 per cent. An addition of ₹ 29,544 in the per capita NSDP of India during this period signified an annual increment of ₹ 923 in the NSDP for every Indian (Table 4.1).

Table 4.1 *India: Per Capita Net State Domestic Product (NSDP), Aggregate Addition and Annual Increment (All in Rupees) by States in 2011–12 and 1980–81 at 2004–05 Prices**

*State***	*2011–12* (₹)	*1980–81* (₹)	*Aggregate addition* (₹)	*Average annual increment* (₹)
Goa	129,397	26,778	102,619	3207
Sikkim	73,704	11,528	62,176	1943
Haryana	61,716	16,206	45,510	1422
Maharashtra	61,468	14,526	46,942	1467
Gujarat	57,447	12,560	44,887	1403
Tamil Nadu	57,093	11,019	46,074	1440
Uttarakhand	52,607	13,288	39,319	1229
Kerala	52,095	13,550	38,545	1205
Himachal Pradesh	49,203	13,859	35,344	1105
Nagaland	46,340	16,317	30,023	938
Punjab	46,325	17,332	28,993	906
Andhra Pradesh***	42,589	9,499	33,090	1034
Karnataka	41,492	10,743	30,749	961
Tripura	39,382	8,722	30,660	958
Mizoram	37,921	10,625	27,296	853
Arunachal Pradesh	35,231	8,857	26,374	824
Meghalaya	34,217	12,191	22,026	688
West Bengal	32,164	9,872	22,292	697
Jammu & Kashmir	28,833	16,474	12,359	386
Rajasthan	28,429	8,433	19,996	625
Chhattisgarh	27,163	11,497	15,666	490
Jharkhand	25,265	11,479	13,786	431
Odisha	24,151	10,227	13,924	435
Madhya Pradesh	23,447	9,823	13,624	426
Manipur	22,739	10,715	12,024	376
Assam	22,420	11,843	10,577	331
Uttar Pradesh	17,980	8,500	9,480	296
Bihar	13,149	5,631	7,518	235
India	41,255	11,711	29,544	923

* Based on standardization of data provided by Central Statistical Organization, New Delhi.

** States are listed in descending order of per capita Net State Domestic Product in 2011–12.

*** Includes Telangana.

Map 4.1

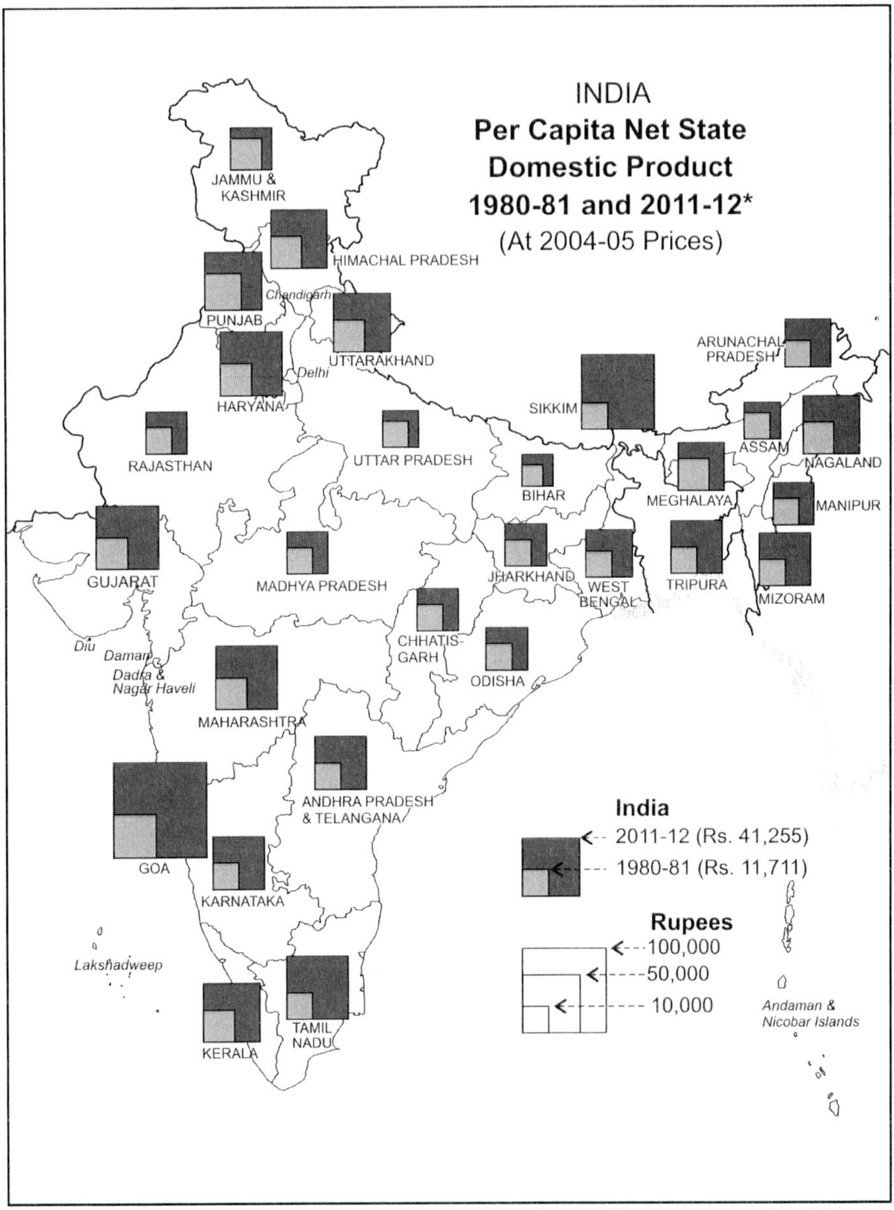

The per capita addition to NSDP during 1980-81 to 2011-12 in India was of the order of nearly ₹ 30,000 in real times; Goa's gain was nearly four times of this and of Bihar, hardly one-fourth.

Source: Central Statistical Organization, New Delhi.

*Data for union territories not available

The growth behaviour of various states, however, differed (Map 4.2). While several surged ahead fast, some were rather sluggish. As a result, the gap between the comparatively well-off and the impoverished ones widened. The per capita NSDP of Goa was five times that of Bihar in 1980–81; this gap had widened to 10 times in 2011–12. Goa's per capita NSDP was 2.3 times of the All-India average in 1980–81; it climbed up to nearly 3.1 times by 2011–12. By contrast, Bihar's ratio to the national average had dipped down from one-half to one-third during the same period. Goa could augment its per capita NSDP by more than ₹ 3,200 every year on an average; the comparable figure for Bihar was a little more than two hundred rupees. The comparative compound annual growth rates of the two states were 5.1 per cent and 2.7 per cent, respectively. While the states in the mode of Goa were leaping forward, those in the nature of Bihar were limping. Contrary to popular perception, the relatively more developed states were marked by a higher degree of variability in their growth rates (Map 4.3). They carried greater scope for their growth rates to fluctuate. The less developed states moved at a consistently slow pace.

What explains the contrast between Goa and Bihar? A small coastal state, with spectacular physical and cultural landscape, Goa is famous as a tourist resort. Proximity and air connectivity to big metropolitan cities like Mumbai, Pune, Bengaluru and Hyderabad are to its great advantage. The peaceful law and order situation has attracted considerable investment from outside. Today it is India's most urbanized state, with 62.2 per cent of its population living in towns and cities. On governance quality, it ranks high. On the other hand, Bihar carries a negative description on several counts. It is noted for a serious land resource-population imbalance. As many as 91.1 per cent of agricultural landholdings here are smaller than one hectare each. No less than 52.8 per cent of the working force derives livelihood as an agricultural labourer, not cultivator, in a semi-feudal context of an agrarian society. The law and order situation is far from desired. The state at 11.4 per cent urban is primarily rural. Above all, devastating floods, subjecting as much as 73 per cent of the state's area to their fury every year, add to the misery of its land, people and economy. There are efforts at improving the situation through extension of physical infrastructure, promotion of construction activity, establishment of industry and strengthening of law and order machinery yet the state has a long way to go before demonstrating a visible transformation. The base itself is meagre and fragile.

Sikkim deserves a special mention for having recorded the highest compound annual growth rate of 6 per cent during 1980–81 to 2011–12 (Table 4.2). This has led to a per capita addition of nearly ₹ 2,000 every year. Benefitting from a remarkable political stability and regular support from the central government, the state has made rapid strides in all spheres since it became a part of India in 1975. The most lucrative source of its income is tourism, coupled with revenue earned through sale of liquor. Earnings of royalty from generation of hydroelectric power are considerable. Marketing of horticultural products outside the state also contribute to its financial

Map 4.2

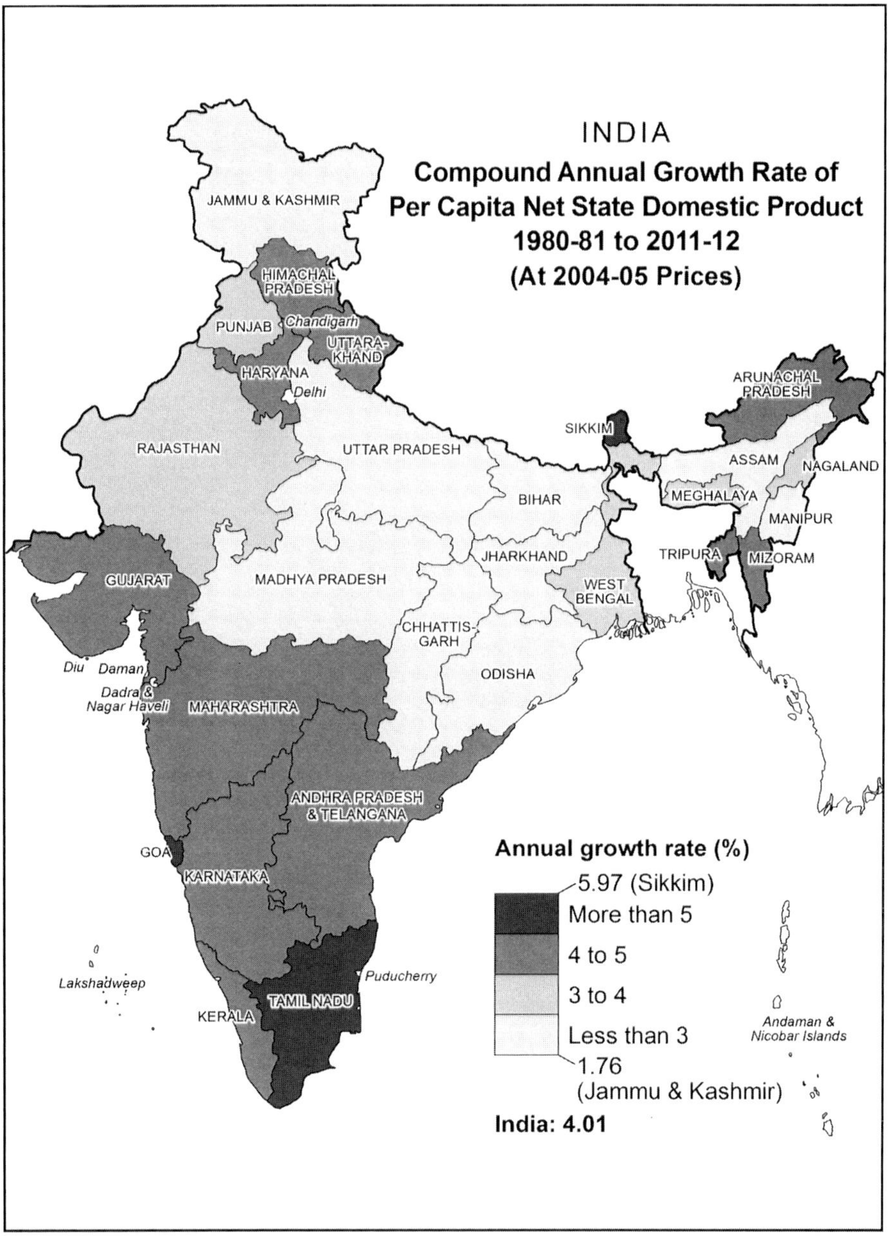

The pace of economic growth slows down as one moves from south to north; hill states are of course an exception by and large.

Map 4.3

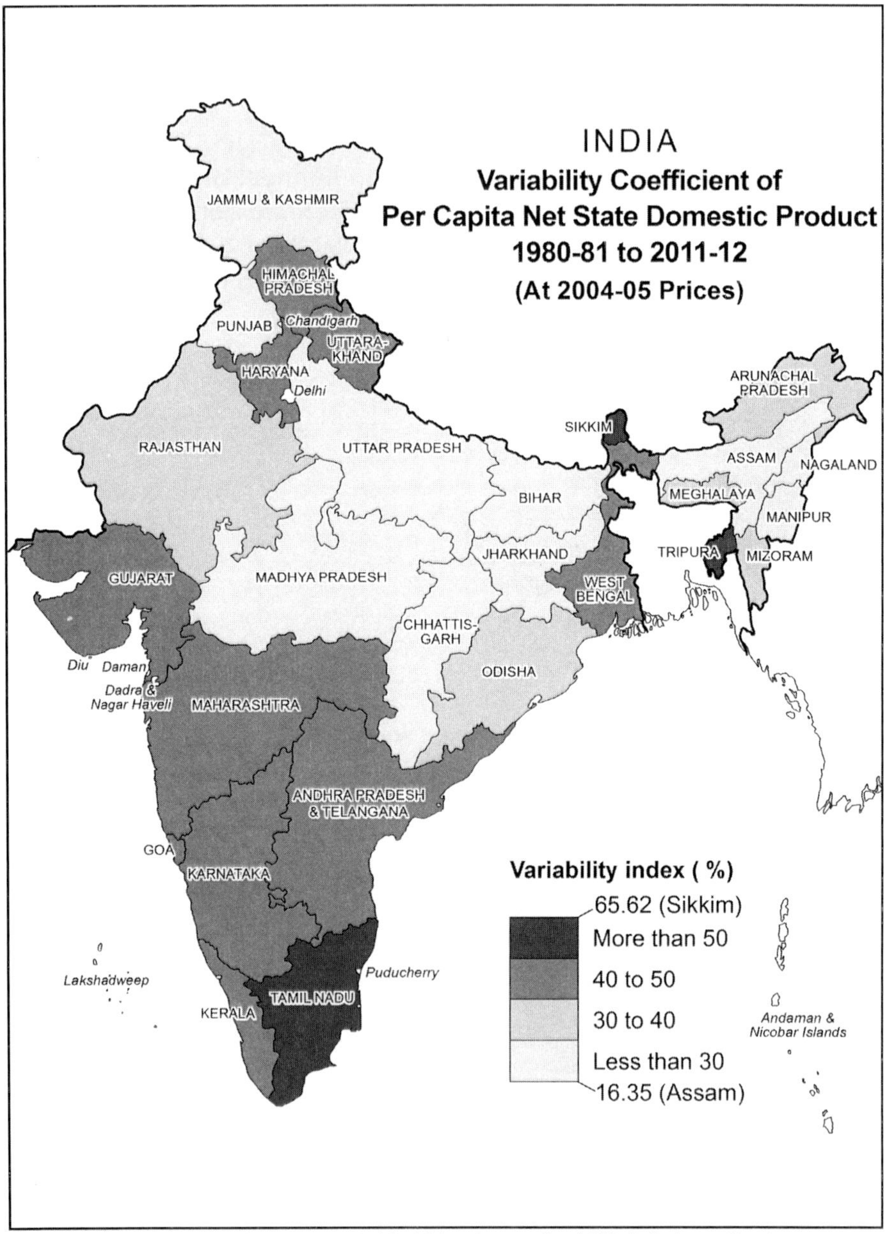

The relatively more developed states are noted for higher degree of variability in their growth rate on year to year basis; the less developed states persist in their sluggish growth behaviour.

kitty. Good governance, skilful management of natural resources, and peaceful law and order situation have helped the state in ranking among the highest on economic vigour in the country.

Table 4.2 *India: Compound Annual Growth Rate and Coefficient of Variability of Net State Domestic Product (NSDP) during 1980–81 and 2011–12 and Ratio between Per Capita NSDP in 2011–12 and 1980–81 at 2004–05 Prices by States**

*State***	*Compound annual growth rate*	*Coefficient of variability (%)* ^	*Ratio of 2011–12 and 1980–81 NSDPs*
Sikkim	5.97	66	6.39
Tamil Nadu	5.28	52	5.18
Goa	5.05	47	4.83
Gujarat	4.87	48	4.57
Tripura	4.82	54	4.51
Andhra Pradesh***	4.80	47	4.48
Maharashtra	4.61	47	4.23
Arunachal Pradesh	4.41	39	3.98
Uttarakhand	4.39	49	3.96
Karnataka	4.31	44	3.86
Kerala	4.30	48	3.84
Haryana	4.27	42	3.81
Mizoram	4.06	39	3.57
Himachal Pradesh	4.04	43	3.55
Rajasthan	3.87	36	3.37
West Bengal	3.76	40	3.26
Nagaland	3.32	26	2.84
Meghalaya	3.28	37	2.81
Punjab	3.12	28	2.67
Madhya Pradesh	2.76	27	2.39
Chhattisgarh	2.72	28	2.39
Odisha	2.72	31	2.36
Bihar	2.69	24	2.34
Jharkhand	2.50	22	2.20
Manipur	2.38	23	2.12
Uttar Pradesh	2.37	21	2.12
Assam	2.01	16	1.89
Jammu & Kashmir	1.76	19	1.75
India	4.01	–	3.52

* Based on standardization of data provided by Central Statistical Organisation, New Delhi.

** States are listed in descending order of the compound annual growth rate.

*** Includes Telangana.

^ As measured by year to year growth rate during 1980–81 to 2011–12.

Gujarat and Maharashtra in West India; Kerala, Tamil Nadu and Andhra Pradesh in South India; hill states of Uttarakhand and Himachal Pradesh in North-West India and Haryana, a large part of which is located in the National Capital Region, are also noted for compound annual growth rates exceeding 4 per cent. On the agro-industrial development map of India, Gujarat and Maharashtra make a bold appearance as bright spots. These two states enjoy several structural advantages, including ports-studded coast line, fairly laid out physical infrastructure and direct connectivity with most parts of India. A strong tradition of entrepreneurial skill, cooperative disposition and investment propensity are a part of their economic life. The administrative machinery is also credited for being relatively efficient. Among 52 metropolitan cities in India, 13 are located in these two states. Nearly half of the population is urban by residence (Table 4.3).

Table 4.3 *India: Percentage of Urban Population, Cultivators, Agricultural Labourers and Agricultural Workers by States, 2011*

*State**	*Percentage of*			
	Urban Population	*Cultivators*	*Agricultural Labourers*	*Agricultural Workers*
Goa	62.17	5.8	4.6	10.4
Mizoram	52.51	47.2	8.6	55.8
Tamil Nadu	48.45	12.9	29.2	42.1
Kerala	47.72	5.8	11.4	17.2
Maharashtra	45.23	25.4	27.3	52.7
Gujarat	42.58	22.0	27.6	49.6
Karnataka	38.57	23.6	25.7	49.3
Punjab	37.49	19.5	16.0	35.5
Haryana	34.79	27.8	17.1	44.9
Andhra Pradesh**	33.49	16.5	43.0	59.5
Manipur	30.21	39.5	9.6	49.1
West Bengal	31.89	14.7	29.3	44.0
Uttarakhand	30.55	40.8	10.4	51.2
Nagaland	28.97	55.2	6.5	61.7
Madhya Pradesh	27.63	31.2	38.6	69.8
Jammu & Kashmir	27.21	28.8	12.7	41.5
Tripura	26.18	20.1	24.1	44.2
Sikkim	24.97	38.1	8.4	46.5
Rajasthan	24.89	45.6	16.5	62.1
Jharkhand	24.05	29.1	33.9	63.0
Chhattisgarh	23.24	32.9	41.8	74.7
Arunachal Pradesh	22.67	51.5	6.2	57.7
Uttar Pradesh	22.28	29.0	30.3	59.3
Meghalaya	20.08	41.7	16.7	58.4
Odisha	16.68	23.4	38.4	61.8
Assam	14.08	33.9	15.4	49.3
Bihar	11.30	20.7	52.8	73.5
Himachal Pradesh	10.04	57.9	4.0	61.9
India	31.16	24.6	30.0	54.6

Source: Census of India, 2011.

* States arranged in descending order by percentage of urban population.

** Includes Telangana.

Kerala, Tamil Nadu and Andhra Pradesh, each is a success story in its own turn. A sound foundation of social development, especially in the spheres of education and health, was a priority for Kerala. On such a base of social development, the state raised a structure of diversified economy and an extended service sector. Hardly 17.2 per cent of the working force is in cultivation and agricultural labour as compared with 54.6 per cent in India. Raising and processing of plantation produce, such as coconut, cashewnut, coffee and rubber, for export is a notable economic activity. The most lucrative source of Kerala's earning is the remittances from abroad, especially by emigrants to the Middle East. These are said to be contributing about one-fifth of the state's NSDP. The growth of secondary and tertiary sectors of economy is reflected in the pace of urbanization. Almost half of the state's population is urban.

Tamil Nadu is also nearly half urban in its demographics. The state has decades old history of dispersed industrial development based upon electricity as the major energy source. Knowledge-based service sector has made a big headway in recent years. Chennai has emerged as one of the major information technology centres in the country, and also as an important hub of automobile industry in its neighbourhood. Indeed the successive state governments of Tamil Nadu have been strongly committed to economic upliftment and social welfare of the people. Highly subsidised are the daily needs of the people, especially rice, wheat, sugar and kerosene. The presence of a relatively symmetrical society was of immense support to this process.

Andhra Pradesh benefitted no less from a strong regional sentiment in scheme of things, political, economic and social in nature. The state government made, over the years, earnest efforts to attract irrigation and power projects, public sector industry, and other development activities funded by the central government. The emergence of Hyderabad as a major information technology hub, industrial cluster and educational centre is a manifestation of its vitality. Telangana was carved out of former Andhra Pradesh in 2014, with Hyderabad resting with the new state. The reorganized Andhra Pradesh is now developing a separate capital at Amravati, located between Vijayawada and Guntur. The indications are in favour of the two states sustaining their economic stamina in a competitive mode.

Maharashtra and Gujarat, two West Indian states, are distinguished by a high degree of economic enterprise. While Maharashtra had a background of industrialization since colonial days, Gujarat started making rapid strides after Independence. Herein was the outstanding role of the state government in favour of industry, infrastructure extension and upgradation and promotion of cooperatives. The economic aggressiveness of Gujarat could be compared with that of East Asian countries. Significant investment by its diaspora has also been a great contributory factor.

The North-Western states of Himachal Pradesh and Uttarakhand have also been high on economic rise. These are among the special category states and thereby beneficiary of liberal financial support from the central government. At their own level, they made every effort to augment their finances through promotion of tourism, commercial production of fruits and vegetables and royalty on hydroelectric power. Both the states are known for a long tradition in army service and their additional earnings through the in-service and ex-servicemen are not insignificant.

Likewise North-Eastern states of Tripura, Mizoram and Arunachal Pradesh are noted for a commendable economic advancement notwithstanding their remote location and limited connectivity with other parts of India. They also belong to the special category states group and hence their budget deficits are taken care of by the central government. The peaceful conditions restored therein have proved advantageous to their development process. Tripura, with a large section of population as emigrant from Bangladesh, followed a path of social development in terms of education, health and infrastructure to raise a strong economy. Mizoram likewise has been making a steady progress, especially through its agricultural transformation. Today a majority of its population is urban. Arunachal Pradesh is not lagging behind in harnessing its hydroelectric potential and strengthening the infrastructure base.

On the other extreme, Jammu & Kashmir recorded the lowest compound annual growth rate of 1.8 per cent during 1980–81 to 2011–12. This is attributed to difficult political situation in the state, particularly since 1989 when ongoing phase of turmoil started. An adverse effect on the economy through a setback to tourism in a big way was on expected lines. The extension of physical infrastructure slowed down. The private sector has also been shy of investing here due to persistent uncertain conditions of law and order. The restrictive land policies of the state, which disallowed purchase of land by outsiders, constrained the entry of investment.

Uttar Pradesh, Bihar and Assam in North India; Madhya Pradesh, Chhattisgarh, Jharkhand and Odisha located to their south, and Manipur, in North-East India, all together accommodating half-a-billion people of India, marked a sluggish compound annual growth rate of less than three per cent. The performance of their respective neighbouring states, namely West Bengal, Rajasthan, Meghalaya and Nagaland was only a shade better with a slow economic growth rate of 3 to 4 per cent. The annual increment in the per capita NSDP of most of these states was less than ₹ 500 each.

The vast Ganga-Brahmaputra plain, carved into the states of Uttar Pradesh, Bihar, West Bengal and Assam, is ascribed several negative attributes defying the sacredness of its river systems, fertility of alluvial soils and abundance of water supply. Reeling under severe population pressure, with vast majority of landholdings smaller than one hectare, and scarce employment avenues outside agriculture, this elongated belt has taken the form of a poverty trough. Poverty itself had a cumulative causation syndrome. Lack of desired quality of governance hampered the pace of development. The private sector investment was diffident because of poor quality of infrastructure and weak condition of law and order. Equally the utilization of financial resources devolved by the central government left much to be desired. A redeeming feature is the prevalence of an acute political awareness of the people. If properly harnessed, it can be turned into a movement for overall development.

The middle belt of India, comprising Rajasthan, Madhya Pradesh, Chhattisgarh, Jharkhand and Odisha, is also marked by a compound annual growth which was below the national average. Part of this could be explained by difficulty of its dissected terrain or by considerable cover of unattended forests, or by persistent isolation of tribal communities in several areas. Herein is located the red corridor or Naxal-affected hotspot of India linked to the outrage of the tribals against usurpation of their land in the name of development, exploitation of natural resources and deficit of governance. Nature's bounty turned into a bane. Poverty persisted, the tribal community was radically organized, and aggressive protests followed. Such conditions were detrimental to rapid economic growth. Irrigation remained a low priority, extension of transport facility was hampered, and provision of educational and health facilities was inadequate. Things are changing now. There is steady improvement in governance. Law and order situation is not as bad as before. There is an effort toward creating a better future.

Likewise the slow economic growth rate of Manipur, Nagaland and Meghalaya in the North-East testifies that lack of peace is a sure source of vulnerability. The terrorist activity linked to insurgency in these states has been disruptive of daily life of the people and was a disincentive to investment. To their disadvantage is also a peripheral location. A boost to India's international trade with Bangladesh and Myanmar can provide a stimulus to their economy. They are, as of now, recipient of illegal immigrants from Bangladesh and at times of insurgents from Myanmar. Things have to change to promise better days for these small, remote, ethnic states of India.

Most worrisome is the case of Punjab. Once eulogized as a model state in being a pioneer of the Green Revolution in wheat and rice, a hub of small scale industries and a qualifier of being second highest in per capita NSDP in 1980–81 in India after Goa, the state has fallen on bad days as far as economic growth rate is concerned. It recorded a compound annual growth rate of only 3.1 per cent during 1980–81 to 2011–12. This was much below the national average of 4 per cent. The addition to the state's per capita NSDP during these years was also on the lower side of the national average. In 2011–12, Punjab ranked 11th among the states of India in terms of per capita NSDP.

The fact is that Punjab could not sustain much less build on the gains of the Green Revolution. It could not wean itself away from the wheat-rice rotation towards a more diversified cropping pattern. This proved detrimental to its water and soil resource base. There was a regular rise in the cost of agricultural production and income to the agriculturalists started falling.

Likewise the industry in Punjab was not successful in competing with industry in the neighbouring states of Haryana and Himachal Pradesh as well as in the National Capital Territory of Delhi. The liberal imports from China also had a depressing effect on the demand for industrial products of Punjab. Meanwhile, Punjab industry had to bear the brunt of exorbitant price of land and high rates of electricity. Above all, the difficult political situation in Punjab in the 1980s and the infirmities of associated governance impaired the state's economy. The greatest irony was that the state could not benefit from remittances from abroad in terms of investment in direct productive activities as much as it could. Many a Non-Resident Indian opted to invest outside in states like Gujarat, Haryana and Himachal Pradesh rather than in the home state. Punjab proved rather weak on the merits of peace and good governance in the first half of the period under reference.

The above observations on the economic growth behaviour of various states are vividly reflected in the ratio between their respective per capita NSDP in 1980–81 and 2011–12. India's per capita NSDP became 3.5 fold during this period. The living standard of an average Indian improved in real terms to this extent during the span of three decades or of a generation.

Sikkim's per capita NSDP multiplied by 6.4 times, of Tamil Nadu by 5.8 times and of Goa by 4.8 times. The multiple factor of the NSDP of Gujarat, Maharashtra and Andhra Pradesh was also higher than 4. Tripura in the North-East belonged to the same group. On the other extreme downhill were the states of Jammu & Kashmir, with a multiple factor of 1.8 times, Assam of 1.9 times and Uttar Pradesh of 2.1 times. The Punjab picture was also dismal with only 2.7 times rise in NSDP. This was only somewhat above the figure of 2.3 times for Bihar and 2.4 times for Odisha.

The data relating to average annual increment in the NSDP of various states portrays the scenario more vividly (Map 4.4). Goa recorded the highest annual increment of ₹ 3,207, followed by Sikkim at ₹ 1,943. The states of Maharashtra and Gujarat in Western India; Tamil Nadu, Kerala and Andhra Pradesh in South India; the hill states of Uttarakhand and Himachal Pradesh in the North-West India and Haryana, which is in contiguity with the National Capital Territory of Delhi, all were noted for an annual increment of ₹ 1,000 to ₹ 1,500 in their NSDP. Bihar, on the other hand, found itself located at the bottom with its NSDP increasing on an average by ₹ 235 every year. Jharkhand, Odisha, Chhattisgarh, Madhya Pradesh and Uttar Pradesh in the Middle and North India; Jammu & Kashmir in the North-West India and Assam and Manipur in the North-East were the other states where the annual rise in the NSDP was less than ₹ 500. The increment figure ranged between ₹ 500 and ₹ 1,000 for the remaining states. Contrary to the popular perception of Punjab being a prospering state, the average annual increase in its NSDP was only ₹ 906 as compared to the national average of ₹ 923.

The regional pattern of economic progression in India is obvious enough. The West Indian states are the sprint runner today, followed by the South Indian states. The states in the middle belt of India are emerging in the

Map 4.4

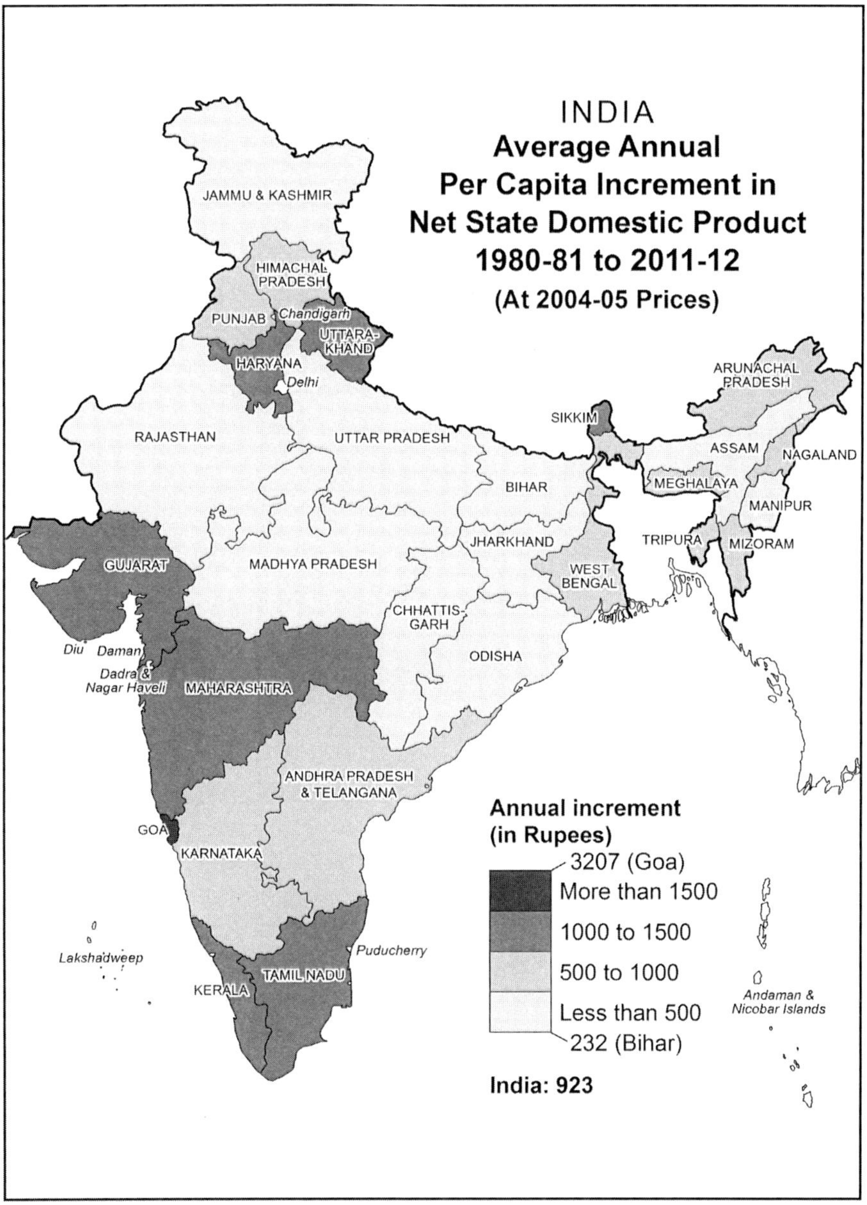

The per capita NSDP or income of an Indian increased by Rs. 923/- per year on an avearge during 1980-81 to 2011-12 in real terms; for Goa this figure was more than Rs. three thousand and for Bihar less than Rs. three hundred.

nature of breaking out ones. Similar is the story of peaceful states in the North-East, more specifically Sikkim, Arunachal Pradesh, Mizoram and Tripura. The hill states of Himachal Pradesh and Uttarakhand are to be applauded for the same reason. All the union territories are also on the path of rapid economic growth. On the other hand, the Great Ganga-Brahmaputra plain is yet to display a hopeful spectacle. Revival of its vitality is awaited.

On the whole, it seems that good governance, peaceful law and order conditions and locational advantages were critical to the process of economic rise of different states. High per capita energy consumption, dense network of metalled roads and favourable credit-deposit ratio were invariably a great stimulus. States which favoured English at the school level of education were better placed for promotion of science, technology and professional courses and hence progressed faster. Newly carved out states exhibited an extra zeal for demonstrating their economic vigour. Emigration from a state was a factor in strengthening its finances through remittances. The economic development map of India has been undergoing a considerable change over time. There is a need to revise the conventional stereotypes on this count.

Contribution of Different States to Net State Domestic Product: 1980–81 to 2011–12

Here is an attempt to measure the relative contribution of various states to the nation's economic performance. The methodology adopted was as follows. As a first step, the NSDP of India, at constant prices of 2004–05, was noted for the years 1980–81 and 2011–12 and difference between the two was worked out. This represented the addition to the nation's NSDP during this period. Second, on similar lines, the difference in the NSDP of every state for the years 1980–81 and 2011–12 was calculated. This was the contribution made by respective states to their aggregate addition in the nation's NSDP. Third, the figure for each state was computed as percentage of the nation's aggregate figure. This stood for the percentage contribution of various states to augmentation in the nation's kitty during the period from 1980–81 to 2011–12. Fourth, the percentage share of the population of each state in India's total in 2011 was found out. Finally, the ratio between the percentage contribution of each state to the addition in the nation's NSDP during the period from 1980–81 to 2011–12 and its percentage share in nation's population in 2011 was calculated. This was meant to neutralize the role of population size of a state vis-a-vis its contribution. If the statistic was higher than one, it showed that the contribution was higher than its share of population and vice versa (Table 4.4).

The contribution of Goa was more than three times relative to its population size; of Sikkim more than two times; and of Maharashtra nearly two times (Map 4.5). Gujarat too was high ranking on this count. All the West and South Indian states made notable contributions to the increment in the nation's earnings. The same was true of all the states in the North-East, barring Manipur. Likewise, the states in the North-West, with the exception of Jammu & Kashmir, belonged to the group of significant

Map 4.5

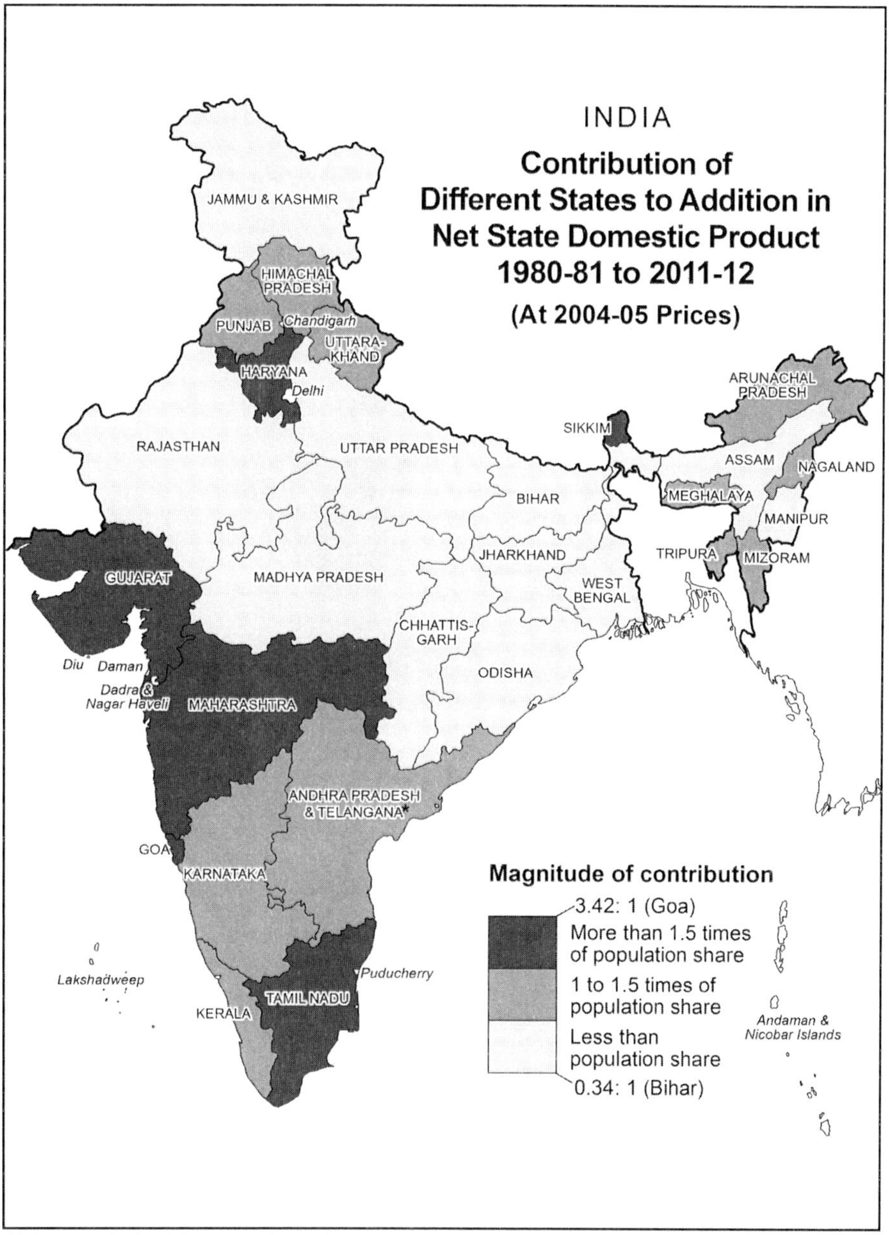

All the states in South India and West India, along with most of them in North-West India, contributed significantly more to the addition in nation's kitty vis-a-vis their share in total population.

contributors. It needs to be added that, in absolute amount, the bigger states made contributions which were many times that of the smaller states.

Table 4.4 *India: Percentage Contribution of Different States (in percentage) to Rise in Net State Domestic Product (NSDP) during the period from 1980–81 and 2011–12 and their Percentage Share in the Country's Total Population in 2011**

State**	Percentage share in		Difference in percentage points	Ratio of share in NSDP addition and population
	Addition to NSDP	Population		
1. Goa	0.41	0.12	0.29	3.42
2. Sikkim	0.11	0.05	0.06	2.20
3. Maharashtra	17.60	9.43	8.17	1.87
4. Haryana	3.82	2.13	1.69	1.79
5. Gujarat	8.60	5.08	3.52	1.69
6. Tamil Nadu	10.12	6.06	4.06	1.67
7. Uttarakhand	1.26	0.85	0.41	1.48
8. Kerala	3.88	2.81	1.07	1.38
9. Himachal Pradesh	0.79	0.58	0.21	1.36
10. Nagaland	0.23	0.17	0.06	1.35
11. Mizoram	0.12	0.09	0.03	1.33
12. Karnataka	6.36	5.13	1.23	1.24
13. Punjab	2.90	2.33	0.57	1.24
14. Andhra Pradesh***	8.76	7.10	1.66	1.23
15. Tripura	0.36	0.31	0.05	1.16
16. Meghalaya	0.27	0.25	0.02	1.08
17. Arunachal Pradesh	0.13	0.12	0.01	1.08
18. West Bengal	7.06	7.67	–0.61	0.92
19. Rajasthan	4.86	5.76	–0.90	0.84
20. Jammu & Kashmir	0.76	1.05	–0.29	0.72
21. Chhattisgarh	1.53	2.15	–0.62	0.71
22. Jharkhand	1.83	2.77	–0.94	0.66
23. Odisha	2.24	3.52	–1.28	0.64
24. Madhya Pradesh	3.66	6.10	–2.44	0.60
25. Manipur	0.14	0.24	–0.10	0.58
26. Assam	1.40	2.62	–1.22	0.53
27. Uttar Pradesh	7.86	16.77	–8.91	0.47
28. Bihar	2.94	8.74	–5.80	0.34

* Based on standardization of data provided by Central Statistical Organisation and Census of India, New Delhi.

** States are listed in descending order of their relative contribution to the NSDP.

*** Includes Telangana.

By contrast, the contribution of Bihar was just one-third in relation to its share in population, of Uttar Pradesh less than one-half, and of Assam slightly more than one-half. Madhya Pradesh, Odisha and Jharkhand were noted for a contribution which was less than two-thirds of their share in population. West Bengal, Rajasthan and Chhattisgarh also fell below their mark in this regard. All these states in North and Middle India are large in population and area size. An all out effort to strengthen their economy is the need of hour.

An equally authentic measure of economic performance of different states is to match the amount of financial transfers, in the form of taxes and grants, they received from the central government and the contribution they made to the increase in the aggregate NSDP during the corresponding period. The data spanning over three decades from the early years of 1980s to 2011–12 was put in service for the purpose. Ratio between the per cent share in the central transfers and the per cent contribution made to the addition in aggregate NSDP by each state during the period was computed and analysed (Table 4.5).

Table 4.5 *India: Per cent Share of Different States in Transfers from the Centre (Tax Devolution plus Grants) during the period from the 6th to the 12th Plans (1980–2012)* and their Contribution to Net State Domestic Product (NSDP) from 1980–81 to 2011–12*

States	*Per cent share in*		*Ratio between share and contribution*
	Central transfers	*Contribution to NSDP*	
Haryana	1.18	3.82	3.23
Maharashtra	6.27	17.6	2.81
Gujarat	3.62	8.6	2.37
Tamil Nadu	5.88	10.12	1.72
Punjab	1.7	2.9	1.71
Karnataka	4.32	6.36	1.47
Goa	0.3	0.41	1.36
Andhra Pradesh**	7.24	8.76	1.21
Kerala	3.38	3.88	1.15
West Bengal	7.55	7.06	0.94
Rajasthan	5.86	4.86	0.83
Uttarakhand	1.61	1.26	0.78
Chhattisgarh	2.42	1.53	0.63
Jharkhand	3.13	1.83	0.58
Madhya Pradesh	7.36	3.66	0.5
Uttar Pradesh	16.37	7.86	0.48
Sikkim	0.23	0.11	0.48
Odisha	4.91	2.24	0.46
Himachal Pradesh	1.87	0.79	0.42
Assam	3.62	1.4	0.39
Meghalaya	0.78	0.27	0.35
Tripura	1.23	0.36	0.29
Bihar	11.05	2.94	0.27
Jammu & Kashmir	2.94	0.76	0.26
Nagaland	1.2	0.23	0.19
Arunachal Pradesh	0.74	0.13	0.18
Mizoram	0.84	0.12	0.14
Manipur	1.02	0.14	0.14

Source: Government of India. 2009–2014. *Report of the Thirteenth Finance Commission*. Vol. 1, pp. 28–29 and National Sample Organization, New Delhi.

* Years 1990–92 was a period of annual plans.

** Includes Telangana.

Most noteworthy is the fact that the two western states of Maharashtra and Gujarat contributed 26.2 per cent to the addition in NSDP while they received hardly 9.9 per cent of the central transfers. This gives a ratio of roughly 3:1 in their favour. If this is added to the contributions made by the four South Indian states of Tamil Nadu, Karnataka, Kerala and Andhra Pradesh, the aggregate works out as 55.3 per cent against 30.7 per cent of central transfers received. This also gives a ratio of nearly 2:1, which is commendable. Contributions of Haryana, Punjab and Goa were also higher than that of their respective shares in central transfers.

On the dismal side, Bihar received 11.1 per cent of the central transfers but contributed barely 2.9 per cent to the addition in NSDP. The respective figures for Jammu & Kashmir were 2.9 and 0.8 per cent respectively. Uttar Pradesh partook 16.4 per cent of the central transfers but added only 7.9 per cent to the NSDP. The story is no different in the case of Madhya Pradesh, Odisha and Himachal Pradesh. Likewise, the aggregate percentage figures for all the eight states of the North-East region were 9.7 and 2.8 respectively. By comparison, West Bengal and Rajasthan made a contribution which was fairly close to their share in central transfers.

The above analysis places the economic performance of the West and South Indian states at a high pedestal. North and Middle Indian states were rather on a weak wicket on the score. Economic health of the states in the North-East region was feeble. Haryana and Punjab in the North-West, of course, presented themselves as bright spots.

Index of Poverty Decline

It is often emphasized that in developing countries like India the quality of development could be better assessed in terms of decline in poverty ratio rather than through the rise in average income level of the people. A rapid rise in per capita income is often a result of a jump in the income level of people in upper strata while the condition of the poor may improve only marginally. Poverty alleviation is a universal imperative. A decline in poverty ratio may not cause a big increase in per capita income because here only small sums are involved. There is no necessary and straight correspondence between the rates of poverty decline and income escalation.

To obtain a comparative view of various states and union territories in respect of their performance on poverty alleviation, the available data on poverty ratio from 1973–74 to 2013–14 was put in service. A poverty decline index was worked out in each case. This was done by subtracting the percentage of population below poverty line in 1973–74 from that in 2013–14 and dividing this difference by the percentage of population below poverty line in 1973–74. The first part of this calculation represented the absolute decline of poverty ratio in percentage points and the second part was meant to refer this decline to maximum possible decline. The resultant indices were in the nature of poverty alleviation success rate. These were multiplied by 100 to convert them in percentage points. The results obtained are given in Table 4.6.

Table 4.6 *India: Index of Poverty Decline during 1973–74 to 2013–14 by States and Union Territories*

States	*Percentage of population below poverty line in*		*Index of poverty decline*	*Rank*
	1973–74	*2013–14*		
Goa	44.3	5.1	89	1
Kerala	59.8	7.1	88	2
Sikkim	50.9	8.2	84	3
Andhra Pradesh*	48.9	9.2	81	4
Uttarakhand	57.1	11.3	80	5
Tamil Nadu	54.9	11.3	79	6
Meghalaya	50.2	11.9	76	7
Jammu & Kashmir	40.8	10.4	75	8
Tripura	51.0	14.1	72	9
Punjab	28.2	8.3	71	10
Himachal Pradesh	26.4	8.1	69	11
West Bengal	63.4	20.0	68	12
Haryana	35.4	11.2	68	13
Rajasthan	46.1	14.7	68	14
Maharashtra	53.2	17.4	67	15
Gujarat	48.2	16.6	66	16
Nagaland	50.8	18.9	63	17
Karnataka	54.5	20.9	62	18
Mizoram	50.3	20.9	58	19
Odisha	66.2	32.6	51	20
Madhya Pradesh	61.8	31.7	49	21
Uttar Pradesh	57.1	29.4	49	22
Jharkhand	61.9	32.6	40	23
Assam	51.2	32.0	38	24
Chhattisgarh	61.8	39.9	35	25
Bihar	61.9	40.7	34	26
Arunachal Pradesh	51.9	34.7	33	27
Manipur	50.0	36.9	26	28
Union Territories				
Andaman and Nicobar Islands	55.6	1.0	98	1
Lakshadweep	59.7	2.8	95	2
Puducherry	53.8	9.7	82	3
Daman and Diu	54.9	9.9	82	4
Delhi	49.6	9.9	80	5
Chandigarh	28.0	21.8	22	6
Dadra and Nagar Haveli	46.6	39.3	16	7
India	54.9	21.9	60	

Source: Compiled and processed data available from the Planning Commission of India, now NITI Aayog, and Reserve Bank of India, New Delhi.

* Includes Telangana.

Map 4.6

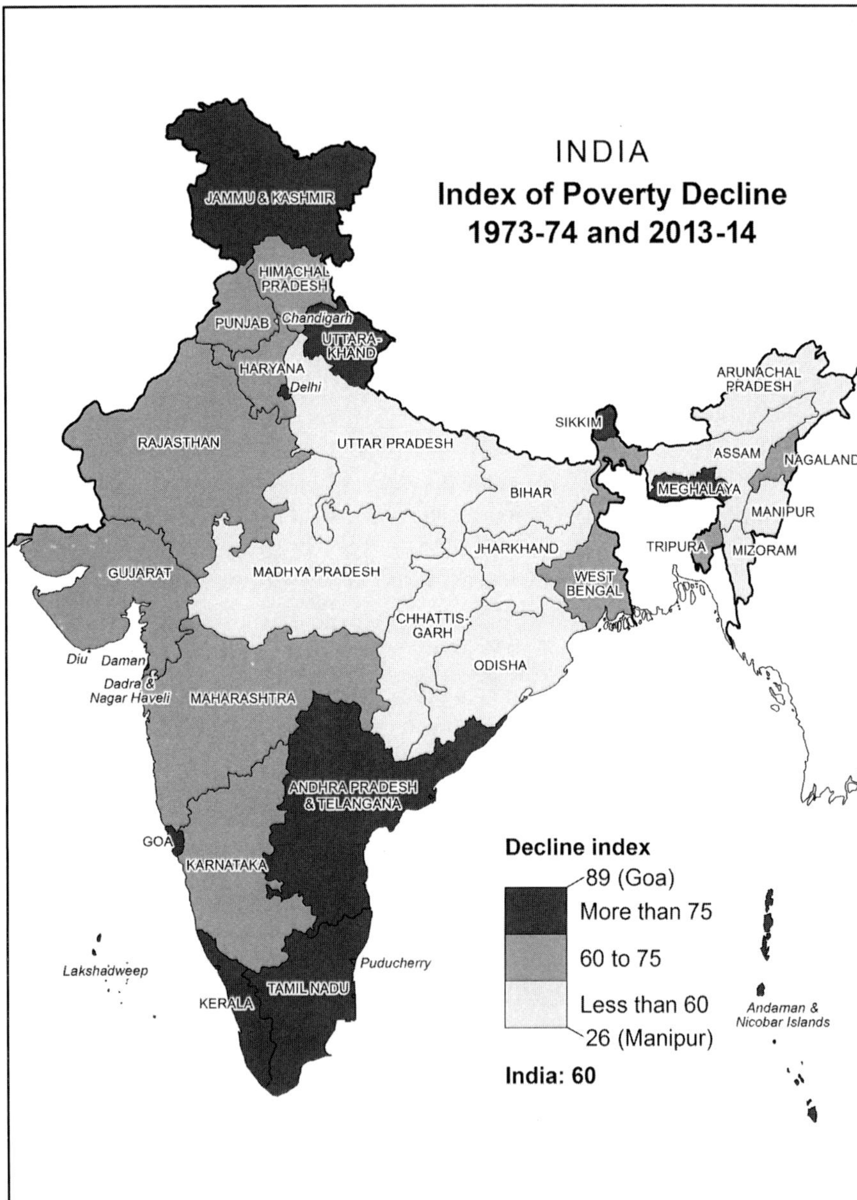

The South Indian states and those in Western Himalayan Region made a significant dent on poverty, essentially by following social welfare policies.

Source: Planning Commission (now NITI Ayog) and Reserve Bank of India, New Delhi

During four decades since 1973–74, India could bring down its poverty ratio from 54.9 per cent to 21.9 per cent. This gives an average decline rate of 0.8 per cent points per year. Statewise performance differed. Goa together with the South Indian states of Kerala, Andhra Pradesh and Tamil Nadu recorded a commendable success in poverty alleviation (Map 4.6). This could be attributed to robust economic growth in Goa and to pro-poor social welfare policies in the case of South Indian states. A steep decline in the poverty ratio of Sikkim was also an outcome of its rapid strides in economic growth. The role of the government policies in favour of the poor was much more evident in the hill states of Jammu & Kashmir, Himachal Pradesh and Uttarakhand. The fall in the poverty ratio in Punjab was commensurate with the overall economic well-being.

Meanwhile, Uttar Pradesh, Bihar, Madhya Pradesh and Odisha, along with Jharkhand and Chhattisgarh, persist as an extensive poverty zone. The decline in poverty ratio has been of the lowest order in this part of India. All these states started with a massive base of poverty and the situation is taking time to improve. Poverty decline in Maharashtra, Gujarat and Haryana was not consistent with the growth rate of their economy. The same has been the case of Karnataka. The metropolitan cities of all these states are regular recipients of migrants from other states.

Some broad aspects of spatial picture of poverty decline may be highlighted again. Greater success in poverty alleviation was achieved by the South Indian states as also by states in the North-Western region. This is attributed to social welfare policies they followed in all earnestness, in addition to their better performance on economic front. North Indian states as also the Middle Indian ones have to go a long way before they can win the battle against poverty. As a group, all the union territories are to be credited for a greater success in poverty alleviation. A meaningful combination of social welfare policies and economic growth offers a fast lane for poverty alleviation in any state or union territory.

Index of Development Level

The preceding discussion on the spatial patterns of economic performance and poverty decline tempts one to explore the regional variations in overall development level in India. This calls for a more comprehensive view of things beyond the considerations of economic growth and poverty decline. One essential aspect here would be to define development in geographical parlance.

For our purpose, development may be equated with the vitality of a regional system. This formulation subsumes the parameters of economic well-being, social harmony, political maturity, ecological balance and a sustained progression. All this has to be mutually-reinforcing.

Which could be the possible measures of the relative development levels of various states and union territories? These are expected to address various dimensions of development, subject to availability of requisite data.

The present study believes that the following eight indicators meet such conditions:

(i) Per capita net state domestic product, to represent economic well-being and efficiency in the system;

(ii) Poverty decline index, as a measure of social welfare and equity;

(iii) Percentage of non-agricultural workers in rural areas, to capture the degree of diversification of rural economy and rural transformation;

(iv) Percentage of literate females, as an index of status of women, and further to social development;

(v) Infant mortality in reverse, to ascertain life survival chances and access to healthcare facilities;

(vi) Percentage of households with computer/laptop facility, to confirm technological advancement;

(vii) Per capita energy consumption, to make evident the functional vigour of the system and

(viii) Percentage of urban population, to epitomize all round progress toward modernization.

Harnessing data from a variety of sources, such as the Central Statistical Organization, Census of India and National Institution for Transforming India (NITI Aayog), a statistical exercise was run to arrive at the development level of various states and union territories of India. These data were processed, the relative weight of different indicators was determined, and composite score of development was calculated in each case. Adopting 100 as the base for India, the scores of different states/union territories were standardized. The results obtained are presented in Table 4.7.

On composite index of development, Goa emerges as far ahead of all other states. It is closely followed by the union territories, by and large. Kerala and Tamil Nadu in South India; Punjab and Haryana in the North-West India; Sikkim and Mizoram in the North-East; and Maharashtra in the West India are also at a relatively high level of development (Map 4.7). Barring Maharashtra and Tamil Nadu, all these states are comparatively small in size. Smallness appears as more favourable. This could not be said about the per unit cost of development which is likely to be less in larger states.

Again Gujarat on the western coast; Karnataka and Andhra Pradesh in South India; the hill states of Jammu & Kashmir, Himachal Pradesh and Uttarakhand; West Bengal in the east; and Tripura, Nagaland and Manipur in the North-East belong to the next category on development level. They are high on certain parameters of development but lag behind on others. Evidently the different parameters of the development process are not advancing at the same pace in their case.

At the low rung of development are located the North and East Indian states of Uttar Pradesh, Bihar and Assam; the middle belt states of Odisha, Chhattisgarh, Jharkhand, Madhya Pradesh and Rajasthan; and North-East states of Arunachal Pradesh and Meghalaya. Bihar finds a place at the bottom among these states. Most of the states in the group are large in size.

Table 4.7 *India: Composite Development Scores of States and Union Territories, 2011*

States	*Development score*	*Rank*	*Union Territories*	*Development score*	*Rank*
Goa	315	1	Chandigarh	297	1
Kerala	181	2	Dadra and Nagar Haveli	296	2
Punjab	139	3	Daman and Diu	278	3
Tamil Nadu	137	4	NCT of Delhi	268	4
Haryana	136	5	Lakshadweep	198	5
Sikkim	135	6	Puducherry	188	6
Maharashtra	132	7	Andaman and Nicobar Islands	141	7
Mizoram	121	8	India	100	
Gujarat	120	9			
Manipur	118	10			
Karnataka	117	11			
Uttarakhand	117	12			
Jammu & Kashmir	110	13			
Himachal Pradesh	107	14			
Nagaland	104	15			
West Bengal	102	16			
Tripura	101	17			
Andhra Pradesh*	100	18			
Arunachal Pradesh	93	19			
Meghalaya	87	20			
Assam	83	21			
Jharkhand	82	22			
Rajasthan	81	23			
Odisha	76	24			
Chhattisgarh	74	25			
Uttar Pradesh	72	26			
Madhya Pradesh	68	27			
Bihar	56	28			

* Includes Telangana.

Some salient features of the development contours of the map of India cannot be missed. Within South India, Kerala and Tamil Nadu are more developed than Karnataka and Andhra Pradesh. In the case of Western India, development level declines from south to north in respect of Goa, Maharashtra and Gujarat. North-West Indian hill states are at a comparatively higher level of development than the North-East states, and within the North-East, the ones located at a distance from Assam are better placed on the development board. The core of backwardness in North India is located in Bihar and that of Middle India in Madhya Pradesh. Notably the newly carved out states, namely Jharkhand, Chhattisgarh and Uttarakhand, are at

Map 4.7

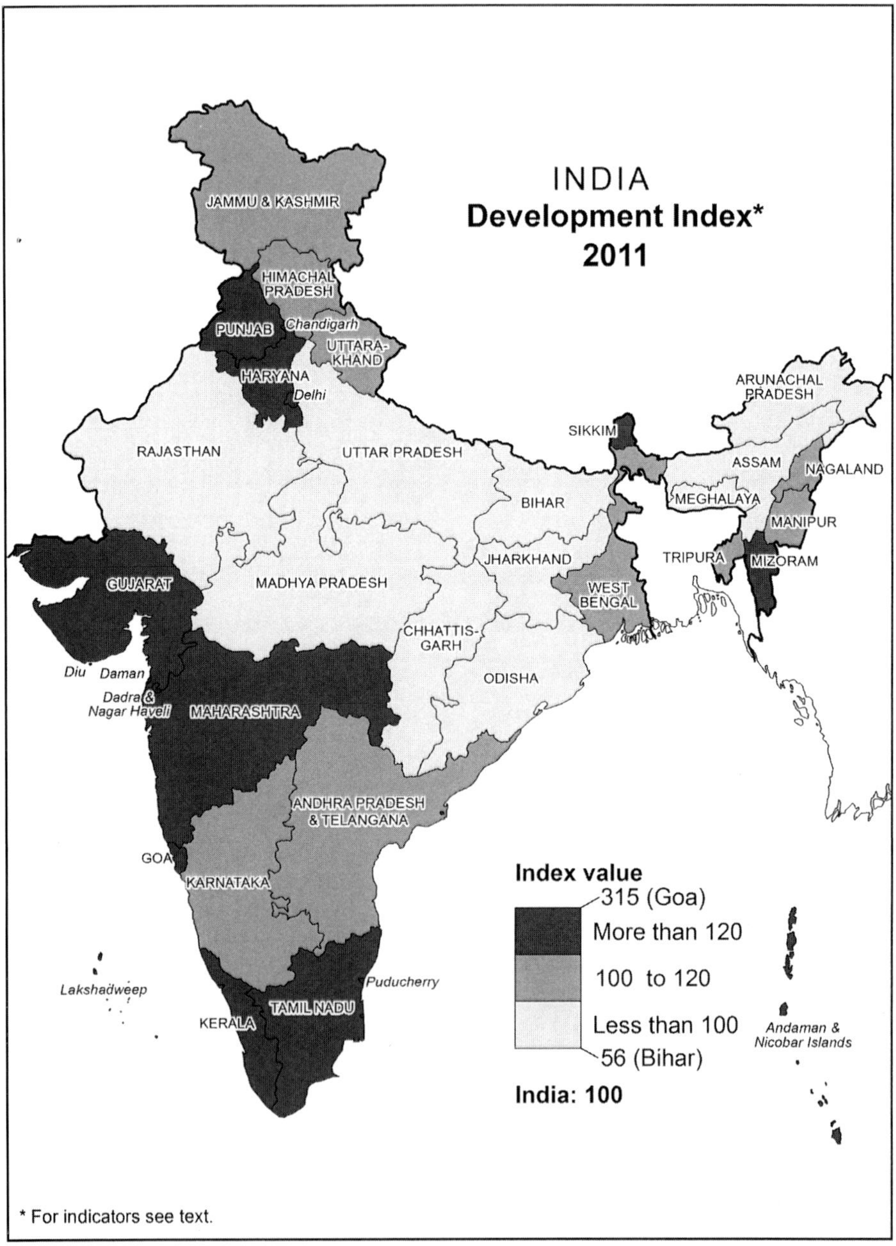

The heartland of India remains weak on development index.

somewhat higher level of development than their parent states. All the union territories stand out high on the development map of India.

It needs to be emphasized that this development map, which is the end product of processes operating over long time, may not necessarily reflect the evolving economic performance map of India today. The middle belt, which ranks low on development, is now a vibrant case. Punjab, which emerges as high on development level, is currently in a sluggish tone. Jammu & Kashmir has slowed down on economic front but Odisha has acquired fresh vigour. Economic drive of Uttarakhand and Himachal Pradesh is not much reflected in their development level. The spatial picture of economic change in India is subject to the quality of governance and associated policy thrust on development issues.

Quality of Living Space

The development level finds an association with the quality of living space. In the context of India, this quality can be referred to three sets of factors: (i) status of housing conditions, represented by the percentage of households living in *pucca, kutcha* or semi-*pucca* houses; (ii) availability of living space, measured by percentage of households living in two or more rooms, percentage of households having separate bathroom and percentage of households having separate kitchen; and (iii) provision of amenities, in terms of percentage of households having toilet within the house; the facility of treated water supply, LPG/PNG as cooking fuel and electricity for lighting. Using data for these indicators, as made available by the Census of India 2011, and applying the same technique as for computing the development index, the quality of living space was worked for all the states and union territories of India. Table 4.8 provides the results as obtained.

The quality of living space in India is marked by striking regional variations. Union territories are noted for higher quality of living space than the states (Map 4.8). The quality index is the highest for the National Capital Territory of Delhi, followed by Chandigarh and Puducherry. Dadra & Nagar Haveli is at the bottom among union territories but its index score is higher than the all-India average.

Among the states, Goa occupies the top position and Bihar is at the lowest step of the ladder. Indeed there is a wide locational scattering of the states distinguished by relatively high quality of living space. These include Punjab, Haryana, Himachal Pradesh and Uttarakhand in the North-West India; Sikkim and Mizoram in the North-East; and Kerala, Maharashtra and Gujarat marking the western coastal belt. The South Indian states of Tamil Nadu, Karnataka and Andhra Pradesh also carry scores which are on the higher side of the national average.

On the other hand, the North and Middle Indian states of Rajasthan, Uttar Pradesh, Madhya Pradesh, Chhattisgarh and Jharkhand, in addition to Bihar already mentioned are below the national average. The same is true of the East Indian states of Assam, West Bengal and Odisha. Tripura and Meghalaya in the North-East belong to the same genre.

Table 4.8 *India: Index of Quality of Living Space by States and Union Territories, 2011*

States	*Index*	*Rank*	*Union Territories*	*Index*	*Rank*
Goa	188	1	NCT of Delhi	190	1
Punjab	157	2	Chandigarh	190	2
Kerala	147	3	Puducherry	172	3
Himachal Pradesh	143	4	Daman and Diu	149	4
Haryana	142	5	Lakshadweep	142	5
Sikkim	139	6	Andaman and Nicobar Islands	137	6
Gujarat	137	7	Dadra and Nagar Haveli	122	7
Uttarakhand	136	8	India	100	
Maharashtra	134	9			
Mizoram	132	10			
Karnataka	126	11			
Tamil Nadu	126	12			
Jammu & Kashmir	114	13			
Andhra Pradesh*	113	14			
Nagaland	105	15			
Manipur	101	16			
Arunachal Pradesh	97	17			
Rajasthan	86	18			
Tripura	82	19			
Meghalaya	82	20			
Uttar Pradesh	79	21			
West Bengal	78	22			
Assam	73	23			
Madhya Pradesh	72	24			
Chhattisgarh	60	25			
Jharkhand	55	26			
Odisha	54	27			
Bihar	46	28			

* Includes Telangana.

It follows that South India enjoys higher quality of living space than North India. Within South India, Goa excels and in North India, Punjab occupies a similar place of pride. Among the hill states in the North-West, Himachal Pradesh is better placed than others and the same is true of Sikkim in the North-East. Dismal is the picture of the heartland of India. Union territories, of course, emerge as comparatively better places to live. In her research based on 2001 Census of India data, Wadhera (2008: p. 243) had discovered per capita income, urbanization level and infrastructure status as the three most critical determinants of the quality of living space in India.

Map 4.8

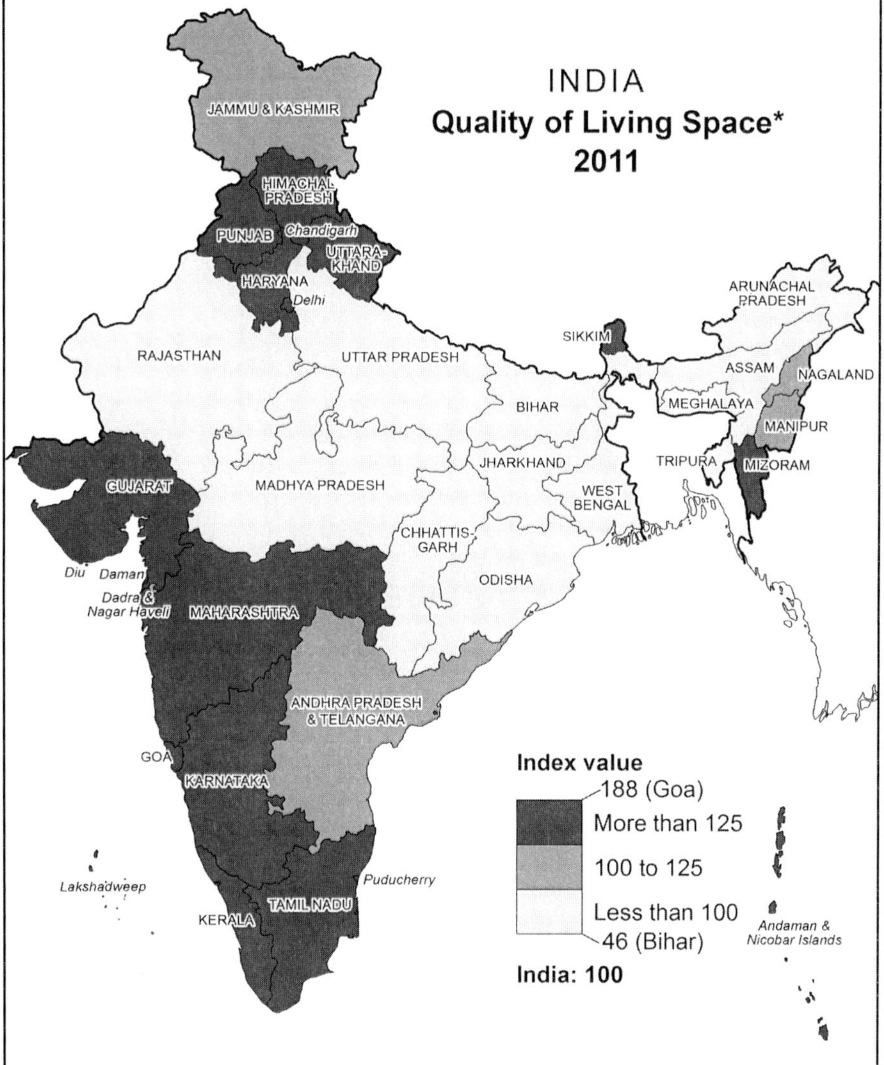

* For indicators see text.

The South, West and North-West India outperform North, Middle and North-East India on the quality of living space.

Economic Dynamism: A Synthesis of Measures

The foregoing analysis focused on five measures of comparative economic dynamism of various states and union territories in India. The first was their 'per capita NSDP and its compound annual growth rate' during 1980–81 to 2011–12. An assessment was made of the relative improvement in economic well-being of the people in different parts of India. At the same time it was considered necessary to work out the contribution of each state to the rise in the national NSDP over the given period. This second measure of 'additive contribution' was meant to identify states which were giving stronger push to the economy of the country. Soon it was realized that an increase in per capita NSDP could be a result of a bigger increase in the income level of the well-off and the poor may have been only a small beneficiary. Therefore, 'decline in poverty ratio' was deemed as the third critical measure of economic dynamism. The fourth measure taken up was under the title 'level of development'. This was consistent with an assumption that this would be a reliable outcome of its economic dynamism. Finally, 'the quality of living space' was adopted as the fifth measure of economic dynamism. The basic idea was that economic dynamism is both a cause and effect of the 'quality of living space' of the people.

The data on these parameters revealed that the following 10 states were higher than the national average on all the five measures (Map 4.9):

South India	(i)	Kerala
	(ii)	Tamil Nadu
	(iii)	Karnataka
	(iv)	Andhra Pradesh
West India	(v)	Gujarat
	(vi)	Goa
North-West India	(vii)	Haryana
	(viii)	Himachal Pradesh
North-East India	(ix)	Sikkim
	(x)	Mizoram

By contrast, the following five states were below the national average on all the five measures:

North India	(i)	Bihar
	(ii)	Uttar Pradesh
Middle India	(iii)	Chhattisgarh
	(iv)	Jharkhand
	(v)	Odisha

The following four states were relatively higher than the national level on four measures but lower on one measure (as mentioned in the parenthesis):

(i) Punjab (compound annual growth rate)
(ii) Maharashtra (poverty decline)

Map 4.9

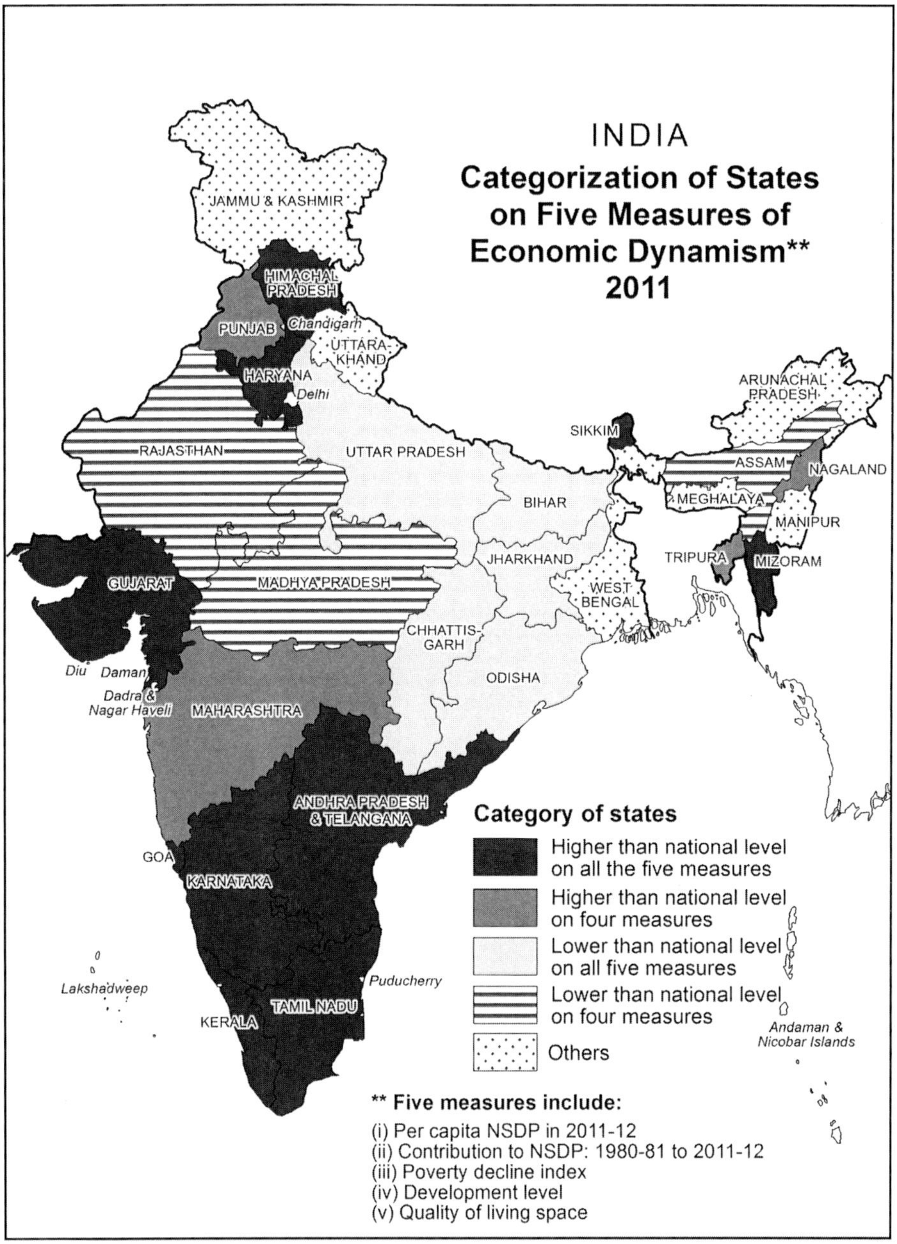

The South and West Indian states stand out as extensive zones of economic dynamism.

(iii) Tripura (quality of living space)
(iv) Nagaland (compound annual growth rate)

By comparison, the following three states were lower than the national level on four measures but higher on one measure (as listed in the parenthesis):

(i) Assam (poverty decline)
(ii) Madhya Pradesh (poverty decline)
(iii) Rajasthan (poverty decline)

The following four states were higher than the national average on the count of three measures but lower on two measures (as listed in parenthesis):

(i) Jammu & Kashmir (compound annual growth rate and contribution to NSDP)
(ii) Uttarakhand (poverty decline and contribution to NSDP)
(iii) Arunachal Pradesh (poverty decline and contribution to NSDP)
(iv) Manipur (compound annual growth rate and contribution to NSDP)

Finally, the following two states were lower than the national average on three measures but higher on two measures (as mentioned in parenthesis):

(i) West Bengal (poverty decline and development level)
(ii) Meghalaya (poverty decline and contribution to NSDP).

The contours of 'economic dynamism' on the map of India are evident enough. The four South Indian states constitute together an extensive economically dynamic zone. Indications are that they are doing well not only in terms of economic growth but also in governance and social welfare. Paradoxical this part of India is marked for both outmigration to other parts of India and emigration to other countries. This represents an urge to avail of lucrative employment opportunities available anywhere. By comparison, the states in West India are also distinguished by economic dynamism and these are destinations of significant inmigration to their industrial-urban concentrations. They are, of course, in the company of South Indian states in terms of emigration. By contrast, the North Indian states are suffering from intense resource/population imbalance, infirmities of social structure on caste lines, and complexities of governance. The states in their contiguity towards the south are rich in natural resources but they are in wait of their optimal utilization for acquiring economic momentum. They are showing signs of acquiring vibrancy through improved governance. In the case of hill states in both North-West and North-East India, peace is the key to economic dynamism. Peace goes with good governance and that determines its vigour. The peaceful states and their politically disturbed neighbouring states in these two regions present a contrast to each other in economic dynamism. Finally, one cannot miss the vigorous economic dynamism of the National Capital Region, which covers the nation's capital and parts of its neighbouring states. Outstanding economic dynamism is evidently metropolitan, coastal and selectively hilly.

References

Acemoglu, Daron and James Robinson. 2012. *Why Nations Fail: The Origins of Power, Prosperity and Poverty*. New York: Crown Business.

Davies, Sara and Martin Hallet. 2002. *Interactions between National and Regional Development*. Hamburg: Institute of International Economics.

Ellis, Peter and Mark Roberts. 2015. *Leveraging Urbanisation in South Asia*. Washington, D.C.: World Bank.

International Monetary Fund. 2014. *World Economic Outlook Database*. Washington, D.C.

Krishan, Gopal. 1989. Trends in Regional Disparities in India. *Asian Profile*. Vol. 17, No. 3, pp. 243–261.

LeFranc, Genevieve. 2015. *The Daily Reckoning*. An email Newsletter, August 5.

O'Sullivan, Arthur and Steven M. Sheffrin. 2003. *Economics: Principles in Action*. New Jersey: Pearson Prentice Hall.

Stiglitz, Joseph E., Amartya Sen and Jean-Paul Fitoussi. 2010. *Mis-Measuring Our Lives*. New York: New York Press.

Wadhera, Bharti. 2008. *Regional Variations in the Quality of Living Space in India*. Chandigarh: Panjab University (Unpublished Ph.D. Thesis).

Williamson, J.G. 1965. Regional Inequality and the Process of National Development: A Description of the Patterns. *Economic Development and Cultural Change*. Vol. 13, No. 4, pp. 3–45.

5

Rise of the Middle Class

A class is a group of people who are similar in their economic standing and social status. They share a common lifestyle, consumption behaviour, political leaning, cultural bearing and opportunity circuit. Classes are marked by both continuity and change depending upon the milieu a society provides for upward mobility.

One has to distinguish between class and caste. While the former is based primarily on materialistic considerations of possessions, power and prestige, the latter is essentially hereditary or biological in character. The two are not exclusive to each other though defined on different lines. Caste system, in all probability, was fossilization of class system at a particular stage in Indian history. Now in reverse when social stratification would take the form of class system in entirety, the influence of the hereditary group or caste is expected to be neutralized. The status of an individual is expected to depend upon one's own rather than inherited properties (D'Souza, 1967: p. 197). Reality has emerged in a somewhat different way in the post-Independence India. The constitutional safeguards for the backward sections of society, the scheduled ones to mention, have given a new lease of life to caste (Srinivas, 1957: p. 529). The process received further stimulus from constitutional provision of reservations for caste-based backward classes.

Class is to be differentiated also from status groups (Ferreira et al., 2013). The former is an economic stratification of society and the latter social categorization. In the vocabulary of political economy while the class is a part of the production system, the status belongs to the consumption domain. After all lifestyle and consumption always go together.

In the field of class analysis, an enquiry into class structure is one component. Other facets of class analysis include class formation that is evolution of classes as organized actors; class struggle, which represents the conflicts between interests of different classes; and class consciousness wherein members of a specific class become aware of their socially perceived role and act in conformity. Class structure is, of course, pivotal to overall logic of class analysis (Wright, 1997: p. 3).

Social scientists delineate the class structure in a variety of ways. On economic lines, the gradation is drawn as the rich, middle and poor. The criterion is evidently income and wealth. Sociologists opt for the terminology of the elite, middle and subaltern. The basis is socio-economic status and political consciousness. In popular parlance, the categorization goes as the upper, middle and lower classes.

Traditionally, in continental Europe, middle class was placed intermediate between nobility (landlords in the countryside) and peasantry (landless labourers working for the landlord), and was termed as bourgeoisie. In the United Kingdom, middle class was seen as situated between the upper class and the working class. In Marxist text, middle class is below the ruling class and above the proletariat. The underlying construct in this case is that of power and authority linked to production relations and production factors (Zweig, 2002/2012: p. 2). The Americans, who pay much less attention to the class question than Europeans do, have an additional terminology to offer. They call the poor as underclass, being subordinate, needy and dependent.

Composition of Middle Class

At Northern Arizona University, United States, Joshi (2010) offers a course on *Worlding the Middle Class: Readings in World History*. This course explores how, why and with what effect the middle class as category has travelled across the world. He observes that though perceived as alike by scholars and layfolks all over, the middle class seems to refer to discrete sociological groups in different countries. In the United States, for example, the middle class has become almost a synonym for the 'common people'. In the United Kingdom, as in many other parts of the world, this category refers to elite group. In socialist countries, they are called bourgeoisie. In India, they are observed as a new economic caste. In developed countries, the division is between the elite and the middle class; in developing countries it is between these two together and the poor. The societal fault lines differ in the two contexts.

The formation, expansion and spread of the middle class is a subject of stimulating inquiry. This has been a major socio-economic and political project of modernity in different parts of the world in varying modes. In the developed realm today, it was a product of the industrial revolution; in the colonized world it has been a byproduct of colonial practices; and in most of the African countries, it followed the spread of education by the Christian missionaries. In the case of India, the British policy of introducing western education, promoting capitalist enterprise and creating new professions during the colonial days was the main cause of emergence of middle class (Misra, 1963). The spread of the welfare state and associated promotion of public sector after the World War II gave a spur to this process.

Frank (2016) links the expansion of middle class at large with production regime of goods of mass consumption, such as radio, television, automobile and mobile. The emergence of consumer societies and rise of middle class have progressed hand in hand with each other. Meanwhile, poverty alleviation has also been an objective of every government. The exit gate of poverty is the entry point for the middle class.

Ushering in of the 21st century has been accompanied by a rapid rise of the middle class. Going by the share of urban population at the global level, the *Economist* (3–9 September, 2011) informs that half of the world population could be categorized as middle class. In Africa, this is around 33 per cent, in Latin America about 70 per cent and in China nearly 90 per cent. Such estimates are, of course, subject to the way the middle class is defined. For stance, a report prepared by the European Union Institute for Security Studies (2012: p. 28) puts the share of middle class population in the world's total at 26 per cent in 2009 which would rise to about 40 per cent in 2020 and nearly 60 per cent in 2030. Obviously a far stricter definition of middle class has been adopted in this case.

What is the underlying dynamics of recent proliferation of middle class worldwide? A pivotal factor is the empirical superiority of capitalism as an ideology. There is an all round effort at upward economic mobility. Earlier the divide between the elite and masses led to propagation of socialism, now the differentiation between the elite and middle class is giving a spurt to capitalism (Sridharan, 2004: p. 405). Goods and services are being produced in bigger quantity and greater variety for mass consumption. There is a race for rapid expansion of industrial and service sectors in all countries, particularly through incentives to private sector for investment. A heightened demand for skilled labour and professional expertise is a common feature. In response, technical and managerial education received a big boost. Urbanization picked up at a pace faster than before. A combination of geopolitical, technological and market forces at the end of the twentieth century had levelled the global field in a way that it enabled more people than ever, from more places than ever, to enter the middle class (Friedman, 2008: p. 66).

The process of emergence and expansion of the middle class was not the same in different countries of the world. Significantly it depended upon the way they defined their superiors and inferiors (Lopez and Weinstein, 2012: p. 378). As a product of industrial revolution, modern middle class is said to have England as its birth place. This class started its career here as a subordinate of the landed aristocracy. In France, the forerunners of the 1789 Revolution found a place for themselves as middle class with the destruction of the feudal class. In Germany, the middle class placed itself as distinct and higher than the poor. In Argentina, the whiteness of the *criollos*, born of persons of local Spanish ancestry with fair complexion, set them apart as middle class vis-à-vis the pure Spanish feudal lords above and non-white peasants below. The middle class as a world family has a horde of species linked to ecologies of a variety of social structures tempered by historical antecedents.

Who specifically belongs to the middle class? The composition of this sociological group is not the same in different countries of the world. This is subject to their political system, stage of development and structure of economy. In the United States, for example, the middle class is composed of small business owners, white collar workers, supervisors, managers and professionals. They serve as a buffer between capital and labour. In Latin American Countries, middle class persons are typically in formal employment rather than self-employed. In India, by comparison, middle class comprises all those who are in organized sector, public or private; own a modest scale business or industry with a capacity to hire a helper or workers; and relatively well-off farmers, artisans and service providers in rural areas. The middle class in India is largely urban and partially rural.

It is worth recalling that for most part of the world history, an overwhelming majority of people was poor. They formed the main mass of humanity. Only a tiny section at the crust was rich. The middle class was virtually non-descriptive. Now a revolutionary change is taking place. The poor world of the past is gradually getting transferred into the middle class world which is highly consumption driven, aware and articulate. Over such a scenario, the business community is understandably glad because of massive increase in demand for all variety of goods and services. On the other hand, the corridors of power are in constant worry in anticipation of likely political fallout triggered by the lack of capacity or failure of the government to meet the rising expectations, particularly of the educated, aspiring and disappointed youth belonging to the middle class. Paradoxically though itself a product and part of the government to a great extent, its rage against the government is not infrequent. Already visible around are such 'local mutinies' with an increasing frequency especially on issues pertaining to service delivery, inflation and employment.

Middle Class Activism

What explains the current sudden assertion and vigorous political activity on the part of the middle class? The boldest expression of all this has been the Arab Spring, which originated as an aggressive movement of the people against government in Tunisia on 8 December 2010, and spatially diffused through the Arab League countries. Similar is a story common to several other countries. The middle class outcry had dislodged the military regime in South Korea in early 1980s. The same thing happened in Taiwan against the authoritarian rule which ended in 1987. Today the middle class in China is restive and more vocal than before.

For long, the middle class was quiescent. The policies pursued by governments were to their advantage, by and large. They were getting a variety of services, including education, health, energy, transport and others, at a subsidized rate in the name of the poor by the welfare state. Most state funding was sucked by the middle class (Micklethwait and Wooldridge, 2014: p. 11). Over time the situation changed when the governments started reinventing themselves through economic reforms. This referred particularly to cutting of government jobs and reduction in subsidies on essential services, such as education, health, water supply, electricity and transport, as well as items of daily need, such as cereals, sugar, petrol and cooking gas. The middle class got deprived of several special benefits but had in the mean time acquired a capacity to pay higher for these services and items. Now they clamoured for their supply ensuring regularity and quality. An expression of their rage against any infirmity of the kind was not uncommon on the platform or even on the road. They were averse to payment of bribe which had become rampant in the system. A combination of ambition and anxiety became operational. The divide between public policy and public opinion came on the surface. Such turmoil recorded a wide and rapid spread wherever micro-blogging services were available to the people.

The rise of the middle class in Europe in the mid–nineteenth century had caused turbulence almost everywhere in the continent. The Bolshevik and Chinese revolutions were also spearheaded by discontented and angry middle class. They certainly had massive support of peasants, industrial workers and the poor. Today the middle class people are restless because of the failure of governments in meeting their rising expectations. They are fighting against abuse of power, irrespective of the fact it happens under authoritarian rule or democratic regime. They are much more technologically empowered to share their messages with each other with speed and spread.

Marx pointed out that in bringing about revolutions in the past, such as the French Revolution, the bourgeoisie or middle class played a pivotal role. Paradoxically the growth of this very class, in the opinion of the Marxists, has been responsible for stalling the success and spread of the communist revolution. The middle class is now in alignment with capitalism. Such a system offers them opportunities for personal advancement in life and also promotes consumerism consistent with their life dream. Added to this is a penchant for democracy which promises freedom in pursuing one's life goals. The rise of middle class is in a true sense democratization of economic power in a society (Huntington, 2016: p. 249). Above all, the middle class today does not look to the government as a provider of free welfare but as an efficient manager of the scheme of things. It expects the government to ensure law and order, lay requisite infrastructure, provide quality services, and generate jobs, along with a ready access to them.

The middle class thereby looks at the government as a problem solving and development ensuring mechanism. Today though their anger against it is worldwide yet the middle class fixation for the government is abiding. They do not find its any alternative for management of the complex societies as evolved. Even the more efficient private sector and the home-grown voluntary organizations look to it for patronage. Government is taken as a given fact and living experience.

Measuring the Middle Class

How to quantify the share of middle class in total population? The assignment is difficult because there is no unanimity on qualitative parameters of this class. These differ in tandem with the income level, occupational structure and educational status of a country, among other things. The way a middle class person is perceived in the United States is not the same as in India. The contexts vary.

In the United States, for instance, four strands of thinking have been responsible for the promotion of the idea of middle class. These include: (i) culture of materialism; (ii) disenchantment with ideology of socialism; (iii) a strong urge for upward mobility and (iv) fascination for media coverage (Jacobs, 1961/1989: pp. 17–18). An entry into the middle class is a life's dream for those at the lower ladder. It is all about power – political and cultural – in this country. This is subject to the educational level one attains. A possession of college degree makes all the difference. Those who are with college education are nicknamed as cauliflowers and others cabbages. Cauliflowers capture the jobs which enjoy higher status and fatter remuneration. A college graduate in the age group of 25–32 years earns 63 per cent more than a counterpart without a college degree, as reported by the *Economist* (29 October–6 November 2015). They constitute the middle class. In the words of a former President of the United States, they are the ones who work hard and play by rules. They earn enough to own a house, procure health insurance and send their children to college.

Historically the working class in the developed world experienced an upward mobility to the middle class with the rise in their income, acquisition of higher levels of education and gradual shift of economy from industrial sector to service sector. The ushering in of a democratic process at large, decline in fascination for socialism and commitment with a tilt in favour of identity assertion took this process further (Fukuyama, 2014: p. 436). What matters is a self-perception as belonging to the middle class.

The middle class in India, by comparison, is noted for common aspirations and ambitions of a rising standard of living, good governance and celebration of India's diversity (Zakaria, 2013: p. 9). They generally are not defined by caste or by location, urban or rural, but by consumption behaviour. They have requisite financial resources to purchase modern gadgets like refrigerators, television sets, cars and what not (Ablett et al., 2007: p. 271). In terms of family, they share a common dream of raising only two children, one son and one daughter. A decent job for the son and a status husband for the daughter would fulfil another fond wish in their life. For themselves, they would be content to raise a personal home as a blissful abode on retirement.

At the level of an individual, the considerations of self-definition, variety and quantum of material possessions, and the command of authority become critical in fixing his or her place in the middle class. Educational level and occupational background are important to consider. A stock has also to be taken of the value system and lifestyle. The economic values of a middle class person centre on income, savings and investment. Social values can be listed as education, health and security. Psychological values confirm a belief in hard work and achievement. Political values favour stability, justice and modernity. And life values cherish small families, parental care and a permanent residential base.

At the collective level, however, the proportion of middle class is usually estimated on the basis of income. Birdsall et al. (2000) considered those households as belonging to the middle class whose income ranged between 75 and 125 per cent of their country's median income. They acknowledged that this measure may not represent any fixed notion of middle class. The technique, however, does capture the middle strata in terms of the income specific to each country. The Asian Development Bank is more precise on this count. It considers a person belonging to the middle class if having a daily income of $ 2 to $ 20 as calculated on the basis of purchasing power parity of the US dollar in 2005. This amount of earning will leave an individual with one-third of the income for discretionary spending after paying for food and shelter.

By comparison, McKinsey Global Institute placed a household of the developed world in a middle class group if its annual income fell in the range of $ 23,000 to $ 181,000 on the basis of purchasing power parity in 2007. These figures are consistent with the per capita income in these countries and work out roughly as $ 60 to $ 500 per day on household basis.

For developing countries, the limits of income for identifying the middle class have been relaxed somewhat on realistic lines. Banerjee and Duflo (2011) placed households living on $ 2 to $ 10 per day in 2008 as belonging to middle class. Martin Ravallion at the World Bank had initially placed these limits in the range of $ 2 to $ 13 at the 2005 purchasing power parity. The two figures are close to each other.

In India, the National Council of Applied Economic Research brought out an elaborate report under the title *The Great Indian Middle Class* in 2004. It was based on a sample survey of 300,000 households in 2001–02. The data pertained to their income level which allowed the categorization of all the households into the following categories in terms of their annual income in rupees: (i) Deprived – less than ₹ 90,000; (ii) Aspirers – ₹ 90,000 to 2,00,000; (iii) Seekers – ₹ 2,00,000 to half-a-million rupees; (iv) Strivers – half-a-million to one million rupees; (v) Near Rich – one million to two million rupees; (vi) Clear Rich – two million to five million rupees; (vii) Sheer Rich – five million to 10 million rupees; and (viii) Super Rich – more than 10 million rupees. The middle class was defined as belonging to the Seekers and Strivers categories. In other words, they fell in the annual income level of ₹ 2,00,000 to one million rupees at 2001–02 prices. The number of people belonging to middle class was placed at 57 million. This figure was projected to grow to 153 million by 2009–10. The whole exercise was essentially meant to capture those who were potential buyers of a car.

Earlier in 1996, the Centre for the Study of Developing Societies had conducted a survey to estimate the size of middle class in India. They considered an individual as hailing from middle class, if he or she: (i) described himself/herself as belonging to middle class; or (ii) resided in a house built of brick and cement; or (iii) had a white collar job; or (iv) satisfied the following two criteria: (a) 10 or more years of formal education; and (b) ownership of three out of the four assets including motor vehicle, television, electric generator and non-agricultural land property. By these standards, 20 per cent of India's population was assessed as belonging to middle class in 1996. Notably, a majority of the middle class, as defined by the survey, came from backward classes, scheduled castes, tribals and religious minorities.

There is evidently no agreement over the criteria and indicators to be harnessed for identifying the middle class. These tend to be country and context specific. Income level enjoys the primacy in general. Occupation and education level are two other favourites. Assets for use or possession and images of prestige are still other markers. Having adopted any or all of these criteria, a search for their representative indicators is to follow. Decisions are also to be taken about the range of income level to capture the middle class; the kind of occupations to be included; the critical dividing line to differentiate the educational status; and the kind of assets to be recorded. These will not be the same in different countries.

There are scholars who would like to go by a different route while looking for the middle class. They would discern their presence by the nature and amount of power and authority wielded. Middling authority between the capitalist and working classes rather than the middling income is adopted by them as the criterion. Hence, the professional people, managers and superiors who serve the capitalist class and have authority over the working class are included in this group. The same is the case with those who are in government service, wielding authority in accordance with their rank but essentially serving the system. The small business owners, who may hire help to assist them but remain dependent upon the government in several ways with limited authority, also fall in the category of middle class. This signifies that whenever we talk about classes, this cannot be done without referring to the matters of power and authority.

Some scholars would like to recognize the middle class people by their behavioural or psychological traits. Sandwiched between tradition and modernity, they are destined to live with and resolve conflicts in their moral values and lifestyle toward a higher goal. They are seen as agents of efficiency and functionality, highly aspiring, striving and achieving. They cause transformation. The real change in developing societies takes place when the poor start entering the middle class. Hence what we need is a new populist ideology that offers a realistic path to healthy middle class societies and robust democracies (Fukuyama, 2012).

Middle Class in India

Today India defines itself as an emerging world power, fast track economy and rising middle class (Marshall, 2015: p. 170). The history of its modern middle class begins with the colonial period. Surendranath Banerji had viewed it as the impact of western culture on Indian Society at the first go (Torri, 1991). Till the end of the nineteenth century, the size of middle class was very small, hardly 0.3 per cent of total population or just 0.7 million. The members of this class hailed mainly from families who traditionally had served in royal courts or princely state capitals. They were the ones who were forerunners in acquiring western education. The professional upper castes, such as Kayasthas of North India, Chitpavan Brahmins and Chandrasenya Kayastha Prabhus of Maharashtra and Nagars of Gujarat made a significant presence among them. The same was the case with Punjabi Khatris, Kashmiri Pandits and South Indian Ayer and Ayengar Brahmins (Sheth, 1995: p. 199).

The Brahmins seemed to have made an early entry into the middle class by virtue of their already existing educational base. This was as true of Tamil Brahmins as of the Konkani ones. With the territorial expansion of the British colonial rule, the Bhadrolog Bengalis, Parsees, Christian communities and upper crust of the Muslims also joined the service of their masters. The descendants of big landlords, families of hereditary accountants, and those in army acquired the character of middle class. Education was a common thread to all of them and practically every one among them spoke, wrote, or knew English. They lived a kind of professional life structured with British Raj (Walsh, 2011: pp. 144–45).

There was a slow and steady increase in the numerical strength of middle class in India during the first half of the twentieth century. On an estimate, they could be put at about 10 per cent of the total population at the time of independence (Varma, 1998: p. 26). Included among them were those in government service; qualified professionals, such as doctors, engineers, lawyers and journalists; teachers in schools and institutions of higher learning; business entrepreneurs and well-to-do traders; partially or fully educated among the agriculturalists; white collared employees in the private sector and substantial section of university students. In the domain of public sector, most of them were employed in government departments, railways, postal services, education and defence.

The size and proportion of middle class experienced a steady enlargement after Independence. This was associated primarily with spurt in development activity, expansion of the government set-up and spread of education. The welfare state tried to improve the lifestyle and standard of living of people through promotion of agriculture, industry, education, health and transport facilities. Urbanization process was also making headway. Meanwhile the Green Revolution in parts of India enjoying the benefit of irrigation led to the rise of income in rural areas. Remittances received from emigrants abroad from some specific regions of the country were an economic boon to the families left behind. The per capita income of an average Indian doubled in real terms or at constant prices by the closing years of 1980s. This was a result of a compound annual growth rate of economy by 4 per cent vis-à-vis the corresponding growth rate of population by 2 per cent rendering a net annual increase of 2 per cent in the per capita income of the people. The rise in overall income of the country uplifted some of the poor to the category of middle class. The share of this class in total population of the country was inching toward 20 per cent by the close of 1980s.

The adoption of new economic policy in terms of liberalization, privatization and globalization in early 1990s marked a critical break in the history of post-Independence India. It gave a spurt to economy through the vigour of private sector. This was titled as *India Unbound* by Das (2000). Liberalization loosened the shackles of government controls over setting up of business and caused a burst of entrepreneurialism in industrial and service sectors. Privatization unloaded the burden of public sector and made available a wider play field for the private sector to operate and demonstrate its effective skill in management. Globalization opened wide both the entry and exit gates for not only imports and exports but also attracted sizeable investment through multinationals. Consumers were beneficiary of a huge variety of goods, especially gadgets and automobiles, of brand quality.

Meanwhile the service and industry sectors had expanded to 60 per cent and 26 per cent of total economy by 2013–14 as compared to 30 and 18 per cent respectively in 1950–51. The share of agriculture was reduced to 14 per cent from earlier status of 52 per cent in 1950s. The per capita income of an average Indian multiplied three times in real terms during the span of just two decades of 1991 to 2011. A transition from a manual to non-manual work, acquisition of a regular job, possession of a motorized vehicle and installation of a tubewell on the agricultural farm, among others, are the markers of gradual entry of the poor into the middle class. The small family culture and increasing frequency of both husband and wife getting into employment were the supportive demographics of the process. The middle class expanded as a result. It is estimated that around one-third of India's population today carries this description. The World Bank had estimated the size of middle class at 264 million in 2005 or about 25 per cent of the total. In that light, the present figure seems to be quite reliable.

Here it would be pertinent to refer to the findings of the Lok Surveys, carried out in 2014 and reported by the *Hindu* newspaper in its 9 December 2014 issue. Almost 50 per cent of India's population perceived themselves as belonging to the middle class. This exaggerated self-image is consistent with the general tendency of the Indians to be status conscious and over rate their social standing.

A point of curiosity arises here. If middle class partakes one-third of India's population, nearly one-third is below the poverty line, and the upper class is a thin crust, where do we account for the remaining about one-third of the population? In all probability they are in the grey zone between the middle class and the poor. They could be described as indeterminate lowest rung of the middle class or upper end of the poor.

Conforming to the global pattern, the middle class in India has been in the forefront of most of the political, social, economic or regional movements. The national movement for freedom from the colonial rule was spearheaded by people belonging to this class. This very class became closely connected with nation-building process in the post-Independence era through work in government institutions, media and business (Khan, 2007: p. 87). Equally significant has been their modernizing role in promotion of education and regulation of family size.

On the other hand, in early 1960s, it was the middle class in South India who aggressively opposed adoption of Hindi as the national language and was successful in retention of English as an official language along with Hindi. In 1990, the members of the middle class in North India and Gujarat were most vociferous opponents of reservation for backward classes in government jobs and educational institutions of higher learning. They were also the ones to agitate for creation of new states, such as Jharkhand, Uttarakhand, Chhattisgarh and Telangana, as well as for reservation of jobs for the natives in states like Meghalaya, Himachal Pradesh and Maharashtra. For long perceived as politically apathetic, middle class has been highly demanding at times and are most activist today. Evidently middle class has been exhibiting two contrasting tendencies. They tend to be inclusive when societal issues, such as empowerment of women, at large are involved but can be highly exclusive when their group interests are threatened, as in the case of employment in organized sector.

Many scholars believe that middle class is emerging as a homogenizing factor of the Indian society. They suggest that the rise of a new middle class will allow India to transcend its various diversities of caste, language and religion (Varshney, 2013: p. 65). The commonality of their existential dreams, similarity in the lifestyle and regular intermingling by virtue of education, occupation and mobility bring them together on the platform of functionality. All this is conducive to soaking them in the same hue.

One cannot, however, ignore a dissenting voice on such an assessment. Jodhka and Prakash (2016) point out that middle class is a heterogeneous group in India. It is marked by differentials of caste, religion and region which break the homogeneity of this group. They add that this fact of diversity within middle class is necessary to understand while analyzing the political culture as specific to different parts of the country. A search for unity in such diversity is a potential theme for research.

One germane point of enquiry would be the similarities, and more so differences, in the nature of middle class in varying backgrounds. How does a middle class person in Tamil Nadu differ from the one in Punjab, or in Kerala from that in Himachal Pradesh, or in Goa from that in Delhi, or in rural areas of Andhra Pradesh from those in rural areas of Gujarat? How do their life style, political preferences and existential dreams converge or diverge from each other? Which stereotypes do they carry about each other? The middle class in

South India has a tendency to claim that they do not wear their wealth on sleeves or intellect on hats, as their counterparts in North India do. The impact of local tradition and culture is expected to be strong in early stage of formation of the middle class. Equifinality may emerge in the long run.

There is a fresh evaluation of the welfare policies that India followed for decades after Independence. Some believe that the country was late in adoption of new economic policy. A prolonged reliance on distributive measures for the poor has proved counterproductive since the welfare benefits, meant for them, were cornered by the non-poor. In effect, a conscious policy in favour of middle class would have been a fast track to the end of poverty. Such an argument finds a favour from the reality that for moving fast, the rich already have the capacity but not necessity and the poor have the necessity but not the capacity. It is the middle class which combines the both. For India to develop in an exclusive way, what is needed is a big bulge of middle class (Lahiri, 2014: p. 43).

There is a discordant note as well. Ballard (2012: p. 563) questions the glorification of the middle class as a model of progressive society or as a natural force of development or as a bulwark of democracy, good governance and modernity. Middle class culture is essentially consumption based and its production requirements are exploitative of natural resources, especially land, forest and water. All this results in deprivation of the poor. The middle class virtues do not get directly translated into development of others. Hence it would not be reasonable to believe that the road to the end of poverty passes through an extended territory of the middle class.

Whatever may be the dynamics, the empirical reality is that eventually the different parts of the world are marching toward a predominant middle class society. This can be called global middle class. The expectations are that in such a world there will be less of economic inequality, a subdued social conflict and a tamed political instability. The present middle class uproar is a transitional phase. There is a need to devise an effective strategy which will facilitate a strife-free transformation of the poor-predominant world to a middle class one.

Regional Pattern of the Middle Class

The share of middle class in the population of a region is a sure indicator of its vitality. Energetic and enterprising by nature, members of this class are valued as catalyst element of society. The traditional middle class may have been strong on ethics; the modern one is street smart, ambitious and mobile. A faster rate of societal change is in the offing.

Data on estimates of middle class are available only at the national level. Figures differ widely, as noted earlier. Such a situation arises because of lack of unanimity over the very definition of middle class. On the top of all this, there is non-availability of these data by states/union territories in India. Such a situation creates a serious constraint for any spatial analysis. The problem is to be resolved by adopting meaningful surrogate indicators.

A *pucca* house could be reckoned as a representative indicator of a middle class household. The assumption is that the lower class is not in a position to afford a *pucca* house. They live in a *kutcha* or *semi-pucca* house. A *pucca* house is a possibility with the non-poor. This indicator, however, does not enjoy a universal application. In several parts of India, such as the Western Himalayas, Rajasthan desert, and Kathiawar plateau, a *pucca* house is a climatic necessity for everyone, bypassing the factor of economic affordability. Moreover, under state welfare schemes of government, thousands of households belonging to scheduled castes in rural areas and those uprooted from slum localities in urban areas have been resettled in *pucca* dwelling units. Forty five per cent of households in India were reported as living in a *pucca* house as per the 2011 Census. This figure defies the likely share of middle class households in India. All of them could not be taken as belonging to middle class. Hence, this indicator was dropped from consideration in the present study.

Instead, the households enjoying the trinity of daily living facilities, namely electricity, treated water supply and sanitation (separate toilet) in the house, were assessed as belonging to the middle class. According to the 2011 Census of India, 36.2 per cent of households met this description. This would put the share of middle class households in the country at a level somewhat higher than one-third. The range at the state/union territory level was wide, from the lowest in Bihar at 10.5 per cent to the highest in Punjab at 77.10 per cent among states, and from 22.30 per cent in Lakshadweep to 87.10 per cent in Chandigarh among union territories (Table 5.1).

In a number of union territories and states, more than half of the households are beneficiary of this trinity of facility group. Most of the union territories are in a leading position on this count. The developed states of Punjab, Haryana, Goa and Gujarat are not far behind. These are followed by hill states like Himachal Pradesh, Uttarakhand, Sikkim and Mizoram. The South Indian states of Tamil Nadu, Andhra Pradesh and Karnataka as also Maharashtra find a place higher than the national level (Map 5.1).

By comparison, Kerala and Lakshadweep surface as a surprise. They are relatively low on the ensemble of these facilities. The predominance of well within the premises, as a source of domestic water supply, obviates the necessity of a formal system of tap water supply. This statistical vagary has been responsible for a drop in their trinity facility status.

In contrast, the states like Bihar, Jharkhand and Chhattisgarh are located at or near the bottom on this indicator. The story of Uttar Pradesh, Madhya Pradesh and Rajasthan is in the same idiom. Most of these states are large in population or area size. Some of them have a significant proportion of tribal population. All of them deserved far more serious attention by their respective governments in provision of essential facilities like treated water supply, sanitation and electricity, among other things. The consequence is there for everyone to see.

Table 5.1 *India: Percentage of Households with Electricity, Safe Drinking Water and Toilet Facilities by States and Union Territories, 2011*

States	*Percentage*
Punjab	77.10
Sikkim	74.20
Goa	70.00
Himachal Pradesh	65.20
Haryana	63.70
Uttarakhand	60.60
Mizoram	55.50
Gujarat	54.50
Tripura	52.90
Maharashtra	45.90
Andhra Pradesh*	45.40
Arunachal Pradesh	44.80
Tamil Nadu	44.10
Jammu & Kashmir	43.90
Karnataka	43.80
West Bengal	40.80
Nagaland	36.80
Manipur	32.70
Kerala	30.80
Rajasthan	30.00
Meghalaya	27.70
Uttar Pradesh	24.30
Chhattisgarh	24.30
Jharkhand	15.30
Odisha	14.50
Bihar	10.50
Union Territories	
Chandigarh	87.10
Delhi	85.40
Daman & Diu	77.20
Puducherry	66.20
Andaman & Nicobar Islands	63.80
Dadra and Nagar Haveli	53.40
Lakshadweep	22.30
India	36.20

Source: Census of India, 2011.
* Includes Telangana.

A salient feature of a middle class household in India is the use of LPG/PNG (liquefied petroleum gas/pipelined natural gas) as a mode of cooking fuel. This cooking fuel is relatively expensive in Indian context and calls for requisite financial affordability. It is also pro-gender in favour of females who are to manage the kitchen and hence is linked to a special kind

Map 5.1

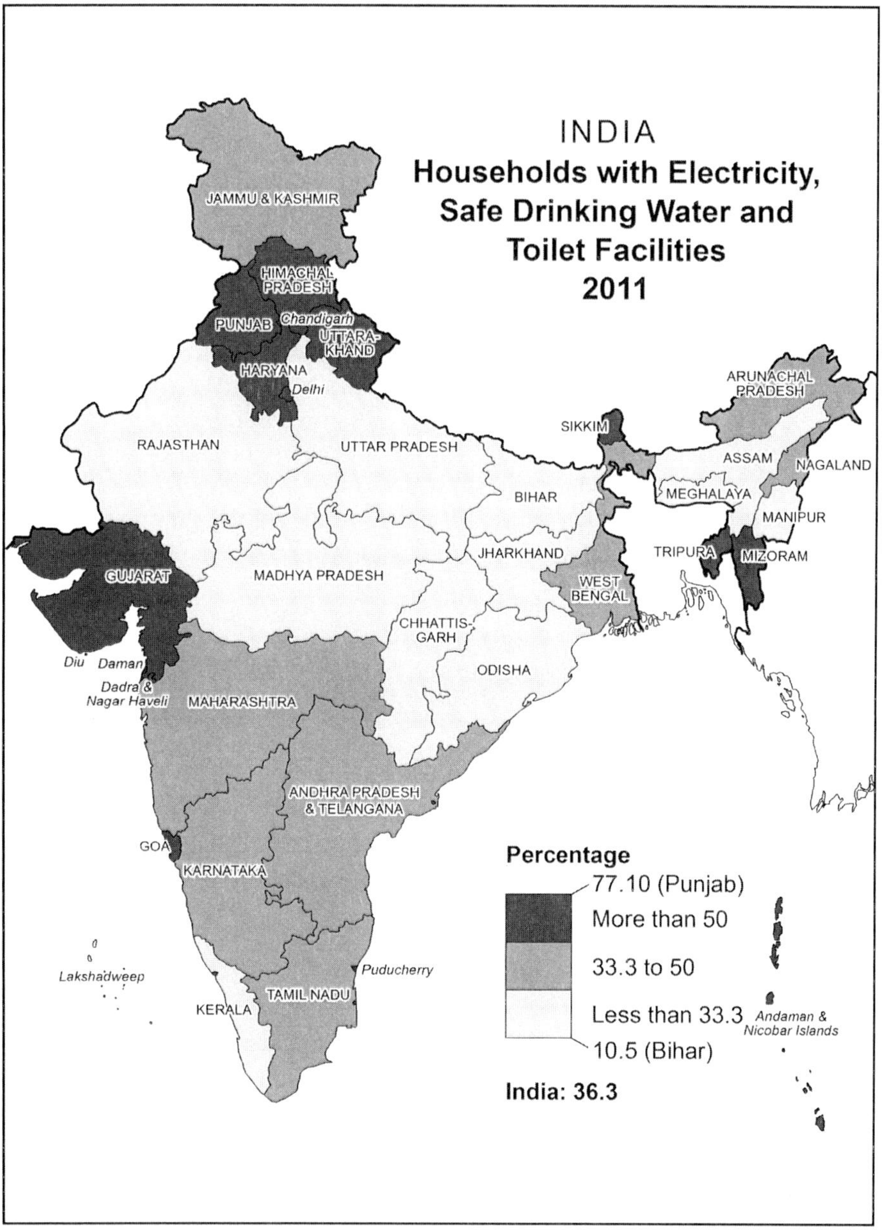

All the union territories and the states in North-West and West India are best placed on the package of electricity, safe drinking water and toilet facilities.

Source: Census of India, 2011

of sensitivity in a male dominated society. The use of LPG/PNG is more suited to small families, particularly in which both husband and wife are in a regular job, and are constrained by time. To them LPG/PNG's 'switch-on switch-off' mode is not only a convenience but also a necessity of daily life. All such details align with the lifestyle and mental make-up of the middle class. Hence, it is a reliable indicator to that effect.

The 2011 Census of India recorded 28.6 per cent of the households in the country using LPG/PNG as fuel for cooking (Table 5.2). Inferentially, nearly one-third of the households in the country qualify as belonging to middle class on this parameter. The percentage of such households is relatively high in three categories of area: (i) more urbanized and developed coastal states in the West and South India and the Punjab-Haryana region in the North-West; (ii) the hill states of Jammu & Kashmir, Himachal Pradesh and Uttarakhand in Western Himalayas and Sikkim and Mizoram in Eastern Himalayas; and (iii) all the union territories (Map 5.2). In the National Capital Territory of Delhi, nine out of every 10; in Goa three out of every four and in Punjab and Mizoram more than one-half of the households fall in this category. On the other extreme, in Bihar and Odisha, not even one in every 10 households can claim such a standing. Almost a similar picture obtains in most of the North and Middle Indian states as well as in many of the North-East ones.

Table 5.2 *India: Percentage of Households Using LPG/PNG for Cooking by States and Union Territories, 2011*

States	*Percentage of households*
Goa	72.70
Punjab	54.50
Mizoram	52.90
Tamil Nadu	47.90
Uttarakhand	44.20
Haryana	44.00
Maharashtra	43.40
Sikkim	41.30
Himachal Pradesh	38.60
Gujarat	38.30
Kerala	35.80
Andhra Pradesh*	35.80
Karnataka	32.50
Jammu & Kashmir	31.60
Manipur	29.70
Arunachal Pradesh	29.20
Rajasthan	22.80
Nagaland	20.00
Assam	19.00
Uttar Pradesh	18.90

Cont'd...

Map 5.2

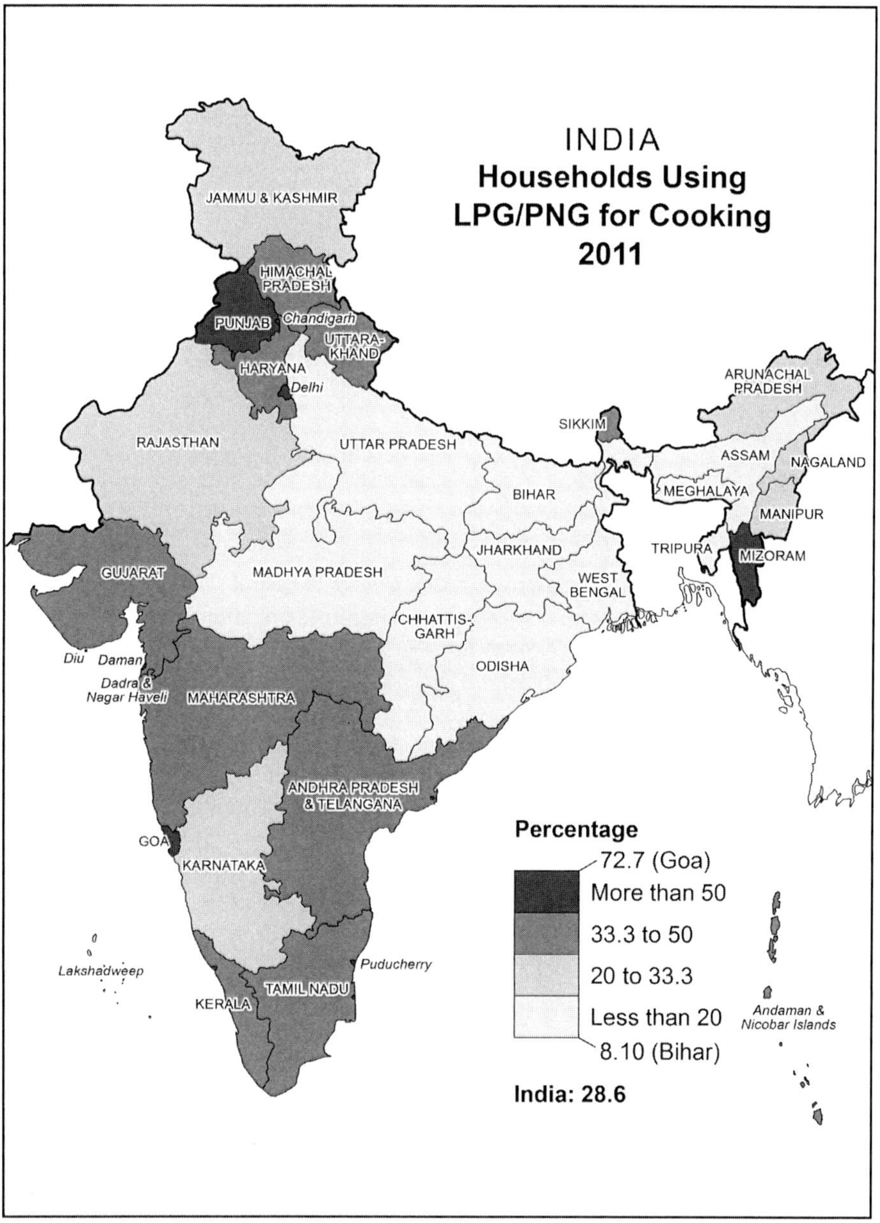

The spatial pattern of the use of LPG/PNG for cooking finds a significant association with the levels of income, urbanization and literacy.

Source: Census of India, 2011.

...Cont'd

West Bengal	18.90
Madhya Pradesh	18.20
Tripura	17.60
Meghalaya	11.90
Jharkhand	11.70
Chhattisgarh	11.20
Odisha	9.80
Bihar	8.10
Union Territories	
Delhi	89.90
Chandigarh	71.60
Puducherry	70.50
Daman and Diu	53.00
Andaman and Nicobar Islands	44.50
Dadra and Nagar Haveli	39.80
Lakshadweep	16.60
India	28.60

Source: Census of India, 2011.
* Includes Telangana.

By and large, a person with an educational level of at least matric/secondary school background hails from a middle class in the Indian context. This level of education is an entry point for admission in a college, university or technical institute. Also, it is an essential qualification for getting a job in the formal sector. In all probability such a person has a working knowledge of English language together with some understanding of other subjects and languages.

On this measure, 31.1 per cent or almost one-third of population can claim to constitute the middle class. This figure represents the educational status of India's adult population in 15-plus age group in 2011. It lies in the midst of and in proximity to those for the two indicators discussed above. All the union territories, with one-third to more than one-half of their population in this group, occupy the top positions (Table 5.3). The South Indian states are better placed than the North Indian ones on this count, with the exception of Punjab and Haryana. The hill states of Jammu & Kashmir, Himachal Pradesh and Uttarakhand are also noted for a comparatively higher degree of achievement on this indicator. By comparison, the states located in the Middle and East India as also in North-East region mark a low score in this regard (Map 5.3).

A cross-study of ranks of various states and union territories on three indicators analysed in this section is quite revealing. Union territories carry relatively high ranks on every indicator. All of them are significantly urban, have large share of their population in administrative, educational, health and other services and are recipient of educated, skilled and professional personnel from other areas. These factors contribute to their inclusion in the reservoir of middle class population.

Table 5.3 *India: Percentage of Persons Aged 15+ with at Least Matric/Secondary School Education by States and Union Territories, 2011*

States	*Percentage*
Goa	48.16
Kerala	47.85
Himachal Pradesh	45.17
Punjab	41.22
Haryana	40.52
Manipur	39.57
Tamil Nadu	39.52
Maharashtra	39.33
Uttarakhand	39.18
Karnataka	36.44
Jammu & Kashmir	34.91
Andhra Pradesh*	32.82
Gujarat	30.61
Nagaland	28.56
Mizoram	28.18
Uttar Pradesh	28.16
Sikkim	27.85
Arunachal Pradesh	27.21
Jharkhand	25.36
West Bengal	24.07
Assam	23.88
Odisha	23.29
Tripura	23.28
Rajasthan	23.12
Bihar	22.92
Madhya Pradesh	22.69
Chhattisgarh	22.32
Meghalaya	21.29
Union Territories	
Chandigarh	58.25
Delhi	54.40
Puducherry	50.37
Daman and Diu	41.32
Andaman and Nicobar Islands	37.59
Dadra and Nagar Haveli	33.93
Lakshadweep	33.78
India	31.07

Source: Census of India, 2011.
* Includes Telangana.

On the other hand, the less developed states, such as Bihar, Uttar Pradesh, Madhya Pradesh, Odisha, Chhattisgarh and Jharkhand, are at or near the bottom in rank on all the three indicators. The slow pace of socio-economic development, semi-feudal structure of society as a historical legacy and low level of urbanization are the factors accounting for such a situation. Bihar is a case in point. It is at the bottom of all the three

Map 5.3

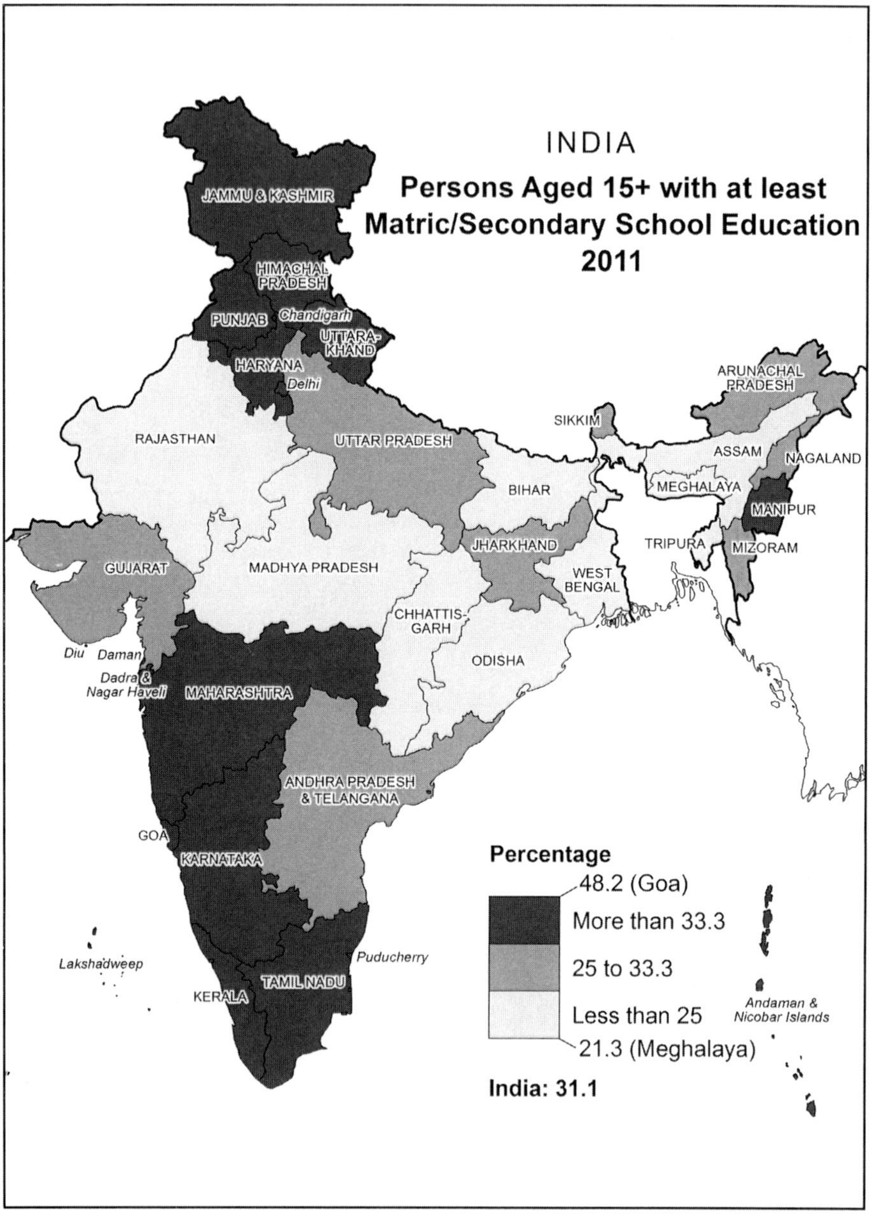

Persons Aged 15+ with at least matric/secondary school education belong to the pool of English knowing people and have access to a wider world of opportunities.

Source: Census of India, 2011.

indicators. A gross distortion in land distribution linked to a semi-feudal social structure is a bane for the state. Poverty is pervasive and a serious constraint for upward social mobility. The expansion of middle class here is a slow process.

Staggering are the differences in ranks of some states on the three indicators. Kerala, for example, holds 25th rank on percentage of households having the trinity of facilities of electricity, safe drinking water and sanitation; 17th rank on percentage of households using LPG/PNG as cooking fuel and 5th rank on adult educational level. The respective ranks on these three indicators for Gujarat are 13, 16 and 20; for Sikkim 5, 13 and 24; and for Mizoram 12, 7 and 22. Such differences indicate that various processes underlying formation of a middle class are operating at varying pace in these states.

To obtain a composite picture, the average of percentages on the three indicators for different states and union territories was worked out. A figure of 32 per cent was obtained. The methodology may not be flawless, as it does not differentiate between the relative weight of the indicators, but gives a fairly reliable idea about the share of middle class population. Almost one-third of India's population in 2011 was testified as belonging to the middle class on such a reckoning.

Goa (63.6%) and Punjab (57.6%) are the two states where majority of population belongs to the middle class (Table 5.4). The former is coastal and latter inland. Both are marked by high per capita income and urbanization level; both have a long tradition of emigration to the developed world; and both are marked by a total fertility rate of two or less. While Goa is strong on tourism sector, Punjab holds a place of pride in being a pioneer in the Green Revolution.

Practically all the union territories are marked by a distinct middle class character in their social structure (Map 5.4). National Capital Territory of Delhi (76.6%) and Chandigarh (72.3%) excel even Goa in this respect and Puducherry (62.4%) is a close companion to it. The union territory of Daman & Diu (57.17%) is also marked by a majority of its population belonging to middle class; and Andaman & Nicobar Islands (48.6%) is close to entering into this category. Dadra & Nagar Haveli (42.4%) has benefitted from its proximity to Mumbai, notwithstanding the fact that a majority of its native population is tribal. Lakshadweep (24.2%) is the only union territory where formation of a middle class society is taking time. An overwhelming majority of its population is Muslim and tribal by demographics.

On the 'middle class' map of India, a north-south divide is evident. The South Indian states have a relatively high proportion of one-third to one-half of their population as middle class while several North Indian states are noted for a proportion of less than even one-fourth on this count. The states in Western India, with 40 to 50 per cent of their population qualifying as middle class, are in the company of South Indian states.

Table 5.4 *India: Estimated Percentage of Middle Class Population Based on Composite Index and Percentage of Urban Population by States and Union Territories, 2011*

States	*Percentage of*	
	Middle Class Population	*Urban Population*
Goa	63.62	62.17
Punjab	57.61	37.48
Himachal Pradesh	49.66	10.03
Haryana	49.41	34.88
Uttarakhand	47.99	30.23
Sikkim	47.78	25.15
Mizoram	45.43	52.11
Tamil Nadu	43.84	48.40
Maharashtra	42.88	45.22
Gujarat	41.14	42.60
Kerala	38.15	47.70
Andhra Pradesh	38.10	33.36
Karnataka	37.58	38.67
Jammu & Kashmir	36.80	27.38
Manipur	33.99	32.45
Arunachal Pradesh	33.74	22.94
Tripura	31.26	26.17
Nagaland	28.45	28.86
West Bengal	27.92	31.87
Rajasthan	25.31	24.87
Uttar Pradesh	23.79	22.27
Assam	22.76	14.10
Madhya Pradesh	21.86	27.63
Meghalaya	20.30	20.07
Chhattisgarh	18.11	23.24
Jharkhand	17.45	24.05
Odisha	15.86	16.69
Bihar	13.84	11.29
Union Territories		
Delhi	76.57	97.50
Chandigarh	72.32	97.25
Puducherry	62.36	68.33
Daman and Diu	57.17	75.17
Andaman and Nicobar Islands	48.63	37.70
Dadra and Nagar Haveli	42.38	46.72
Lakshadweep	24.23	78.07
India	31.96	31.15

Source: Composite Index (see text) and Census of India, 2011.
* Includes Telangana.

The coastal regions of South India constitute extensive elongated belts of middle class population. Here are located several metropolitan cities, port cities and industrial towns. These places are actively connected not only with their interior hinterlands but also with the outer world, including through emigration on a significant scale.

Map 5.4

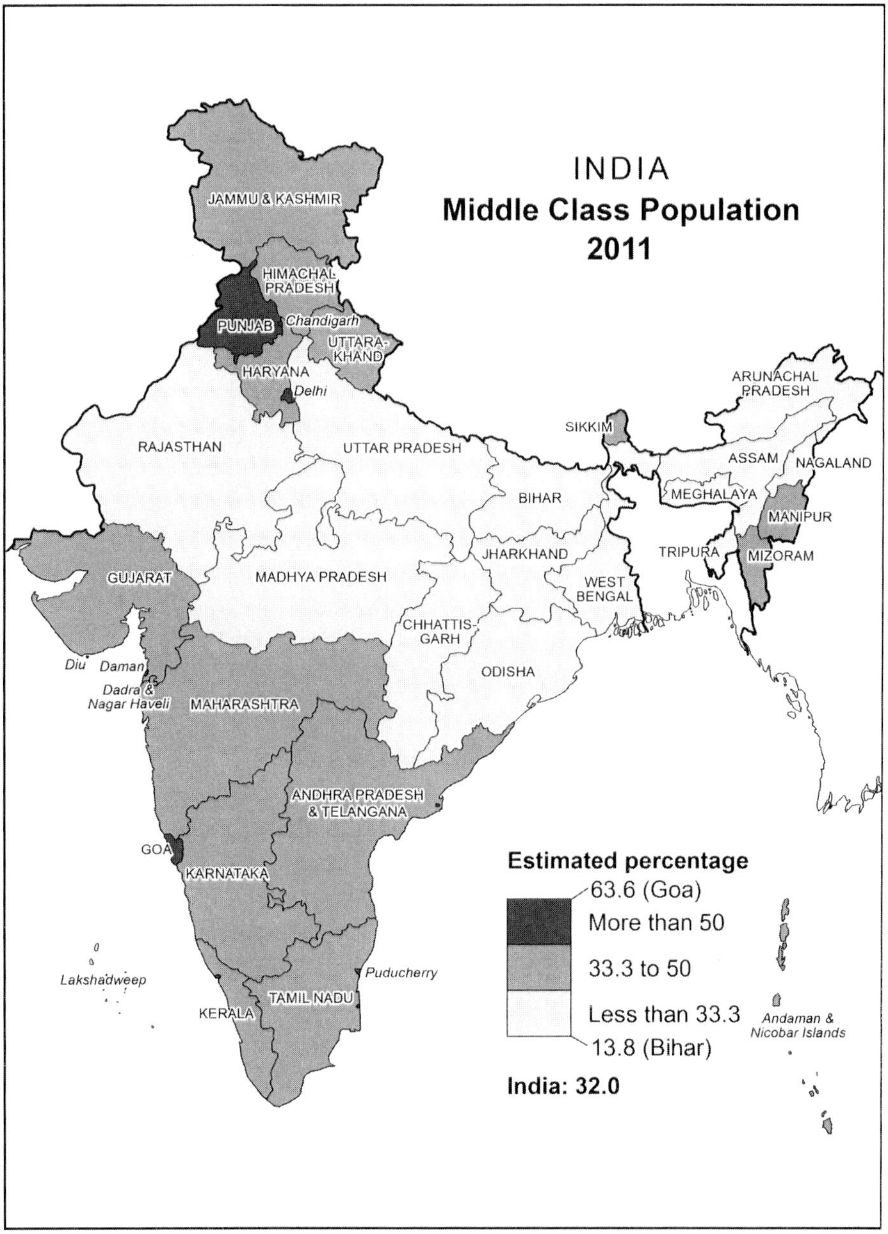

About one-third of India's population belongs to the middle class; Goa and Punjab, in addition to most of the union territories, have a majority of their population in this category.

Source: Census of India, 2011

The agro-industrial green revolution areas of Punjab, Haryana and Western Uttar Pradesh constitute a major contiguous inland concentration of middle class population. Massive rural-urban commuting was instrumental in gradual spread of middle class in rural areas as well. This was more typical of the rural tracts characterized by long tradition in army service or emigration to other countries or availability of large scale infrastructural facilities. At the heart of the green revolution areas is located the National Capital Region of Delhi. The entire area is distinguished by relatively high degree of urbanization, diversification of rural economy and associated income levels.

A number of hill states like Himachal Pradesh, Uttarakhand, Jammu & Kashmir and Sikkim are also noted for comparatively high proportion of middle class population despite the fact these are at a lower level of urbanization than the national average. The income level here is, of course, significantly higher than that of an average Indian. This is attributed to their status as 'special category of states' which entitles them to liberal devolution of funds from the central government not only for development projects but also for meeting the salaries of the relatively large number of government employees' vis-à-vis population. Considerable additional income occurs to these states through tourism, sale of horticultural products and royalty on generation of hydroelectricity. Such a play of economy and governance has been vital to expansion of middle class in these states.

One cannot miss the dismal fact that in Bihar hardly 13.8 per cent of the population could acquire the status of middle class. The situation is no better in Odisha (15.9%), Jharkhand (17.5%) and Chhattisgarh (18.1%). Madhya Pradesh (21.9%), Assam (22.8%) and Uttar Pradesh (24.8%) too have long miles to go before they raise a sizeable mass of middle class. All these states are predominantly rural. The society in their case has a thin upper crust of well-off, educated, urban people sited on a vast mass of the poor, predominantly agricultural, rural masses. Poverty is endemic to several parts of these states.

The incidence of middle class is neutral to the factor of demographic homogeneity or heterogeneity. Punjab and Assam are both diverse in terms of religious composition but differ in their share of middle class population. Kerala and Odisha are both homogeneous on linguistic parameter but stand apart on percentage of middle class population. Himachal Pradesh and Madhya Pradesh have the same Hindi as their state language but strongly differ in terms of share of middle class. Importance given to English at the level of school education seems to be having a strong association with the formation of middle class.

The regional variations in incidence of middle class are a portrayal of comparative vitality of different parts of India. The size and rise of middle class has been concomitant with the urbanization process, more so with growth of metropolitan cities, especially if they happen to be national or state capitals. There is a virtual equivalence between the percentage of urban population and that of middle class population in India (Table 5.4). At the same time, one observes relatively significant concentration of middle class in rural areas of the Green Revolution states. Several hill states, despite low level of urbanization, are also noted for comparatively high proportion of middle class as associated with employment in public sector. An over-riding fact is that the formation and growth of middle class during the colonial and post-colonial periods till the adoption of new economic policy in early 1990s in to be attributed to the public sector. In the current phase, the role of private sector has become more pronounced, especially in relatively developed parts of India. The eminence of public sector continues in the case of special category states.

References

Ablett, J. et al. 2007. *The Bird of Gold: The Rise of India's Consumer Market*. Mumbai: McKinsey Global Institute.

Ballard, Richard. 2012. Geographies of Development: Without the Poor. *Progress in Human Geography*. Vol. 36, No. 5, pp. 563–572.

Banerjee, Abhijit and Esther Duflo. 2011. *Poor Economics: A Radical Thinking on the Way to Fight Global Poverty*. New York: Public Affairs.

Birdsall, Nancy, Carol Grahm and Stefano Pettinato. 2000. *Stuck in the Tunnel: Is Globalisation Muddling the Middle Class?* Washington, D.C.: Centre on Social and Economic Dynamics, Brooking Institution, Working Paper No. 14.

Das, Gurcharan. 2000. *India Unbound*. New Delhi: Penguin.

D'Souza, Victor S. 1967. Caste and Class: An Interpretation. *Journal of Asian and African Studies*. Vol. 2, No. 3–4, pp. 192–211.

European Union Institute for Security Studies. 2012. *Global Trends 2030: Citizens in an Interconnected and Polycentric World*. Paris: EUISS.

Ferreira, Francisco H.G. et al. 2013. *Economic Mobility and the Rise of Latin American Middle Class*. Washington, D.C.: The World Bank.

Frank, Trentmann. 2016. *Empire of Things: How We Became a World of Consumers: From the Fifteenth Century to the Twenty-First Century*. New York: Harper Collins.

Friedman, Thomas L. 2008. *Hot, Flat and Crowded: Why We Need a Green Revolution*. New York: Picador/Farrar, Straus and Giroux.

Fukuyama, Francis. 2012. The Future of History: Can Liberal Democracy Survive the Decline of the Middle Class? *Foreign Affairs*. Vol. 91, No. 1, pp. 53–61.

——. 2014. *Political Order and Political Decay: From the Industrial Revolution to the Globalisation of Democracy*. New York: Farrar, Straus and Giroux.

Huntington, Samuel. 2016. Will More Countries Become Democratic? *Political Science Quarterly*. Vol. 131, No. 2, pp. 237–266.

Jacobs, Jane. 1961 and 1989. *The Death and Life of Great American Cities*. New York: Vintage Books.

Jodhka, Surinder S. and Asseem Prakash. 2016. *The Indian Middle Class*. New Delhi: Oxford India.

Joshi, Sanjay (ed.). 2010. *The Middle Class in Colonial India*. Oxford: Oxford University Press.

Khan, Yasmin. 2007. *The Great Partition: The Making of India and Pakistan*. New Haven: Yale University Press.

Lahiri, Ashok K. 2014. The Middle Class and the Economic Reforms. *Economic and Political Weekly*. Vol. 49, No. 11, pp. 37–44.

Lopez, A. Recardo and Barbara Weinstein (eds). 2012. *The Making of Middle Class: Towards a Transnational History*. Durham and London: Duke University Press.

Marshall, Tim. 2015. *Prisoners of Geography: Ten Maps Explain Everything About the World*. New York: Scribner.

Micklethwait, John and Adrian Wooldridge. 2014. *The Fourth Revolution: The Global Race to Reinvent the State*. New York: Penguin.

Misra, B.B. 1963. *The Indian Middle Class: Their Growth in Modern Times*. Oxford: Oxford University Press.

Sheth, D.L. 1995. The Great Language Debate. In Upendra Bakshi and Bhiku Parekh (eds), *Crisis and Change in Contemporary India*. New Delhi: Sage Publications.

Sridharan, E. 2004. The Growth and Sectoral Composition of India's Middle Class: Its Impact on the Politics of Economic Liberalization. *India Review*. Vol. 3, No. 4, pp. 405–428.

Srinivas, M.N. 1957. Caste in Modern India. *Journal of Asian Studies*. Vol. 16, No. 4, pp. 529–548.

Torri, Michelguglielmo. 1991. The Myth of a Westernised Middle Class. In John L. Hill (ed.), *The Congress and Indian Nationalism: Historical Perspectives*. London: Curzon Press, pp. 18–55.

Varma, Pavan K. 1998. *The Great Indian Middle Class*. New Delhi: Viking.

Varshney, Ashutosh. 2013. Federation: Promise and Peril. In Mckinsey and Company (ed.), *Reimagining India*. New York: Simon and Schuster, pp. 60–67.

Walsh, Judith E. 2011. *A Brief History of India*. New York: Checkmark Books.

Wright, Erik Olin. 1997. *Class Counts: Comparative Studies in Class Analysis*. Cambridge: Cambridge University Press.

Zakaria, Fareed. 2013. The Rediscovery of India. In Mckinsey and Company (ed.), *Reimagining India*. New York: Simon and Schuster, pp. 3–9.

Zweig, Michael. 2000 and 2012. *The Working Class Majority: America's Best Kept Secret*. Ithaca and London: Cornell University Press.

6

Management of Multiculturalism

In writings on multiculturalism, it is often mentioned that the concept was first introduced in 1970s in Canada, Great Britain and the United States. These countries were facing the issue of assimilating the immigrant communities in the mainstream. The effort was to make themselves free of any streak of fragmentation (Garcia, 2008).

A development of a parallel idea also needs to be noted. Huntington (1996) propounded the thesis of 'clash of civilizations', primarily on religious and cultural lines. He envisaged a serious conflict between the West and the Rest of the world as the momentous feature of global politics in the twenty-first century. The emerged reality is that today there is a sharper struggle within rather than between civilizations, be it Christian or the Muslim or others. Sen (1999: p. 15) emphatically lays bare diversity within most cultures in the world. He questions the veracity of Huntington's thesis by arguing that the western culture is no less diverse within.

Multiculturalism is, indeed, a powerful political movement of our time that challenges the dominance of western culture in general (Tuan, 1989: p. 279). A multicultural society is one marked by coexistence of several cultures where each cherishes its own distinctiveness. The presence of diverse cultures in an area gets manifest in a variety of modes of worship, ways of living and configurations of landscape. At times this can be a source of conflict, a cause of segmentation, and a reason of separation too. This is true of most parts of the world, including Europe.

Indian scholars are said to have joined such a discourse only in the later years of 1990s. It is contended on the contrary that India has a long civilizational history of living with multiculturalism. Celebration of diversity has been a part of its inner geography through time. On gaining freedom from the yoke of colonial rule, the country designed a multicultural polity as a mark of its cultural vitality.

Evolution of the Idea

The ongoing discourse on multiculturalism has much longer history than indicated above. It had its first origin in the domain of political science. Scholars like Laski (1917), Truman (1951) and Shils (1962) referred to situations wherein conflicting interests of diverse groups called for a resolution.

Furnivall (1945) coined the term 'plural societies'. He had in mind a colonial context which was marked by a ruling European minority and a subjugated indigenous majority. Rangoon in Burma, Penang in Malaya and Jakarta in Indonesia were home to plural settings under the colonial rule. Indeed such are extreme situations wherein a European minority and the native majority functioned in a mode of a ruling elite and subjected masses. All plural societies may not be of this kind. These essentially represent the coexistence within a nation state of impervious social segments or cultural collectivities, each aware of its ethnic and other particularism (Dogan and Pelassy, 1984: p. 50). A hierarchical division among them is not essential. India today is one such case. Hence one has to avoid the pitfall of ethnocentrism or a belief in intrinsic superiority of a specific group while analyzing the composition of a society.

There are other variants of thought on the theme. Despres (1967: p. 22) distinguishes three distinct types of societies – homogeneous, heterogeneous and plural. Going beyond his analysis of a plural society in the colonial British Guiana, comprising the English, Indians, Chinese and Portuguese, we may illustrate his threefold classification of societies by taking present day examples. A homogeneous society exists when most of its members belong to a single set of institutions, which may be defined as formal and informal social norms that structure social interactions. This is true of China in a broad sense. A heterogeneous society is a one where people belong to different kinds of institutions at the local and regional levels but do not form conflicting cultural groups at the national level. Switzerland is a fine example of the kind. A plural society, by comparison, is characterized by some cultural schism at the national level. Lebanon offers itself as an illustration.

One of the early books raising the question of 'What is pluralism?' was edited by Kuper and Smith (1969). It highlighted that the issue of pluralism emerges in societies which are marked by diversity of cultures, institutional practices and hierarchical structures. Such differences get translated in multiple affiliations and put heavy pressure on the functioning of liberal democracy. A constant effort to manage such cleavages is any government's prime obligation.

Based on the degree of complexity, Geertz (1963) identifies five types of multi-ethnic situations: (i) asymmetrical duality with one large group and the other small, such is the case of Sinhalese and Tamils in Sri Lanka; (ii) symmetrical duality with both groups almost equal, such as Javanese versus Outer Islands people in Indonesia; (iii) asymmetrical multiplicity of one large and several smaller groups, for example Malayais, Chinese and Indians in Malaysia; (iv) multiple ethnic fragmentation, as illustrated by South Africa, Philippines and Nigeria; and (v) complex conglomeration, as in the case of Republic of Congo, which offers a count of around 250 separate tribal – linguistic groups. India is characterized by a relatively even gradation of groups in importance, from several large ones through many medium-sized ones to a number of small ones, with no clearly dominant and no sharp cut-off points (Brass, 1974: p. 11).

The concept of pluralism in the spirit of political geography is propounded by Kliot and Waterman (1983). The theme is treated under two organizational principles. The first is devoted to the context of diversity as a social reality and the second engages with the political manifestation of pluralism on religious, ethnic and class lines. Pluralism, thus, lends itself to both social analysis and political action.

On the basis of his study of the Caribbean demographic scene, Clarke (1984: pp. 52–54) identifies three variants of pluralism: structural (Trinidad), social (Puerto Rico) and cultural (Jamaica). The conceptual and empirical distinction between these terms may be illustrated by examples from other parts of the world. Structural pluralism is produced when population aggregates are incorporated into society on differing legal or political basis. Citizens and refugees do not have the same legal status in a society and thereby they introduce structural pluralism. This is the case of Syrian refugees in Germany. Social pluralism is on the lines of an exogenous elite ruling over indigenous colonized masses. South Africa presented such a scenario after Independence. Cultural pluralism is invariably associated with ethnic variety defined in terms of conflicting interest groups based on race, religion, language or caste operating in the context of democratic polity. This is the India of today. An additional institutional pluralism may also be mentioned. It divides people into different groups on the basis of their education, occupation and income level. In the United States, for example, people are formally classified into two categories of those who went for university education and others who stopped at school education.

Industrialization, urbanization, education, transportation and communication are expected to homogenize a society. The ethnicity-based tradition would give way to modernity characterized by democratization, secularization, equality and economic growth. Western Europe is cited as an example. This may not take place in reality. The development process often stokes competition and jealousy among rival groups. Ethnicity may re-emerge as a new socio-economic and political force, wherein group or religious interests come into clash. Even totalitarian methods of integrating a population, as in the case of former Soviet Union, prove ineffective. Such a strategy often fosters a deep cleavage between public and private lives of people. They may obey the laws and norms of the imposed dispensation but only in a superficial manner. The inner self continues to survive. Indeed any attempt at depluralizing a society is to be questioned.

Multiculturalism, Pluralism and Interculturalism

There is a need for clarification on the concepts of multiculturalism, cultural pluralism and interculturalism. Multiculturalism is a civilizational idea while pluralism is a political concept. Many a times these are used inter-changeably. A belief in equality neutral to racial, religious, regional and other considerations is basic to multi-culturalism. By comparison, pluralism offers a strategy to actualize all this through an action script.

Under the umbrella of multiculturalism different groups are expected to project themselves as one political entity. India is multicultural, where several groups coexist and there is consciousness of distinctiveness on the part of each. Multiculturalism has nation-state as its container wherein diversity of cultures is nurtured, all cultures receive equal place, and state does not discriminate between different cultures. It does not require the presence of a dominant cult.

As a part of her *Pluralism Project* at Harvard, Eck (2006) raises the question: 'What is pluralism?' She emphasizes that pluralism is not diversity alone but an energetic engagement with diversity; it is just not tolerance but seeking of understanding across lines of difference; it is not relativism, but an encounter of commitments. Pluralism is based on dialogue, both speaking and listening. It demands a conscious effort at dealing with diversity or multicultural context.

Pluralism does entail a multitude of problems. It is seen as closely associated with segmentation, tribalism and communalism based on consciousness of legal provisions. These pose obstacles in the path of national integration. Cleavages get defined and not only constrain effective administration but also lead to the question of even the right to existence of some minorities. No wonder pluralistic countries view assimilation and nation-building as a critical imperative.

One may distinguish also between multiculturalism and interculturalism. While multiculturalism attempts to promote a variety of cultures on equal footing, interculturalism is a call for assimilation in place of segregated existence of various cultural groups in a nation-state. This is going beyond the idea of multiculturalism which is considered as distinguisher rather than integrative of different cultures. Interculturalism is devised to cultivate inter-ethnic understanding, tolerance and civility. Several projects have been designed on interculturalist lines in the United Kingdom. Similar are the efforts in Germany. France has been working the same way. The idea is to challenge the emerging tendency of identity politics.

Rattansi (2011: p. 7) questions the validity of criticism against multi-culturalism as causing social segregation and disharmony. This is said with particular reference to Islamic radicalism in Europe. He believes that multi-culturalism allows immigrant minorities to retain their cultural identity. He recognizes the pitfalls of multiculturalism and acknowledges its rarity in actual existence. Interculturalism is favoured by him as a desired path.

In essence, the idiom of multiculturalism found wide currency as a device to manage diversity of cultures and subcultures within a nation-state. This had a background of several factors operating together. Prominent among these included a consciousness about the power of democracy, an increasing faith in secularism, and above all, a reaction to the homogenizing influence of western culture through globalization. Multiculturalism was a measure to counter hegemonic tendencies linked to dominance of one religion, language, domicile, or culture in the functioning of the nation-state (Madan, 2009).

Resolution of Multiculturalism

A variety of strategies have been adopted to deal with the multiethnic or multicultural situations. These could be grouped under two categories: 'conflict resolution' and 'territorial rearrangement'. Under the first category, for example, the United States invokes the 'melting pot' sensibility wherein heterogeneous immigrant groups are encouraged to merge into the mainstream for creating an ever harmonious cultural whole. This has given rise to an American way of life, mental make-up and ideology. Canada goes by 'salad bowl' mode wherein every cultural component is favoured as a distinct entity and is considered as an ingredient of the whole. The broad division of the country into English speaking, French speaking and Inuit (Eskimo) realms is a testimony to this. The same could be said about Belgium which is a 'mosaic' of Dutch or Fleming speaking, French or Walloons speaking, and German speaking territories.

Malaysia follows 'conglomerate' approach in which regional Malay loyalties are satisfied through rotation of presidency among the old sultanates. Lebanon presents an interesting case of 'consociational arrangements'. It is a segmented democratic system under which political power is shared on ethnic basis. Here the president has to be Christian, prime minister a Sunni Muslim and speaker a Shia Muslim. A pragmatic path has been adopted.

The other route is territorial re-arrangement. This is illustrated by break-up of the former Soviet Union, Yugoslavia, Czechoslovakia, and nearer home Pakistan. The Partition of the Indian subcontinent in 1947 was on similar lines. Ethnic considerations were dominant in each case.

For effecting harmony, multiculturalism must find some cementing force. The hope that the appeal of 'humanism' will work has been belied. Democracy was and continues to remain another hope on this front but multiculturalism itself has been hard on democracy since in many cases the ethnic groups as also the castes take the form of vote banks or identities. Secularism was another way out but it was on a weak wicket when religion of the majority was assertive and that of minority reactive. In all probability, the answer lies in the cultivation of a culture of mind which readily accepts otherness, honours diversity and has a non-dogmatic worldview.

A successful multicultural society is one where minority groups feel that they are allowed to claim more than one identity simultaneously –

Indian and Muslim by religion, Indian and Punjabi by language, Indian and Mizo by tribe. Such an approach is more crucial for developing countries where federalism and localism coexist with capitalism and globalization. Federalism seeks wider economic space through capitalism and localism is keen to assert its identity vis-à-vis the homogenizing forces of globalism. The basic task is to glue together the three ascending spatial scales of localism, federalism and globalism. This is made possible when there is a firm adherence to egalitarian liberal democracy as an ideology.

On the sideline, there is a skeptical perspective on multiculturalism. The idea is seen as an ideological device to promote ethnicity at the cost of class. A discourse in favour of multiculturalism is seen as skirting the issues related to class struggle. The question of ethnic identity gets projected as more critical than poor-rich dichotomy. This leads to persistence of the traditional hegemony of the bourgeoisie as a dominant socio-cultural group (Richmond, 1991). A debate on the primacy of sociological ordering of the society on ethnic lines or economic ordering in terms of income and wealth disparity is a natural corollary of such a line of thinking. This boils down to the task of ensuring harmony between ethnicity and economic growth to deliver social justice.

The Indian Panorama

Heterogeneity is a hallmark of Indian reality. There are hardly any areas which could be described as ethnically homogenous. All regions of India had started becoming multi-ethnic, multi-religious and multilingual in the pre-colonial period (Singh, 2011: p. 10). This was an outcome of interregional and intra-regional mobility caused by continuing flow of people from across the borders and intermixing of people within following periodic change in the internal political landscape of the country. The process intensified during the colonial and post-colonial periods due to migration flows associated with development activities.

By and large, communities remained linked to territorial ecology. Singh (1992), in the *Survey of People of India,* made a count of 4,635 communities based on caste, occupation, locality and such like other considerations. If equitably distributed, these will be only about 30 kms apart. About 70 per cent of these belonged to general category, 16 per cent to scheduled castes and 14 per cent to scheduled tribes. The variety of communities is of higher order in the South and North-East India than in North, North-West and West India.

As such several internal cleavages sharply divide the subcontinent of India (Frankel, 1984: p. 20). These are based on religion, language and region. Mass protest movements could be organized around such sensitive affiliations. The regionalist movements have been most frequent and vociferous. At times these took the form of secessionist demands. Appeals combined promises of economic upliftment with promotion of socio-cultural aspirations. There has never been a time since Independence when one or the other such demand was not voiced by some segment of population (Brass, 1974: p. 3).

India has been described as a series of 'parallel ethnic structures', each of which is characterized by an internal hierarchical order (Weiner, 1967). The predominant pattern is one of division in which each religious, tribal or linguistic group contains within itself a complete societal division on sectarian, clan or caste lines. The relative status differs within each case. The downtrodden scheduled castes are no exception to this. Some consider themselves superior to others, within their own generic group.

Three successive manifestations of all this may be noted. The Indian subcontinent was partitioned on religious lines in 1947; the country was reorganized on linguistic lines in 1956; and practically every state is directly or indirectly pursuing the 'sons of the soil' policy. The catch phrase 'sons of the soil' is a nativist movement against the inmigrants or immigrants from outside. The avowed purpose is to protect the available limited opportunities in job market, investment avenues and educational field for the local people which they see as being captured by better educated, highly skilled and exceedingly enterprising migrants from other areas. In urban areas, it is a typical middle class phenomenon. In rural areas, it is generally a protest of the locals against the state sponsored settlement of displaced persons from outside.

A comprehensive analysis of nativist movements in five regions of India, including Assam, Chota Nagpur, Andhra Pradesh, Bombay (now Mumbai) and Bangalore (now Bengaluru) has been provided by Weiner (1978). The discourse is placed in the context of local versus migrant in the opportunity market. Electoral considerations have also emerged as a sensitive factor in this regard. The nativist sentiment against migrants from Bihar and Uttar Pradesh in Mumbai and against immigrants from Bangladesh in Assam supports this observation.

For coping with a situation of bewildering social complexity, internal cultural variety and historical political fragmentation, India had to muster its skill in management of multiculturalism. This is a testimony to its vitality. India has followed the appropriate path for a nation-state by combining ethnicity and development (Sheth, 1989: p. 624). Spatial strategies have been equally effective. The primary reorganization of states on linguistic basis enabled it to satisfy regional aspirations. The national policy structure has been built upon accommodation of linguistic, religious and regional considerations. This is seen as the only way to sustain national integration, enhance the legitimacy of the political system and accelerate the developmental process through containment of social conflicts (Frankel, 1984: p. 20).

The provisions of the Constitution of India have been a critical help. The Article 29 has been framed in the spirit of multiculturalism though this term does not find explicit expression in the document. It grants right to minorities to preserve and promote their culture, language and script. Also, Article

30 guarantees special rights to the minorities to establish their educational, professional and religious institutions and administer them with a high degree of autonomy. Even the Royal Proclamation to the Princes, Chiefs and People of India by Queen Victoria in 1858 had affirmed that there would be no interference with religious traditions. This was a way of honouring the doctrine of multiculturalism (French, 2011).

A heritage of civilizational unity has been of immense value in this respect. Such a unified heritage is best represented in Indian literature. Though, written in many languages, the underpinnings of messages, such as cycle of birth and death, *karma* and associated reward and fate governing human life are a common thread. A pan-India sensibility and the same set of patterns and images of Indian consciousness are discernible (Choudhuri, 1995). A conflict between traditional Indianness and functional modernization is a recurrent theme. Meanwhile, the new regional literature is unfolding the specificity of local areas.

Geography of co-existence is essentially the art of living with diversity. It calls for accommodation of the presence of the other, carrying any definition. Any diversity has to function in the mode of productive complementarity. That is the way to a sustained unity.

Diversity and Development Debate

There are few words in social science literature that are as frequently used as diversity and development. Equally conspicuous is the lack of studies which examine the impact of diversity on development. The *Human Development Report* (United Nations Development Programme, 2004) placed its focus on the theme of cultural diversity. It questioned common perception of incompatibility between diversity and development. The assertion made was that there is no evidence that the two cannot move together.

A closer look at the Report, however, prompts one to question the veracity of this pronouncement which tries to be politically correct. Among the 35 countries ranked as the lowest on Human Development Index, 30 were ethnically highly diverse within. Most of these are located in Africa, where the national borders drawn by the colonial powers pieced together a variety of tribal groups within individual countries and rendered them multiethnic. On the other hand, only 30 countries were found as single-ethnicity cases, where no religious or ethnic minority group accounted for more than 10 per cent of the total population. These were strongly represented among those enjoying the highest of human development index. Included herein are Norway, Sweden, the Netherlands, Japan, Ireland and Austria.

The diversity of a country's demographics is not without a cost (Alesina and Spolaore, 2003). Size of a nation does matter and bigger ones tend to be diverse. Managing ethnic diversity is expensive. Different groups make competing demands on the finite resources of the country and the government is obliged to make compromises to deal with such situations. Optimal decisions may not be taken in the process and the pace of development is likely to be adversely affected.

A report on the development and diversity indices of districts and states in India has recently been prepared by Shariff (2015). The development index in each case was referred to a number of indicators belonging to four criteria of economic development, material well-being, education and health. The diversity index was not computed but the development level of each district/state was further decomposed in terms of scheduled caste/tribe versus all socio-religious communities; other backward classes versus all socio-religious communities; and the Muslims versus all socio-religious communities. The emphatic message of the report is that the Muslims are located at the bottom of the economic and social pyramid, and their condition is worse than that of even scheduled castes and scheduled tribes in many states. One does not, however, find in this report, any analytical framework for examining a relationship between diversity and development but presents a picture of inequality in development level of different socio-religious groups. It simply reinforces in greater spatial details the findings of the Sachar Committee Report (2006).

Historically it is observed that several parts of the world, particularly Europe, witnessed evolution of nation-states on the basis of ethno-nationalism. The underlying ideology favoured ethnically homogeneous societies to ensure internal solidarity, emotional affinity of the people to a common cause and optimal implementation of government programmes (Muller, 2008: p. 31). Over time such a sentiment mellowed down and there was a yearning for a wider arena to capture missed opportunities. This is how the European Union subsuming heterogeneity came to be formed in the interest of all member nation-states.

The process of globalization, international migration and coming together of diverse kinds of people creates situations wherein virtues of heterogeneity become visible. On the basis of data gathered in 44 countries, Anderson and Paskeviciute (2006: p. 799) also affirm that heterogeneity is a necessary ingredient for building a vibrant and stable civil society and democratic life. More creative and efficient decisions are a hallmark of such a context. The greatest obligation of heterogeneous societies is to ensure trust among different communities.

Sowell (2015: p. 141) observes that with its vast array of ethnic, linguistic, caste and other subdivisions, India is a pool of human skills, expertise and perspectives. This should be to its great advantage. An empirical verification of this assertion is the objective of this essay.

Accordingly basic hypothesis of the present exercise is that ethnic diversity or multiculturalism is generative of faster pace of development. A positive relationship between the degree of multiculturalism and level of socio-economic development in different parts of India is envisaged. A multicultural context is premised as generative of more of complementarity than conflict. It protects diversity, fosters tolerance, decentralizes powers and provides more freedom. Progress occurs from the confrontation and resolution of issues, pooling of ideas and adherence to optimal decisions (Morrill, 1983: pp. 74–77). All this requires a dynamic interaction rather than a mere passive coexistence. Needless to add that faith in multiculturalism is essential to India's vitality.

The Indian states are multireligious in a varying degree. Though each has a specific scheduled official language yet these are multilingual too. The interstate migration streams have also led to the presence of a variety of people in each setting. Accordingly, the demographic diversity in this essay has been referred to three parameters of religion, language and domicile.

Religion and Development

A world defined and differentiated by religion and concerned with development is naturally interested in discerning the role of religion in impacting upon the development process. More than religion, a context of religious diversity is of greater relevance to the analysis of the issue at hand. This will indicate the desirability or otherwise of multicultural societies vis-à-vis ethno-national entities.

Going by the estimates made available by the Washington DC-based Pew Research Centre, one-third or 2.4 billion of the 7.2 billion people in the world in 2012 were Christian by religion. No less than 126 countries were Christian majority. In 51 countries, the Christian population was on the higher side of 90 per cent.

By comparison, the Muslims with a numerical strength of 1.7 billion accounted for nearly 24 per cent or roughly one-fourth of the world total. Fifty countries were noted for a majority of Muslim population. Thirty-two countries had more than 90 per cent of their population as faithful to Islam.

The Hindus, nearly 1.1 billion in number, were 15 per cent of the population of the world. Around 97 per cent of them were confined to India alone where they made four-fifths of the country's total population. Nepal and Mauritius were other two countries which could claim a majority of Hindu population. Over 81 per cent of the population in Nepal recorded Hinduism as their faith.

The rest of the world population adheres either to Buddhism, or organized religions like Sikhism and Judaism, or traditional regional or local beliefs or claims to be unaffiliated to any religion or creed. The frequency of unaffiliated persons is relatively high in East Asian, West European and former socialist countries where they make more than 20 per cent of total population. This percentage is 57 in Japan, 42 in Netherlands, 25 in Germany and no less than 52 per cent in China. Around 15 per cent of the world population falls in this group.

A survey of the world literature shows that there has been all-too-plenty of studies separately on religion and development. Analytical efforts at examining the impact of religion on development are not many. This can be referred to some solid reasons. First, religion is a sensitive matter and needs to be handled with care while expounding on its negative aspects vis-à-vis progress of humanity. Second, religion is difficult to define and comprehend in totality. It does not allow any easy formulation of a confident analytical framework. Involved herein are not only the issues relating to specific moral tenets and belief systems of different religions but also their in-practice behavioural adherence and ritual performance. Third, the distinctive role of religious organizations is also to be made a part of any research effort of the kind. They may not share relevant data or information. Above all, religion is deemed as irrelevant to the process of modernization and scientific thinking. It is perceived as apathetic to matters of material development. Hence it may better be left to itself, free from scrutiny by research (Harr and Ellis, 2006: p. 352).

In much of social science writings, religion is generally presented in a negative light. It is seen as a source of conflict between civilizations, a hurdle in evolution of a secular society and an impediment to modernization process. 'Much of religion is not religious'. At the same time, religion is valued for fastening human mind on a moral path. Its reformative, motivational and energizing role is duly acknowledged. In India, Mahatma Gandhi invoked religion as a moral force for winning country's freedom. Same way religion was instrumental in bringing about a positive political change in Poland, South Africa and Iran during the recent decades.

In earlier years of the nineteenth century, Weber (1926, 1930) propounded the idea of austere Protestantism as a factor in the rise of capitalism and stabilization of nation-state in the western world. Protestant ethics stood for a resolve to work hard, fulfil one's life obligations, and ensure savings to facilitate investment at large. This paved the way for smooth journey of capitalism toward economic development.

He had meanwhile held spirituality, disdain for materialism, otherworldliness, belief in fatalism, and lack of rational practices of Hindus as responsible for India's lack of progress and persistence of poverty. The perception of this world as *Maya* or illusion added to this effect. Additionally the rigidity of caste system proved virtually an impregnable barrier to upward mobility of a large section of masses. All such formulations were strongly contested by several scholars. Indians were described as no less materialistic. They worship *Lakshmi*, the goddess of wealth, and *Ganesh*, the god of success, and observe '*navratras*' (nine days of ritual fasting) for worldly gains. India was glorified as a land of prosperity, 'a golden sparrow', for a long span of its history.

Several western scholars were appalled also at the backwardness of the Muslim countries in general. They attributed this to the factor of resistance of Islam to modernization. This they located in a variety of beliefs, social norms and behavioural patterns of the Muslims world over. This view is strongly contested by Islamic scholars. They hold their subjugation by western imperial powers as responsible for this underdevelopment. Else they had a glorious past during the medieval times when Turks were a world power. The turn of events stunted their institutional growth and thwarted the development process (Ragab, 1980: p. 513).

One may come across in social science literature a scattering of such studies linking religion and development but overall there is a paucity of research efforts which measure the outcome of co-presence of several religious communities in a country or region on its development process. How to go about a research exercise to this effect? This can be done by evaluating economic development outcomes with reference to growth rate and investment; social development outcomes in terms of communal harmony and status of women; and institutional development outcomes as reflected in quality of governance and status of law and order.

A negative outcome of religious diversity on economic development was demonstrated by Montalvo and Reynel-Querol (2005), based on their study covering a large sample of 138 countries for which data were analysed for the years 1960–1989. They linked this to a reduction in investment for development. The associated factors were an increase in government expenditure for maintenance of law and order and caution on the part of private sector apprehending the probability of civil conflict.

Likewise, Kodila-Tedika and Agbor (2014), in their study of Sub-Saharan Africa, found that religious diversity was not without a negative effect on investment, and thereby on economic development. On somewhat similar lines was the observation of Eng (2008), based on the Singapore experience. He emphasized the need for a carefully managed diversity-unity balance by the state so as to ensure best of results. Religious diversity cannot be left to government alone. An inter-faith empathy, dialogue and collaboration are essential on the part of the people as well.

The fact is that ethnic diversity works both ways, negative as well as positive. Operational part of its dynamics differs by public sector and private sector. Public sector favours homogeneity because this spares it from digging into complexity, and renders things easy to manage. Diversity makes the administrative process more expensive and this impinges upon the resources available for development investment. By contrast, private sector values diversity. It is seen as widening the scope of investment and also as promoting participation by different groups in complementarity with each other. Diversity is valued for generating vibrancy, variety and plenty. Societies functioning as rainbow are seen as flourishing the most.

Religious Diversity and Development

India is a secular country consistent with its historical legacy of civilizational unity and provisions laid down in the Constitution. It is multi-religious in demographic complexion, with pre-eminence of the Hindus, who account for 79.8 per cent of the total population as per the 2011 Census of India (Table 6.1). The actual number is 966 million, three times the total population of the United States. No less than 172 million are Muslims, representing 14.2

per cent of the country's population. This number almost equals the total population of Pakistan. At 27.8 million, Christians are half in number of the total population of Italy, though they make only 2.3 per cent of India's population. Accounting for 1.7 per cent of the country's population, the Sikhs are 20.8 million, a number which approximates the total population of Sri Lanka. Both Buddhism and Jainism have their birth place in India but the number of their adherents in this country today is hardly 8.4 million (0.7 per cent) and 4.5 million (0.4 per cent), respectively. The remaining about one per cent of India's population belongs to other religions or persuasions or beliefs, such as animism, Zoroastrianism or even atheism.

Table 6.1 *India: Religious Composition of Population, 2011*

Religious community	*Population in million*	*Percentage in the total*
Hindu	966.3	79.8
Muslim	172.2	14.2
Christian	27.8	2.3
Sikh	20.8	1.7
Buddhist	8.4	0.7
Jain	4.5	0.4
Other religions and persuasions	7.9	0.7
Religion not stated	2.9	0.2
Total	1210.8	100.0

Source: Census of India, 2011.

A perusal of data relating to the religious composition of states/union territories of India informs that Hindus are in absolute majority in all states, barring Mizoram, Nagaland, Meghalaya, Arunachal Pradesh, Manipur, Jammu & Kashmir and Punjab, and the union territory of Lakshadweep (Table 6.2). Mizoram, Nagaland and Meghalaya are noted for absolute majority of Christians, Jammu & Kashmir that of Muslims, and Punjab that of Sikhs. In Manipur, Hindus are in relative majority but not in absolute one. The same is the situation of Christians in Arunachal Pradesh (Map 6.1).

India is distinguished not only by considerable religious diversity but more so by a lot of religiosity. Accordingly to a Global Gallup Poll in 2015, nearly 80 per cent of the Indians affirmed that religion plays an important role in their daily life. The comparable figures in percentage are 24, 30 and 65 in Japan, France and the United States respectively. Pilgrimages bring about a half of the total package tours in a year. The number of places of worship of all variety in the country at 3.01 million is more than the number of educational institutions (2.1 million) and health centres (0.7 million) put together. One per cent of occupied census houses in 2011 were recorded as places of worship.

Map 6.1

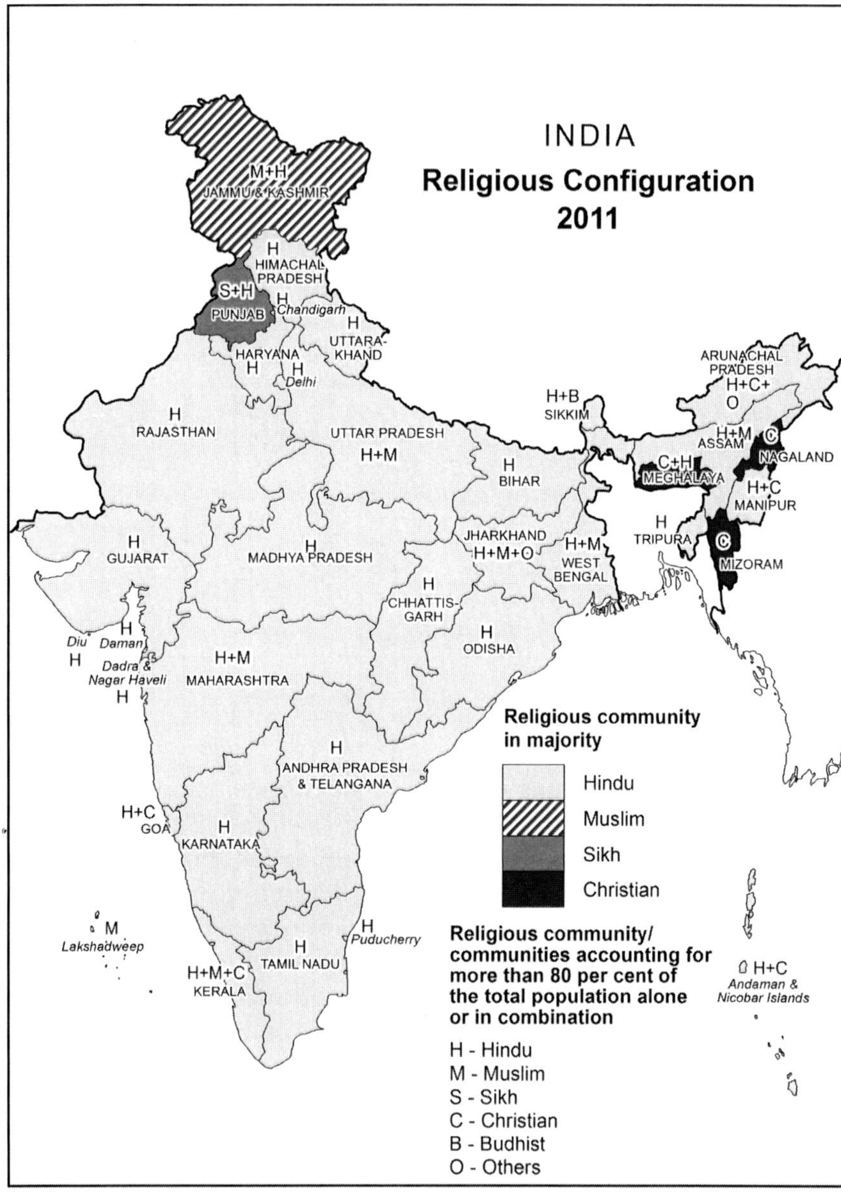

Barring MIzoram, Nagaland and Meghalaya, which are Christian majority; Jammu and Kashmir as well as union territory of Lakshadweep which are Muslim majority; and Punjab, which is Sikh majority; all other states and union territories of India are Hindu majority.

Source: Census of India, 2011.

Table 6.2 *India: Religious Composition of the States and Union Territories, 2011*

States	*Population share in percentage*						
	Hindu	*Muslim*	*Christian*	*Sikh*	*Buddhist*	*Jain*	*Others*
Andhra Pradesh*	88.5	9.6	1.3	0.0	0.0	0.1	0.5
Arunachal Pradesh	29.0	2.0	30.3	0.2	11.8	0.1	26.6
Assam	61.5	34.2	3.7	0.1	0.2	0.1	0.2
Bihar	82.7	16.9	0.1	0.0	0.0	0.0	0.3
Chhattisgarh	93.2	2.0	1.9	0.3	0.3	0.2	2.1
Goa	66.1	8.3	25.1	0.1	0.1	0.1	0.2
Gujarat	88.6	9.7	0.5	0.1	0.1	1.0	0.0
Haryana	87.5	7.0	0.2	4.9	0.0	0.2	0.2
Himachal Pradesh	95.2	2.2	0.2	1.2	1.1	0.0	0.1
Jammu & Kashmir	28.4	68.3	0.3	1.9	0.9	0.0	0.2
Jharkhand	67.8	14.5	4.3	0.2	0.0	0.0	13.2
Karnataka	84.0	12.9	1.9	0.0	0.2	0.7	0.3
Kerala	54.7	26.6	18.4	0.0	0.0	0.0	0.3
Madhya Pradesh	90.9	6.6	0.3	0.2	0.3	0.8	0.9
Maharashtra	79.8	11.5	1.0	0.2	5.8	1.2	0.5
Manipur	41.4	8.4	41.3	0.1	0.2	0.1	8.5
Meghalaya	11.5	4.4	74.6	0.1	0.3	0.0	9.1
Mizoram	2.7	1.4	87.2	0.0	8.5	0.0	0.2
Nagaland	8.7	2.5	87.9	0.1	0.3	0.1	0.4
Odisha	93.6	2.2	2.8	0.1	0.0	0.0	1.3
Punjab	38.5	1.9	1.3	57.7	0.1	0.2	0.3
Rajasthan	88.5	9.1	0.1	1.3	0.0	0.9	0.1
Sikkim	57.8	1.6	9.9	0.3	27.4	0.1	2.9
Tamil Nadu	87.6	5.9	6.1	0.0	0.0	0.1	0.3
Tripura	83.4	8,6	4.4	0.0	3.4	0.0	0.0
Uttar Pradesh	79.7	19.3	0.2	0.3	0.1	0.1	0.3
Uttarakhand	83.0	13.9	0.4	2.3	0.1	0.1	0.2
West Bengal	70.5	27.0	0.7	0.1	0.3	0.1	1.3
Union Territories							
Andaman and Nicobar	69.4	8.5	21.3	0.3	0.1	0.0	0.4
Chandigarh	80.8	4.9	0.8	13.1	0.1	0.2	0.1
Dadra and Nagar Haveli	93.9	3.8	1.5	0.1	0.2	0.3	0.2
Daman and Diu	90.5	7.9	1.2	0.1	0.1	0.1	0.1
Delhi	81.7	12.9	0.9	3.4	0.1	1.0	0.0
Lakshadweep	2.8	96.6	0.5	0.0	0.0	0.0	0.1
Puducherry	87.3	6.1	6.3	0.0	0.0	0.1	0.2
All India	79.8	14.2	2.3	1.7	0.7	0.4	0.9

Source: Census of India, 2011.
* Includes Telangana.

In statistical terms, there is on an average nearly one place of worship for every one square km of area, 1.5 places of worship for every institution of education, around five places of worship for every outlet of health (Table 6.3). The preponderance of places of worship over educational and health institutions is well marked in the whole of Northern Plain, Eastern Coastal states, Western Hill states, Gujarat and Rajasthan. On the other hand, there are three areas where the additive figure for educational and health centres exceeds that of places of worship. First, the North-East, where church alone is in virtual religious command in several areas; second, the central tribal belt, where institutionalized places of worship are not that frequent; and third, large urban places where high population densities do not require as many places of worship as is the case with scattered rural settlements. Contrary to one's expectations, the frequency of places of worship is relatively low in Kerala, Maharashtra and Sikkim, which otherwise are noted for a diversified composition of population (Map 6.2).

Table 6.3 *India: Occupied Census Houses Used as Place of Worship, School/College and Dispensary/Hospital, 2011*

States	*Number of census houses used as*		
	Place of worship	*School/college*	*Hospital/dispensary*
States			
Andhra Pradesh*	191,418	138,574	49,556
Arunachal Pradesh	3,427	5,405	787
Assam	159,818	93,616	21,304
Bihar	166,560	105,439	29,587
Chhattisgarh	62,015	82,634	10,508
Goa	5,964	2,913	1,649
Gujarat	181,854	93,087	39,801
Haryana	33,315	24,364	13,665
Himachal Pradesh	38,199	27,560	7,376
Jammu & Kashmir	49,135	31,843	6,278
Jharkhand	64,336	68,290	12,014
Karnataka	219,915	139,176	42,781
Kerala	105,562	75,480	31,589
Madhya Pradesh	170,240	198,641	27,126
Maharashtra	278,768	213,833	100,885
Manipur	5,724	4,388	724
Meghalaya	7,005	11,584	1,111
Mizoram	3,875	4,879	658
Nagaland	3,168	3,887	941
Odisha	133,789	98,437	17,873
Punjab	63,244	31,228	14,494
Rajasthan	224,269	131,434	36,649
Sikkim	1,407	2,434	324

Cont'd...

...Cont'd

Tamil Nadu	170,553	86,294	49,977
Tripura	10,366	10,692	2,214
Uttar Pradesh	354,421	256,746	80,727
Uttarakhand	33,503	29,949	7,676
West Bengal	257,125	119,465	64,983
Union Territories			
Andaman and Nicobar Isles	1,494	1,058	291
Chandigarh	450	695	366
Dadra and Nagar Haveli	425	711	209
Daman and Diu	555	221	146
Delhi	8,668	9,709	7,853
Lakshadweep	466	328	43
Puducherry	2,282	1,715	1,063
India	3,013,315	2,106,709	683,228

Source: Census of India; 2011.
* Includes Telangana.

A scrutiny of religious diversity vis-à-vis development equation reveals that most of the homogeneous states, namely Odisha, Chhattisgarh, Madhya Pradesh and Nagaland, are at a low or relatively low level of development (Table 6.4). Himachal Pradesh and Mizoram are the exceptions in this group. On the other hand, the states with significant heterogeneity of religious communities, namely Kerala, Goa, Maharashtra and Sikkim are distinguished by high level of development. In case this heterogeneity has a fair component of tribal persuasions, as in Meghalaya, Tripura and Jharkhand, it gets associated with a drop in development level. One major religious majority overall (Hindu) and one urban based minority (Muslim/Christian), as in Gujarat, Tamil Nadu and Karnataka, are associated with high level of development. Rajasthan and Andhra Pradesh are exceptions to this effect. On the other hand, a combination of one overall dominant religious community (Hindu) and one rural based large minority (Muslim), as in Assam, West Bengal, Bihar, and Uttar Pradesh, finds an association with low level of development. In situations, where two religious communities are in significant proportions, as in Punjab (Sikh and Hindu), Jammu & Kashmir (Muslim and Hindu) and Manipur (Hindu and Christian), the conditions are favourable to development. Arunachal Pradesh stands out as an exception in this case. All the union territories are high on development level despite a differing nature of their religious composition. Daman & Diu, Dadra & Nagar Haveli and Lakshadweep are homogeneous, Chandigarh and Puducherry are characterized by one majority and one large minority each, and Delhi and Andaman & Nicobar Islands are marked by heterogeneity. The emerging message is that urban-rural composition of different religious communities is a critical factor in assessing their overall impact on the development process.

Map 6.2

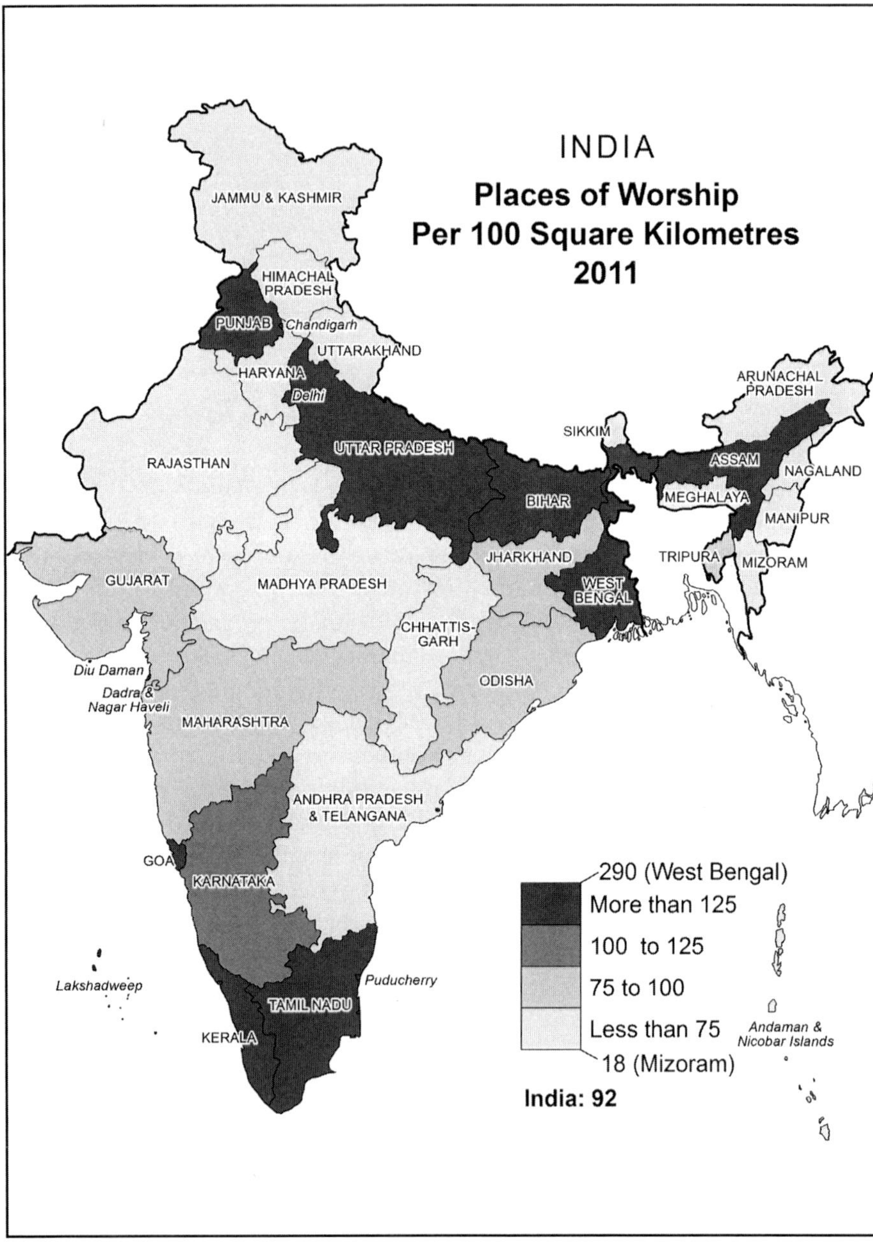

On an average, India has one place of worship for every one square kilometre of area.
Source: Census of India, 2011.

Table 6.4 *India: Religious Diversity Status and Development Level of Different States and Union Territories, 2011*

Category	*States (religious communities)*	*Development level*
Homogeneous	Odisha (Hindu)	Low
	Madhya Pradesh (Hindu)	Low
	Chhattisgarh (Hindu)	Low
	Nagaland (Christian)	Relatively low
	Mizoram (Christian)	Relatively high
	Himachal Pradesh (Hindu)	Relatively high
Significantly heterogeneous	Kerala (Hindu, Muslim, Christian)	High
	Goa (Hindu, Christian, Muslim)	High
	Maharashtra (Hindu, Muslim, Buddhist)	High
	Sikkim (Hindu, Buddhist, Christian)	High
Considerably heterogeneous with a large number following other persuasions	Meghalaya (Christian, Hindu, Other persuasions)	Relatively low
	Tripura (Hindu, Muslim, Other persuasions)	Relatively low
	Jharkhand (Hindu, Muslim, Other persuasions)	Relatively low
One dominant community/one significant urban based minority	Tamil Nadu (Hindu, Christian)	High
	Karnataka (Hindu, Muslim)	Relatively high
	Gujarat (Hindu, Muslim)	Relatively high
	Andhra Pradesh* (Hindu, Muslim)	Relatively low
One dominant community/one significant rural based minority	Bihar (Hindu, Muslim)	Low
	Uttar Pradesh (Hindu, Muslim)	Low
	Assam (Hindu, Muslim)	Relatively low
	West Bengal (Hindu, Muslim)	Relatively low
	Uttarakhand (Hindu, Muslim)	Relatively high
	Haryana (Hindu, Muslim)	High
Two communities in significant proportion	Punjab (Sikh, Hindu)	High
	Jammu & Kashmir (Muslim, Hindu)	Relatively high
	Manipur (Hindu, Christian)	Relatively high
	Arunachal Pradesh (Christian, Hindu)	Relatively low
Category	*Union Territories (religious communities)*	*Development level*
Assorted pattern	Delhi (Hindu, Muslim, Sikh)	High
	Andaman and Nicobar Islands (Hindu, Christian, Muslim)	High
	Chandigarh (Hindu, Sikh)	High
	Puducherry (Hindu, Christian)	High
	Daman and Diu (Hindu)	High
	Dadra and Nagar Haveli (Hindu)	High
	Lakshadweep (Muslim)	High

* Includes Telangana.

All in all, religious heterogeneity in Indian context is favourable to development and homogeneity has somewhat dampening effect. Most encouraging outcome is experienced if two or three religious communities mark a significant presence in a state. Among the minorities, the Sikhs, the Christians and the Jains are noted for a positive impact on development. In the case of the Muslims, the influence is dual. If they are in greater concentration in urban areas, this tends to be pro-development, and if they are largely in rural areas, this gets associated with low level of development. Evidently in all such situations, religion seems to be an associative rather than a causative factor.

Linguistic Diversity and Development

After the resolution of ethnic conflict in consonance with 'two nation' theory, which led to the Partition of the Indian subcontinent into non-Muslim India and Muslim-Pakistan on religious lines in 1947, the issue of managing linguistic diversity emerged as serious in both countries. A dismemberment of India on linguistic lines was apprehended by several western scholars' right since the time it gained Independence. This did not happen. By contrast, the linguistic chasm, among other factors, in the case of Pakistan culminated in fragmentation of the country into Pakistan and Bangladesh in 1971.

The Indian state adopted several sensible policies on democratic lines to meet the situation. Most important was the reorganization of states on geo-linguistic basis in 1956. The states were carved out in a manner that each had a specific majority language and in none of them all the minorities put together equaled or exceeded half of the total population. This was intended to accommodate the linguistic, cultural and historical aspirations of the people in different parts of the country. At the institutional level, a three language formula was enunciated in 1968. It stipulated that every school child in Hindi speaking states would be taught Hindi, English and one of the other languages in the Eighth Schedule of the Constitution and in non-Hindi speaking states every school child will be taught the official language of the state, English and Hindi. The idea was to promote the spirit of nationalism through language learning. At the administrative level, a bilingual or even trilingual 'file notings' in government offices was introduced so as to facilitate the desired communication between the central and state governments.

A striking feature of India's cultural make-up cannot be missed. In terms of religion, the country is marked by a dominance of Hinduism in general coupled with considerable religious diversity within states. In the case of language, by comparison, the country is polyglot in overall terms but most of the states are marked by one dominant language. India does not have a national language, as per provisions of its Constitution. Hindi is the official language of pan-India usage. English is the additional official language. It will retain this status till the time the legislatures of all non-Hindi states and both the houses of the Parliament decide otherwise. The Eighth Schedule of the Constitution lists 22 languages, including Hindi but excluding English. In addition, the Government of India has conferred the status of classical languages to Sanskrit, Tamil, Kannada, Telugu, Malayalam and Oriya. The regional languages of all the South Indian states have acquired the prestige of being classical.

India's linguistic panorama is in fact much more diversified. The 2001 Census of India, which is the latest one to provide data on linguistic composition of the country, lists 122 major languages and 1,599 other languages as spoken by people in different parts of the country. Thirty languages had more than one million speakers each. Hindi and English are the *lingua franca*, a role which was played by Persian during the Mughal period and by English during the colonial period.

A five-layered spatial pattern of Indian languages is not difficult to visualize (Dutt et al., 1985). Hindi, English and Urdu have nationwide spread. Languages with macro-regional extent include Bengali, Tamil, Marathi and Punjabi. By comparison, Gujarati, Kannada, Malayalam, Oriya and Telugu are noted for their regional expanse. Assamese and Kashmiri define themselves as languages limited to the core. Finally, Sindhi is noted as a language without a core. It is sprinkled mainly in large cities of India.

English has evolved as the most important link language in the country. Since India does not have a national language, English enjoys a special status in the domains of higher education, national media and upper levels of judiciary, bureaucracy and business. Knowledge of this language is considered as an entry permit for a white collar job. It carries a special value also for professional education, internet usage and emigration process.

The Census of India does not provide direct data on English knowing or speaking people. This is to be worked out by adding the number of persons who reported English as their mother tongue with those who reported it as second or third in order of their linguistic ability. Going by this technique it is found that there were 125 million or one in every eight persons knowing English in India in 2001. The *India Human Development Report 2005* informs that 28 per cent of the men and 17 per cent of the women in the sample households could at least speak some English. This represents the growing popularity and adoption of English even among the backward sections of society. No wonder the English medium schools, of whatever quality, are mushrooming in both urban and rural India. One could easily reckon that today the share of English knowing persons, in the country is probably one-third of the total population.

Some degree of linguistic diversity is typical of all the states and union territories. This could be attributed to factors like settling of a variety of linguistic groups in an area over time, the methodology of demarcation of states based on district as the basic spatial unit leaving a scope for inclusion of persons having an affinity with the language of the neighbouring state, and the process of inter-state migration. The extent of linguistic diversity differs by states/union territories. A cross-tabulation of data on the extent of linguistic homogeneity/diversity of different states and union territories vis-à-vis their respective development level does not display any consistent relationship. This is a departure from the pattern of religious diversity which, in general, has a positive association with the level of development. Language is certainly a less differentiating factor of the people than religion within states, organized as these were on linguistic basis.

Among seven states in the top quartile in terms of degree of linguistic homogeneity, three (Kerala, Punjab and Tamil Nadu) are at a high level of development, one (Himachal Pradesh) at a relatively high level, one (Nagaland) at a relatively low level, and two (Uttar Pradesh and Rajasthan) at a low level (Table 6.5). In the second quartile, one (Haryana) is at a high level of development, three (Uttarakhand, Mizoram and Gujarat) are at a relatively high level, one (West Bengal) is at a relatively low level, and two (Madhya Pradesh and Bihar) are at low level. In the third quartile, one (Maharashtra) is at a high level of development, one (Karnataka) is at a relatively high level, three (Meghalaya, Tripura and Andhra Pradesh) are at a relatively low level, and two (Odisha and Chhattisgarh) are at a low level. In the bottom fourth quartile, on the parameter of linguistic homogeneity, two (Goa and Sikkim) are at a high level of development, two (Jammu & Kashmir and Manipur) are at a relatively high level, two (Assam and Arunachal Pradesh) are at a relatively low level, and one (Jharkhand) is at a low level. All the union territories, whatever their degree of homogeneity or heterogeneity on linguistic lines, are distinguished by a high level of development.

Evidently every quartile or group defined on the basis of linguistic diversity status is composed of states at varying levels of development, defying a specific role of this factor. This finding can be placed for comparison with the findings of Pool (1972: p. 222). In an analytical study of 133 countries, he tries to verify the relationship between their linguistic diversity and per capita gross domestic product. He observes that linguistic diversity in a country proves a barrier to its economic growth. One can hardly locate any linguistically diverse country which is prosperous. In his view, linguistically homogeneous societies tend to advance faster in education, modernization and economic growth. He adds that his observations are tentative and call for further scrutiny.

One cannot gloss over the fact that a situation of linguistic diversity in a country is different from that within its different parts. The Indian states, for example, may be linguistically diverse vis-à-vis each other and may contain some element of linguistic variety but each of them enjoys power to follow a uniform language policy. This is a scene of regional homogeneity within national heterogeneity.

Table 6.5 *India: Linguistic Diversity Status, 2001, and Development Level of Different States and Union Territories, 2011*

Category	*States (with majority language and percentage of its population)*	*Second and third ranking languages*	*Developmental level*
Top quartile	Kerala (Malayalam; 96.8)	Tamil, Urdu	High
	Punjab (Punjabi; 91.7)	Hindi, Urdu	High
	Uttar Pradesh (Hindi; 91.3)	Urdu, Punjabi	Low
	Rajasthan (Hindi; 91.1)	Punjabi, Urdu	Low
	Tamil Nadu (Tamil; 89.4)	Telegu, Kannada	High
	Himachal Pradesh (Hindi; 89.3)	Punjabi, Kashmiri	Relatively high
	Nagaland (Tribal dialects; 89.2)	Tribal dialects	Relatively low
Second quartile	Uttarakhand (Hindi; 88.0)	Urdu, Punjabi	Relatively high
	Bihar (Hindi, 87.3)	Urdu, Bengali	Low
	Haryana (Hindi; 87.3)	Punjabi, Urdu	High
	Madhya Pradesh(Hindi; 87.3)	Marathi, Urdu	Low
	Mizoram (Mizo; 87.3)	Bengali, Tribal dialects	Relatively high
	West Bengal (Bengali; 85.3)	Hindi, Urdu	Relatively low
	Gujarat (Gujarati; 84.5)	Hindi, Sindhi	Relatively high
Third quartile	Andhra Pradesh* (Telegu, 83.9)	Urdu, Hindi	Relatively low
	Meghalaya (Tribal dialects; 83.4)	Bengali, Nepali	Relatively low
	Odisha (Oriya; 83.2)	Hindi, Telegu	Low
	Chhattisgarh (Hindi; 82.7)	Oriya, Tribal dialects	Low
	Maharashtra (Marathi; 68.9)	Hindi, Urdu	High
	Tripura (Bengali; 67.4)	Hindi, Tribal dialects	Relatively low
	Karnataka (Kannada; 66.3)	Telegu, Marathi	Relatively high
Bottom quartile	Arunachal Pradesh (Tribal dialects; 64.9)	Bengali, Nepali	Relatively low
	Sikkim (Nepali; 63.0)	Hindu, Tribal dialects	High
	Manipur (Manipuri; 60.7)	Tribal dialects	Relatively high
	Jharkhand (Hindi; 57.7)	Bengali, Oriya	Low
	Goa (Konkani; 57.2)	Marathi, Hindi	High
	Jammu & Kashmir (Kashmiri; 54.0)	Dogri, Hindi	Relatively high
	Assam (Assamese; 49.4)	Bengali, Hindi	Relatively low
Category	*Union territories (with majority language and percentage of its population)*	*Second and third ranking languages*	*Development level*
Assorted group	Lakshadweep (Malayalam; 97.9)	Tamil, Konkani	High
	Puducherry (Tamil; 88.5)	Telegu, Malayalam	High
	Delhi (Hindi; 81.0)	Punjabi, Urdu	High
	Daman and Diu (Gujarati; 68.8)	Hindi, Marathi	High
	Chandigarh (Hindi; 67.6)	Punjabi, Urdu	High
	Dadra and Nagar Haveli (Tribal dialects; 40.8)	Gujarati, Hindi	High
	Andaman and Nicobar Islands (Bengali; 26.0)	Hindi, Tamil	High

* Includes Telangana.

Regional Diversity and Development

The linguistic and religious diversity of a state in India is the outcome of several factors operating over time. First is the way boundaries were fixed at the time of its formation. The effort may have been to render a linguistic unity but nothing could be done to perfection. A considerable amount of linguistic diversity as already existing had to be accommodated in varying degree. Second, the historical factor of a variety of social movements and associated conversions of whatever magnitude played its own role in imparting religious diversity to the state as formed. There is hardly any state in which the administrative and religious boundaries are in complete agreement with each other. Finally, the inflow of people from outside the state not only influences the linguistic and religious composition of a state but also introduces a new kind of diversity which is linked to the phenomenon of domicile. This we may call as regional diversity. The demographic complexion of a state remains in a continuous state of change with every fresh inflow or outflow of people.

A state can, thus, be a home to two broad categories of people; native to the state and the outsiders who are the people hailing from diverse areas. Though the contribution of outsiders to the economic dynamism and cultural variety of a state is duly acknowledged yet they are also viewed as competitors in the labour market at large and also as exploiters of the limited opportunities and resources as available. They have to often face the ire of the natives incited by the proponents of the 'sons of the soil' theory.

Regional diversity is essentially an outcome of interstate migration. The 2001 Census of India, which is the latest one to provide data on migration in the country, recorded 42.34 million people as interstate migrants. They made for 4.12 per cent of the total population. This percentage ranged from the highest of 19.56 for Goa to the lowest of 0.81 for Manipur. Among the union territories, Chandigarh recorded the highest percentage of interstate migrants at 59.36 while the figure of 5.80 for Lakshadweep was the lowest. Of the 42.34 million interstate migrants, 16.83 million or about 40 per cent had moved during the preceding 10 years. A significant recent rise in interstate migration is indicated. The spatial pattern of this mobility was in consonance with the already existing base. A stability of the regional diversity pattern is indicated.

Virtually all the states in the top quartile on the parameter of regional diversity, such as Maharashtra, Punjab and Haryana in addition to Goa and Sikkim, are at a high level of development (Table 6.6). A variety of employment opportunities were available here which attracted migrants from other states. Arunachal Pradesh, which is at a relatively low level of development, is an exceptional case in this group. Non-availability of adequate local talent and skill in carrying out new development activities necessitated recruitment of outsiders, especially in educational, technical and administrative fields.

Table 6.6 *India: Regional Diversity, 2001, and Development Level of States and Union Territories, 2011*

Group	*States*	*Percentage share in total population*		*Development level*
		Life time in-migrants	*In-migrants during the last ten years*	
Top quartile	Goa	19.56	8.98	High
	Arunachal Pradesh	15.54	6.58	Relatively low
	Haryana	12.64	5.84	High
	Uttarakhand	10.21	4.16	Relatively high
	Sikkim	9.79	4.15	High
	Maharashtra	8.01	3.34	High
	Punjab	7.20	3.34	High
Second quartile	Jharkhand	6.61	1.87	Low
	Himachal Pradesh	5.67	3.10	Relatively high
	Gujarat	4.97	2.21	Relatively high
	Chhattisgarh	4.65	1.63	Low
	Mizoram	4.34	2.54	Relatively high
	Nagaland	4.30	1.69	Relatively low
	Karnataka	4.00	1.66	Relatively high
Third quartile	Meghalaya	3.97	1.46	Relatively low
	Madhya Pradesh	3.71	1.35	Low
	West Bengal	3.11	0.90	Relatively low
	Rajasthan	3.06	1.28	Low
	Tripura	1.97	1.26	Relatively low
	Assam	1.94	0.46	Relatively low
	Bihar	1.91	0.56	Low
Bottom quartile	Odisha	1.79	0.63	Low
	Uttar Pradesh	1.69	0.65	Low
	Jammu & Kashmir	1.63	0.86	Relatively high
	Andhra Pradesh*	1.35	0.56	Relatively low
	Kerala	1.30	0.72	High
	Tamil Nadu	1.27	0.39	High
	Manipur	0.81	0.19	Relatively high
Assorted	*Union Territories*	*Percentage share in total population*		*Developmental level*
		Life time in-migrants	*In-migrants during the last ten years*	
	Chandigarh	59.36	26.55	High
	Delhi	38.40	15.75	High
	Daman and Diu	38.36	-	High
	Dadra and Nagar Haveli	31.32	-	High
	Andaman and Nicobar Islands	30.18	8.26	High
	Puducherry	27.20	-	High
	Lakshadweep	5.80	-	High

Source: Census of India 2001 and 2011.
* Includes Telangana.

In the second quartile also, most of the states, such as Gujarat, Karnataka and Himachal Pradesh, are at a relatively high level of development. The native population here is noted for relatively high percentage of educated and skilled persons in comparative terms. Inflow of migrants from other states was also of qualified labour and highly specialized personnel. Jharkhand and Chhattisgarh in this group deserve a special mention. The inadequacy of local talent to harness the rich natural resources and carry out a variety of development activities necessitated and attracted a large number of migrants from other states.

All the states in the third quartile, such as Bihar, Madhya Pradesh and Rajasthan, are noted for a small segment of inter-state migrants. These are at a low or relatively low level of development. Similar is the case of states like Assam, Meghalaya and Tripura in the North-East which experienced a large influx of emigrants from Bangladesh as compared to migration from other states of India. West Bengal carries a description of the same kind.

The states in the bottom quartile, marked by the lowest percentage of interstate migrants, are a queer mix in terms of development level. Among these two, namely Kerala and Tamil Nadu, are at a high level of development; another three, Andhra Pradesh, Jammu & Kashmir and Manipur, are at a relatively high level, and the remaining two, Uttar Pradesh and Odisha, are at a low level. Three among these seven states fall in South India. These pose a language barrier for migrants from labour-source Hindi speaking states. Difficult political situation in Jammu & Kashmir and Manipur is a constraint to in-migration. The least developed states of Uttar Pradesh and Odisha have a limited number of employment opportunities to offer for migrants from other states.

All the union territories are at a high level of development. These are a great attraction for migrants in view of not only a variety of economic opportunities but also better quality of life and efficiency of administration. Several central government offices located here bring in public sector employees hailing from different states of India.

In response to a fresh vigour acquired by various states on the development front under the influence of new economic policy, the picture of regional diversity in their case is likely to change somewhat. A research exercise aimed at estimating the net inter-state migration during 2001–11 found that, among the major states, Tamil Nadu and Karnataka in South India; Maharashtra and Gujarat in West India; Punjab and Jammu & Kashmir in North-West India; and Madhya Pradesh in Central India will be net gainers in this process (Table 6.7). On the other hand, Kerala and Andhra Pradesh in South India; Bihar, Uttar Pradesh and Rajasthan in North India; Assam, West Bengal and Odisha in East India; and Himachal Pradesh in North-West India will be net losers. As an outcome, regional diversity in the states located in the West and South India will rise while it would be sustained at a low level in the states falling in North and East India. The demographic complexion of the National Capital Region is bound to become more variegated in years to come.

Table 6.7 *India: Estimation of Net Interstate Migration Rate (Inmigration minus Outmigration per 100 of population) for Major States, 2001–11*

Category	*State*	*Net interstate migration rate*	*Development level*
Positive	Tamil Nadu	+4.92	High
	Maharashtra	+2.70	High
	Haryana	+2.01	High
	Karnataka	+1.68	Relatively high
	Gujarat	+1.64	Relatively high
	Punjab	+0.77	High
	Madhya Pradesh	+0.48	Low
	Jammu & Kashmir	+0.37	Relatively high
Negative	Kerala	–5.41	High
	Bihar	–3.39	Low
	Assam	–2.21	Relatively low
	Andhra Pradesh	–2.02	Relatively low
	Uttar Pradesh	–1.94	Low
	Rajasthan	–1.34	Low
	Odisha	–0.55	Low
	West Bengal	–0.50	Relatively low
	Himachal Pradesh	–0.40	Relatively high

Source: Avijit Mistri. 2015. *Estimation of Internal Migration in India, during 2001–11*. Munich University, Germany.
* Includes Telangana.

A salient message of this essay is that one has to distinguish between the impact of culture and that of cultural pluralism as an analytical tool. The co-existence of several cultural and sub-cultural groups creates a special milieu wherein variety of value systems, lifestyles and interests are to be managed and cohered toward a common goal. The task has its own dividends and difficulties. This generates an additional debate about the supremacy of homogeneity versus heterogeneity in the scheme of things. Any given situation has to be honoured as de facto and optimized in the interest of all. In that light findings here in the Indian context are of special interest. It is learnt that while religious diversity is positively associated with development, the linguistic diversity is neutral to it. The regional diversity, being a product of migration, finds an association with the development process. Variable is the play of different diversities. In overall terms, a positive relationship between cultural diversity and development testifies the country's vitality in managing its multicultural setting.

References

Alesina, Alberto and Enrico Spolaore. 2003. *The Size of Nations*. Cambridge, Massachusetts: The MIT Press.

Anderson, Christopher J. and Aida Paskeviciute. 2006. How Ethnic and Linguistic Heterogeneity Influences the Prospects for Civil Society. *Journal of Politics*. Vol. 68, No. 4, pp. 783–802.

Brass, Paul R. 1974. *Language, Religion and Politics in North India*. Cambridge: Cambridge University Press.

Census of India. 2001. *Language: India, States and Union Territories*. New Delhi: Office of the Registrar General, India.

——. 2011. *The First Report on Religion Data*. New Delhi: Office of the Registrar General, India.

Choudhuri, Indra Nath. 1995. The Indian Literature. In Sachidananda Murty and Amit Dasgupta (eds), *The Divine Peacock: Understanding Contemporary India*. New Delhi: Indian Council of Cultural Relations and Wiley Eastern Limited.

Clarke, Colin. 1984. Caribbean Perspectives. In Colin Clarke, David Ley and Ceri Peach (eds), *Geography and Ethnic Pluralism*. Winchester, Massachusetts: Allen and Unwin.

Danino, Michel. 2011. *Indian Culture and India's Future*. New Delhi: Printworld.

Despres, Leo A. 1967. *Cultural Pluralism and Nationalist Politics in British Guiana*. Chicago: Rand McNally.

Dogan, Mattei and Dominique Pelassy. 1984. *How to Compare Nations: Strategies in Comparative Politics and International Political Economy*. New Jersey: Chatham House Publishers.

Dutt, Ashok K., Chandrakanta Khan and Chandralekha Sangwan. 1985. Spatial Pattern of Languages in India. *Geo-Journal*. Vol. 10, No. 1, pp. 51–74.

Eck, Diana L. 2001 and 2006. *The Pluralism Project*. Boston: Harvard University Press.

Eng, Lai Ah (ed.). 2008. *Religious Diversity in Singapore*. Singapore: Institute of Policy Studies.

Garcea, Joseph. 2008. Postulations on the Fragmentary Effects of Multiculturalism in Canada. *Canadian Ethnic Studies*. Vol. 40, No. 1, pp. 141–159.

Frankel, Francine R. 1984. *Indian Political Economy: 1947–1977*. New Delhi: Oxford University Press.

French, Patrick. 2011. *India: A Portrait*. New Delhi: Penguin.

Furnivall, J.S. 1945. *Colonial Policy and Practice: A Comparative Study of Burma, Netherlands and India*. Cambridge: Cambridge University Press.

Geertz, Clifford. 1963. The Integrative Revolution: Primordial Sentiments and Civil Politics in New States. In Clifford Geertz (ed.), *Old Societies and New States: The Quest for Modernity in Asia and Africa*. New York: The Free Press.

Harr, Gerrie Ter and Stephen Ellis. 2006. The Role of Religion in Development. *European Journal of Development Research*. Vol. 18, No. 3, pp. 351–367.

Huntington, Samuel P. 1996. *The Clash of Civilisations and the Remaking of World Order*. New York: Simon and Schuster.

Kliot, Nurit and Stanley Waterman (eds). 1983. *Pluralism and Political Geography: People, Territory and State*. New York: St. Martin's Press.

Kodila-Tedika, Oasis and Julius Agbor. 2014. Religious Diversity and Economic Development in Sub-Saharan Africa. *Journal of African Development*. Vol. 16, No. 1, pp. 99–117.

Kuper, Leo and M.G. Smith (eds). 1969. *Pluralism in Africa*. Berkeley and Los Angeles: University of California Press.

Laski, Harold. 1917. *Studies in the Problem of Sovereignty*. New Haven: Yale University Press.

Madan, T.N. 2009. *Modern Myths, Locked Minds: Secularism and Fundamentalism in India.* New Delhi: Oxford University Press.

Montalvo, Jose G. and Marta Reynel-Querol. 2005. Ethnic Diversity and Economic Development. *Journal of Development Economics.* Vol. 76, No. 2, pp. 293–323.

Morrill, Richard L. 1983. Dilemmas of Pluralism in the United States. In Nurit Knot and Stanley Waterman (eds), *Pluralism and Political Geography: People, Territory and State.* New York: St. Martin's Press.

Muller, Jerry Z. 2008. Us and Them: The Enduring Power of Ethnic Nationalism. *Foreign Affairs.* Vol. 87, No. 2, pp. 18–35.

Muthiah, S. 1987. *A Social and Economic Atlas of India.* New Delhi: Oxford University Press.

Newman, W.M. 1973. *American Pluralism.* New York: Harper and Row.

Pool, Jonathan. 1972. National Development and Language Diversity. In Joshia A. Fishman (ed.), *Advances in the Sociology of Languages.* The Hague: Mouton Press, pp. 213–230.

Ragab, Ibrahim A. 1980. Islam and Development. *World Development.* Vol. 8, No. 7, pp. 513–521.

Rajagopalan, Swarna. 2001. *State and Nation in South Asia.* Boulder Colorado, United States: Lynee Reinner Publishers.

Rattansi, Ali. 2011. *Multiculture: A Very Short Introduction.* Oxford: Oxford University Press.

Richmond, Anthony H. 1991. Immigration and Multiculturalism in Canada and Australia: The Contradiction and Crisis of 1990's. *International Journal of Canadian Studies.* Vol. 3 (Spring), pp. 87–110.

Sachar, Rajinder. 2006. *Sachar Committee Report.* New Delhi: Ministry of Minority Affairs, Government of India.

Sarangi, Asha (ed.). 2009. *Language and Politics in India.* New Delhi: Oxford University Press.

Sen, Amartya. 1999. Democracy as a Universal Value. *Journal of Democracy,* Vol. 10, No. 3, pp. 3–17.

Shariff, Abusaleh. 2015. *District Development and Diversity Index Report of India.* Washington, D.C.: U.S.-India Policy Institute and Centre for Research and Debates in Development Policy.

Sheth, D.L. 1989. State, Nation and Ethnicity Experience of Third World Countries. *Economic and Political Weekly.* Vol. 24, No. 12, pp. 615–626.

Shils, Edward Albert. 1962. *The Intellectual between Tradition and Modernity: The Indian Situation.* Hague: Mouton.

Singh, K.S. 1992. *People of India: An Introduction.* Calcutta: Anthropological Survey of India.

——. 2011. *Diversity, Identity and Linkages: Explorations in Historical Ethnography.* New Delhi: Oxford University Press.

Smith, M.G. 1979. Some Developments in the Analytic Framework of Pluralism. In L. Kuper and M.G. Smith (eds), *Pluralism in Africa.* Berkeley, Los Angeles and London: University of California Press.

Soffer, Arnon. 1983. The Changing Situation of Majority and Minority and its Spatial Expression: The Case of Arab Minority in Israel. In Nurit Kliot and Stanley Waterman (eds), *Pluralism and Political Geography: People, Territory and State.* New York: St. Martin's Press.

Sowell, Thomas. 2015. *Wealth, Poverty and Politics: An International Perspective*. New York: Basic Books.

Truman, David Bicknell. 1951. *The Government Process*. New York: Alfred A. Knopf.

Tuan, Yi-Fu. 1989. Cultural Pluralism and Technology. *Geographical Review*. Vol. 79, No. 3, pp. 270–279.

United Nations Development Programme. 2004. *Human Development Report*. New York: United Nations.

Weber, Max. 1926 and 1930. *The Protestant Ethnic and Spirit of Capitalism*. London: George Allen and Unwin.

Weiner, Myron. 1967. *Party Building in a New Nation: The Indian National Congress*. Chicago: Chicago University Press.

——. 1978. *Sons of the Soil: Migration and Ethnic Conflict in India*. Princeton: Princeton University Press..

7

The Indian Diaspora

'The sun never sets on Indian diaspora', thus proclaims the *Report of the High Level Committee on Indian Diaspora,* brought out by the Indian Council of World Affairs, New Delhi. It provides data and information on the number and chronicle of Indian diaspora as scattered over different countries of the world. A vivid view of the scatter, historical past and current situation of Indians abroad becomes available. One can glean vitality in their tales of turmoil and triumph.

Diaspora literally means 'dispersal'. The term was initially used for the Jews who moved out of their homeland during eighth-sixth century BC in search of new economic pastures wherever. Now the expression is suffixed to a variety of communities, such as Chinese diaspora, Irish diaspora, Greek diaspora and Indian diaspora, whose members are settled in large numbers outside the countries of their origin. They maintain links back home through visits, marriages and remittances, and also transplant their homeland in some manner in the hostland.

Our discussion here is confined to the Indian diaspora as making a continuing scatter since the colonial era and subsequently during the post-Independence period of Indian history. This can be taken more precisely as effective since 1833. This was the year when the British abolished slavery and were in search of indentured labour from any of their colonies as a replacement of the African slaves to work on their newly raised plantations, railway construction projects and other public works. Indentured labour was subsequently joined by free labour groups and individuals. India, with a large reservoir of the poor, served as a major source.

The Ministry of Overseas Indian Affairs, Government of India, has made available data for the number of Indians settled abroad in 184 countries/political entities in 2011. Such persons are grouped under two categories: Persons of Indian Origin and Non-Resident Indians. Persons of Indian Origin (PIOs) are the ones who are no longer Indian citizens but whose at least one of the parents or grandparents or great-grandparents was a citizen of India, as defined in the Government of India Act 1935, or of other territories which became a part of India thereafter. Non-Resident Indians, by comparison, are residing abroad but have retained Indian passport. Spouses of persons belonging to either of the above two categories are also considered as PIOs. The Indian diaspora, thus, includes Indians naturalized in some other country, Indian citizens abroad and descendants of the two above.

The data in respect of Persons of Indian Origin represents the emigration which largely took place during the colonial period while that pertaining to Non-Resident Indians is indicative of emigration mainly during the post-colonial period. On the basis of the available information, thus, the different countries of the world with Indian diaspora could be classified into the following four categories:

(i) To which emigration from India was predominant during the colonial days but slowed down or ceased thereafter, such as the Caribbean countries;
(ii) To which emigration from India started during the colonial days and continued thereafter, such as the United Kingdom;
(iii) To which emigration from India had a colonial background but the real spurt was recent, such as Australia; and
(iv) To which emigration from India was mainly during the post-colonial years, such as the Middle East.

There are other variants of classification of emigrants too. Exploring diversity within a common identity, Pande (2013) offers a chronological typology of Indian diaspora. The first category represents pre-colonial waves of emigrants who moved to South-East Asia, West Asia and East Africa for trade and culture. The coastal regions of Bengal, Odisha, Andhra Pradesh, Tamil Nadu, Kerala and Gujarat were the major participants. The period following 1833, when slavery was abolished throughout the British Empire, until the World War-II belongs to the second category of diaspora. Included here are emigrants to the West Indies, South-East Asia, East and South Africa and islands in the Indian Ocean. They went as indentured or contract or free passage labourers, by and large. Post-World War-II emigrants constitute the third category. They moved to the developed countries, such as United Kingdom, the United States, Canada and others and also to Gulf countries as skilled labour or professionals. Then there were twice-migrants forming the fourth category. These were the ones who got uprooted from or disillusioned with the first country of emigration and moved to the developed world. Several migrants to East Africa rebuilt their new homes in the United Kingdom, Canada or Australia. The fifth category is constituted by students who sought new educational arenas and employment opportunities in the developed countries. Finally, there was political diaspora, such as some Sikhs, Kashmiris and Tibetan refugees who sought refuge out of India.

At the time of independence, the number of persons born in India but living abroad or descendents of such people was around four million (Davis, 1950: p. 98). In mid-1970s there were an estimated five or six million persons of this description (Tinker, 1977). This number was put at 21 million by the *Report of the High Level Committee on Indian Diaspora*. Today the number of Persons of Indian Origin (PIO's) and Non-Resident Indians (NRIs) is placed at 25 million (Ministry of Overseas Affairs, Government of India, 2015: p. 4). More Indians live outside India than all the people living in Australia.

The 2015 *Survey Report on International Migration*, brought out by the Department of Economic and Social Affairs of the United States, informs that nearly 16 million persons were born in India but were living in some other country. These people are in the nature of Non-Resident Indians by and large. This signifies that among the 25 million Indian diaspora, about two-thirds are Non-Resident Indians (NRIs) and one-third Persons of Indian Origin (PIOs), or children of NRIs.

Indiaspora is, thus, the third dimension of our country, the other two being India (urban) and Bharat (rural). Diaspora is visualized as transplanting Indians, belonging to different regions, all over the globe and interlinking diverse local homelands with a variety of global hostlands. Shukla (2003) has rightly titled the introduction to her book *India Abroad* as 'Geographies of Indianness'. A hybrid Indianness gets reproduced in multifarious forms. In the spirit of topophilia, most of Indian diaspora remains in the mode of long distance nationalists.

Global Spread of Indian Diaspora

Today, the United Nations has 193 countries as its members. No less than 184 countries of the world are home to Indian diaspora in varying numbers. Hence, hardly a few countries are without a representative of this community.

Three countries do not accommodate any Indian diaspora. These include North Korea, which is closed off to the world; Pakistan, which does not give long term visas to Indians; and Bhutan, which does not allow non-Bhutanese to gain citizenship or permanent residency. All of these are Asian countries, two of them neighbours of India.

The number of Indian diaspora is on the higher side of one million in eight countries, with the United States on the top (Table 7.1). In 19 countries, their number ranges from 1,00,000 to one million, and in 33 countries the scatter is between 10,000 to 1,00,000. As such, the size of Indian diaspora is at least or more than ten thousand in 60 countries of the world. The fact remains that more than half of the Indian diaspora is confined to eight countries on the top (Map 7.1). A world regional picture of Indian diaspora is presented below in a tabular and descriptive form.

1. United States
   - 2.25 million in 2015 as compared with one million in 2000 and only 13,000 in 1960.
   - Immigration in waves: first as farm workers migrating southward from British Columbia (Canada); second as educationists, retailers

Map 7.1

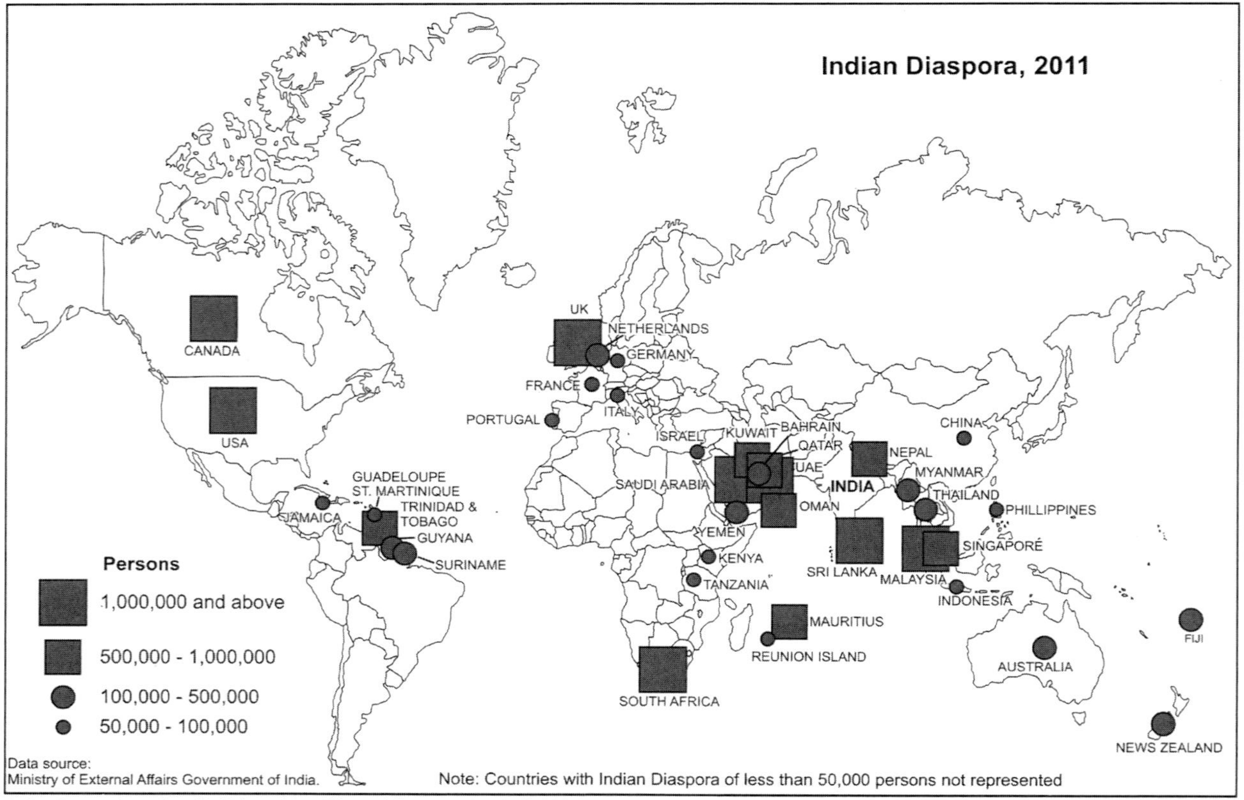

Indian diaspora is scattered in 184 countries of the world but more than half of this is concentrated in eight countries of the United States of America, Malaysia, Saudi Arabia, United Arab Emirates, Sri Lanka, the United Kingdom, South Africa and Canada, each with at least one million persons.

Table 7.1 *Indian Diaspora: Number of Indians Living in Different Countries of the World, 2011*

Sr. No.	*Country*	*Number*	*Sr. No.*	*Country*	*Number*	*Sr. No.*	*Country*	*Number*
1	USA	2,245,239	63	Ghana	7,100	125	Togo	302
2	Malaysia	2,050,000	64	Brunei Darussalam	7,047	126	Iceland	301
3	Saudi Arabia	1,789,000	65	Jordan	7,000	127	Aruba	300
4	UAE	1,702,911	66	Malawi	7,000	128	Comoros	300
5	Sri Lanka	1,600,500	67	Sudan	7,000	129	Lao PDR	300
6	UK	1,500,000	68	Korea (Republic of)	6,732	130	Senegal	300
7	South Africa	1,218,000	69	Panama	6,500	131	Guinea	253
8	Canada	1,000,000	70	Denmark	6,419	132	Bulgaria	250
9	Mauritius	882,220	71	St. Lucia	5,250	133	Burundi	250
10	Nepal	600,000	72	Grenada	5,100	134	Montserrat	210
11	Singapore	590,000	73	Netherlands Antilles	4,500	135	Georgia	200
12	Kuwait	579,390	74	Congo (Dem. Rep. of)	4,000	136	Uzbekistan	200
13	Oman	557,713	75	Cyprus	4,000	137	Venezuela	200
14	Trinidad and Tobago	551,500	76	Ukraine	4,000	138	Bolivia	182
15	Qatar	500,000	77	Afghanistan	3,749	139	Namibia	160
16	Australia	448,430	78	Egypt	3,500	140	Malta	158
17	Myanmar	356,560	79	Finland	3,500	141	Burkina Faso	155
18	Bahrain	350,000	80	Barbados	3,330	142	Andorra	140
19	Guyana	320,200	81	St. Vincent and the Grenadines	3,050	143	Colombia	116
20	Fiji Islands	313,798	82	Kazakhstan	2,550	144	Tunisia	112
21	France (Reunion Island	275,200	83	China (Taiwan)	2,525	145	Mali	102
22	Netherlands	201,000	84	Kyrgyzstan	2,500	146	Equatorial Guinea	100

Cont'd...

...Cont'd

23	Thailand	150,000	85	Poland	2,100	147	Estonia	100
24	Guadeloupe (France)	145,000	86	Angola	1,500	148	Palestine	81
25	Suriname	140,300	87	Cambodia	1,500	149	Lithuania	80
26	Yemen	111,000	88	Liberia	1,496	150	Slovak Republic	80
27	New Zealand	107,000	89	Iran	1,430	151	East Timor	70
28	Indonesia	85,000	90	Argentina	1,400	152	Samoa	70
29	Portugal	80,000	91	Chile	1,200	153	Uruguay	70
30	Israel	78,200	92	Lesotho	1,200	154	Guinea Bissau	60
31	Kenya	75,000	93	Czech Republic	1,050	155	Mongolia	60
32	Italy	71,907	94	Brazil	1,000	156	Honduras	52
33	Germany	70,500	95	Luxembourg	1,000	157	Croatia	50
34	China	67,000	96	Ethiopia	994	158	Vanuatu	50
35	France	65,000	97	Romania	948	159	Slovenia	46
36	Tanzania	54,700	98	Cayman Islands	860	160	Latvia	40
37	Jamaica	53,500	99	Turks and Caicos Islands	810	161	Niger	40
38	Philippines	50,000	100	Papua New Guinea	800	162	Ecuador	34
39	China (Hong Kong)	37,250	101	Vietnam	780	163	Bosnia	30
40	Nigeria	30,000	102	Turkmenistan	700	164	Serbia	28
41	Spain	30,000	103	Syria	650	165	El Salvador	25
42	Maldives	26,001	104	Antigua and Barbuda	630	166	Guatemala	24
43	Austria	25,000	105	Belarus	602	167	Nauru	21
44	Madagascar	22,500	106	Gambia	600	168	Albania	20
45	Japan	22,335	107	Swaziland	550	169	Cuba	20

Cont'd...

...Cont'd

46	Mozambique	21,000	108	Rwanda	540	170	Mauritania	20
47	Uganda	20,000	109	Dominica	530	171	Solomon Islands	20
48	Ireland	19,365	110	Sierra Leone	529	172	Moldova	18
49	Sweden	18,000	111	Azerbaijan	500	173	Nicaragua	16
50	Belgium	16,000	112	Eritrea	500	174	Marshall Islands	15
51	Switzerland	15,577	113	Cote d'Ivore	470	175	Kiribati	14
52	Libya	15,000	114	Algeria	450	176	Palau	14
53	Russian Federation	14,200	115	Armenia	450	177	Dominican Republic	10
54	Zambia	13,000	116	St. Kitts and Nevis	450	178	Macedonia	10
55	Norway	12,828	117	Bahamas	410	179	Costa Rica	9
56	Greece	12,100	118	Morocco	400	180	Korea (DPR)	3
57	Botswana	11,000	119	Paraguay	400	181	Liechtenstein	3
58	Zimbabwe	10,500	120	Tajikistan	369	182	Micronesia	3
59	Bangladesh	10,012	121	Djibouti	350	183	Niue	3
60	Lebanon	10,000	122	Hungary	350	184	Sao Tome and Principe	3
61	Iraq	9,000	123	Turkey	345			
62	Seychelles	8,500	124	Peru	316			

Source: Ministry of External Affairs, Government of India, 2011.

and motel owners after the enactment of Immigration and Nationality Act in 1965 which initiated a new policy on reuniting immigrant families and attracting skilled labour; and as repatriates from the British colonies during the 1960s, from the Caribbeans during the 1970s, and from Fiji Islands during the 1980s; and third as professionals, doctors, engineers and students in 1990s onward till date.

— Regional, religious and linguistic diversity of India represented.
— Major concentration in California, New York, New Jersey, Texas and Illinois states.
— Per capita income of the Indian Americans here higher by 1.5 times of the US average.

2. Canada
— One million in a country of 35 million.
— Punjabis in majority, accounting for 70 per cent of Indian diaspora.
— Many repatriates from the Caribbeans, East Africa and Fiji.
— Liberalization of immigration policy since 1967, which favoured education and skill rather than ethnic background, facilitated influx of immigrants.

3. Australia and New Zealand
— Over half-a-million.
— First arrival during 1800–60 to work as labourers, domestics and camel handlers.
— Punjabi Sikhs and Muslims came as agricultural labourers, hawkers and traders during the latter half of the nineteenth century.
— Sizeable inflow of immigrants from the *Bist Doab* region of Punjab in 1930s.
— Now students and professionals arrive in large numbers aspiring permanent residency.
— In New Zealand, immigration of Indians largely from Fiji islands, Punjab and Gujarat.

4. United Kingdom
— 1.5 million Indians in a population of 63 million or 2.4 per cent of the total.
— Over two-thirds of the Indian community based in Europe is settled in the United Kingdom.
— Historical bond through administration, trade, navigation, education and army.
— Indian diaspora arrived as seamen, soldiers and students before Independence; as blue collar or manual workers after World War II; as repatriates from East Africa in 1960s and 1970s; as doctors to serve in the National Health Scheme set up in 1960s; and as students now in large numbers.
— Gujaratis and Punjabis more numerous.

5. Continental Europe
   - About 0.6 million.
   - Most of the Indian community here is migrant from former colonies of the European powers; now emigration from India is more pronounced.
   - To France from Mauritius, Seychelles, Madagascar, Indo-China and Puducherry (India).
   - To Portugal from Angola, Mozambique and Goa (India).
   - To Netherlands from Suriname.
   - To Austria, nurses from Kerala and labourers from Punjab.
   - To Greece, as labour on the ports.
   - To Germany, Spain, Italy and Scandinavian countries; mostly as professionals and students as well as in dairying, tourism and small business.
6. Caribbean Region
   - 1.2 million persons of Indian Origin in Trinidad and Tobago, Guyana and Suriname.
   - Came as indentured labour in 1836 in Guyana, in 1845 in Trinidad and Tobago, and in 1873 in Suriname.
   - No less than 90 per cent hailed from north Bihar and eastern Uttar Pradesh or the Bhojpuri Region, formerly part of Bengal Presidency.
7. Mauritius
   - Nearly 0.9 million.
   - Persons of Indian Origin account for over-two thirds of the total population of the country.
   - Most of them came as indentured labour after 1833.
   - Largely Bhojpuris, some Tamils and Telegus.
8. Fiji Islands
   - 0.3 million.
   - Arrived as indentured labour in 1879.
   - 75 per cent from the Bhojpuri Region of Bihar and Uttar Pradesh; 25 per cent from Tamil Nadu and Andhra Pradesh.
   - Gradually evolved as an educated, well-off enterprising community.
   - Have been facing manifest hostility since 1999 when the natives captured political power.
   - A tendency to re-emigrate to Australia, New Zealand, United States and Canada common.
9. East Africa
   - 0.2 million.
   - Kenya, Tanzania and Uganda, the former colonies of the United Kingdom, were the destination.

- Influx started in 1860s when about 30,000 workers, mostly Sikhs, were brought here on a three year contract to provide labour for various public works, especially the East African Railways.
- Subsequently joined by Gujaratis as free immigrants; many of them entered into local trade and retailing.
- Outflow of Indian diaspora started in 1960s when the East African countries became free from the colonial rule.

10. South Africa
    - 1.2 million.
    - Beginning was made in 1860 when indentured labour from Madras Province was brought here to work in the Natal region.
    - Meanwhile Gujaratis arrived as free immigrants.
    - Tamils and Telugus from the former Madras Province make two-thirds of the Indian diaspora; the rest came from the former Bombay Province, Saurashtra and Bengal Province.
    - Indians were known as coolies; granted citizenship only in 1962.
11. South-East Asia
    - About 3 million.
    - Large majority of early immigrants came from former Madras Province, Punjab Province and Travancore – Cochin states; now from metropolitan cities.
    - In large numbers in Malaysia, Singapore, Thailand and Indonesia.
    - To Malaysia, indentured labour during 1910–1930, and subsequently as free migrants in a variety of jobs.
    - To Singapore, a penal colony from 1825–1875 when some convicts from India were brought here; indentured labour from Madras Province started arriving since 1833; now a cherished destination for professionals and students.
    - To Thailand and Indonesia, in search of business opportunities.
12. Reunion Islands
    - About 0.3 million.
    - An overseas department or district of France since 1819.
    - France used Puducherry as the base for recruitment of indentured labour, Tamils in majority; Gujaratis arrived as free immigrants.
13. Gulf Region
    - About 6 million.
    - Saudi Arabia 1.8 million, UAE 1.7 million, Kuwait 0.6 million, Oman 0.6 million, Qatar 0.5 million, Bahrain 0.4 million, and so on.
    - Indian migration followed the oil boom in 1970s; gained momentum after migration from South Korea and Yemen slowed down.
    - Majority from South India, especially Kerala
    - In Saudi Arabia, 85 per cent in general labour and technical jobs, 10 per cent in white collar assignments and the remaining in professions.

— Diaspora is not entitled to citizenship even after a life-long stay; Oman is the only country which gives citizenship to foreign nationals; it also guarantees freedom of worship.

14. Israel
    - Nearly 0.1 million.
    - After the formation of Israel as a country in 1948, about 30,000 Jews moved soon after; the subsequent emigration continued from Cochin and Mumbai.
    - Several of them adopted agriculture as a source of livelihood.
15. Former Socialist Countries
    - In small numbers in Russia, East Europe (Poland, Hungary, Czech Lands, Slovakia, Rumania, Albania, Serbia and Bulgaria) and Central Asia (Kazakhstan, Uzbekistan and Turkmenistan).
    - Friendly but not receptive to immigrants.
    - Now students and businessmen are making an entry.
16. Latin America
    - Only a few.
    - The language, distance and lack of historical linkage main barriers.
17. India's Neighbours
    - Nearly 3 million.
    - Sri Lanka 1.6 million; Nepal 0.6 million; Myanmar 0.4 million; China (including Hong Kong) 0.1 million.
    - Immigration policies of neighbours, except of Nepal, not favourable to India.

It follows that most of the Indian diaspora during the colonial times originated from the territories which were under the rule of the British or French or Portuguese and moved to their newly colonized territories in other parts of the world. They were taken as indentured labour to work on sugarcane, tea and rubber plantations, in distant and remote island countries in the Caribbean region, Arabian Sea and Pacific Ocean, or in coastal regions of South-East Asia, East Africa and South Africa. Migration to the mother country of the colonial masters itself was negligible.

The post-Independence decades witnessed a change in this scenario. To begin with there was considerable migration to war ravaged and labour hungry countries of the colonial powers in Europe for reconstruction. Following the oil boom of 1970s, migration to the Middle East countries surged on large scale in the form of semi-skilled or skilled labour. Since the middle of 1960s, consequent upon liberalization of immigration laws, the developed countries like the United States, Canada, Australia and New Zealand became big attractions for the emigrants. This movement was of the educated and professional personnel. Meanwhile emigration to several European countries, such as Netherlands, Germany and Italy also picked up, thanks to the demand for Information Technology professionals. In overall terms, the destinations of the Indian diaspora before Independence were defined by the colonial powers. Today these are of their own choice in

is reflected in diversity of diaspora from Maharashtra which included, among others, naval workers, businessmen, information technology professionals, and students.

Historically Odisha had commercial, cultural and political contacts with South-East Asia, especially Southern Burma, Malaysia and Indonesia in ancient days. During the colonial days, Oriyas were drafted as indentured labour to work in the Caribbean countries, East Africa and South-East Asia. Ganjam district, which was then a part of the Madras Presidency, was one major source of indentured labour. Oriya emigration of engineers and professionals to the developed countries like the United States, Canada and Australia is a recent phenomenon. In the United States, they are concentrated mainly in high-tech industry, services and tourism.

It is not known to many that the pioneer wave of emigration to Mauritius was from the former French territories of Pondicherry (now Puducherry) and Mahe in India. This is as expected because Mauritius at one time was a French colony. Indian immigrants came to this country first in 1736 (Richards, 2016). The French colonies in India, that is Pondicherry, Karaikal, Mahe and Yanam, were a big source of emigration to overseas territories of France, including the Arabian Sea islands of Reunion, Seychelles and Mauritius and the Caribbean islands of Guadeloupe and Martinique. The big surge of emigration from the Bhojpuri region to Mauritius was a sequel to its takeover by the British from France in 1810. The former Portuguese colony of Goa, which was the first to come into interface with the western culture in the colonial era, also recorded significant emigration. Earlier this emigration was directed to Portuguese colonies like Angola, Mozambique and Macau. Now most of the emigrants have the Middle East, the United States and Europe as their destination. About one-third of the households in Goa have at least one member abroad.

In the inventory of Indian diaspora, Punjabis hold a place of being not only massive in number but also wide in scatter. The early South Asian emigrants to Canada and the United States, toward the close of nineteenth century, were from Punjab and 90 per cent of them were the Sikhs. A simultaneous wave of their emigration is noted to East Africa, South-East Asia and Australia. They were in a variety of jobs in different countries, such as carpentry in East Africa, hardware business in Thailand, security police in Malaya, timber felling in Canada and fruit farming in the United States. After Independence, several of them moved to the United Kingdom and the United States, apart from the Middle East, Australia and New Zealand. The major areas of emigration from Punjab include Manjki, Dhak Dona and Sirowal in Doaba; Riarki and Gurdaspur Majha in Majha; and Baggar, Puad (Ludhiana district) and adjoining areas in Malwa (Judge, 2011: p. 30). In the Doaba subregion, 24 per cent of the households have at least one member as emigrant, while the respective figures for the Manjha and Malwa subregions are 12 and 5 per cent (Nanda and Veron, 2015: p. 38). A recent feature of emigration from Punjab deserves a special mention. For long, Kerala was typically recognized for emigration of nurses. Today, Punjab has come up as a hub of training in nursing and emigration of nurses. Initially this emigration of female professionals was directed to the Middle East; today Canada, the United States and New Zealand are the major destinations.

The history of Tamil diaspora is as old as the history of Tamil civilization. This part of India had close commercial and cultural links with South-East Asia during the ancient and medieval periods. Hence, Tamil emigration has been a long well established feature. During the modern times, the Tamil soldiers arrived in Philippines in 1762–1764 under a French chieftain. Many of them were tempted to settle there. Later the British colonial rule was marked by massive Tamil emigration as indentured labour to a variety of destinations in the Caribbean islands since 1860; in Fiji islands since 1880; in Malaysia and Singapore since 1901. Recruiting agencies were initially allowed to take indentured labour for Malaya and Singapore only from the Madras Province (Jayaram, 2004: p. 69). The largest share of emigration during the colonial rule was taken over by the Tamils. Many of them belonged to densely populated districts like Trichinapally, Madurai, Ramnad and Salem, located south of Madras city and hailed from castes low in hierarchy (Tinker, 1977: p. 6). Tamil migration to Sri Lanka has a long history and it became massive during the colonial rule in the form of labour on tea and coffee plantations. Several of them were repatriated to India on Sri Lanka gaining freedom in 1948. After India's Independence, the Tamil migration was directed mainly to the United Kingdom as labourers. Now a large number of them are settled in the United States. Meanwhile, several Tamils, previously settled in Fiji Islands, shifted to Australia and New Zealand over time.

Emigration from West Bengal during the colonial days was mainly to the United Kingdom. The small Indian community in Britain before 1939 included largely Bengalis (Tinker, 1977: p. 8). Calcutta was the capital and most important port city of the British India till 1911. Emigration of some educated persons was a natural outcome. Several Bengali sailors were also tempted to settle in Britain. One cannot also ignore the fact that the first wave of emigration of indentured labour, beginning in 1833, had its source in the 'hill coolie' (an unskilled, cheaply employed worker through indentured system) districts of Bankura, Birbhum and Burdwan of the Bengal Presidency (Jain, 2003: p. 10). The post-colonial years were marked by emigration of Bengalis to North America (the United States and Canada), South-East Asia (Singapore, Malaysia, and Indonesia), and Pacific region (Australia, New Zealand and South Korea). The Bengal diaspora, with their high level of technical and professional competence, had a stronger tendency to emigrate to developed world, both before and after Independence.

The spatial pattern of emigration areas during the colonial times is obvious. These were located mainly in the Bengal, Madras, Bombay and Punjab provinces of the British India. Densely populated districts in proximity of capitals of these provinces were prominent scenes of emigration. Considerable emigration from Pondicherry under the French and Goa under the Portuguese also took place. Princely states did not emerge as a major source of emigration. Now every urban place of some significance, especially the capital cities, has become a springboard of emigration.

The National Sample Survey Organization Report entitled *Migration in India: 2007–08* informs that 9.3 per cent of the urban households have at least one member abroad. In Goa, over half of the urban households belong to this category and in Kerala one-third (Map 7.2). In Punjab and Tamil Nadu, one urban household in every seven, in Andhra Pradesh and Karnataka one in every eight, and in Gujarat one in every 10 had at least one emigrant. Surprisingly the incidence of urban emigration from West Bengal and Maharashtra is considerably less than expected. The super-metropolitan cities of Kolkata and Mumbai must be absorbing a number of professionals who could be a potential candidate for emigration. By comparison, 4.9 per cent of the rural households in India had at least one migrant abroad (Panagariya, 2013: p. 325). The frequency of such households was one in every three in Kerala, one in every four in Punjab, and one in every five in Goa. In the case of Tamil Nadu, one in every eight households carries this description. Andhra Pradesh is also noted for considerable proportion of such households. All these states, barring Punjab, are coastal in location.

Table 7.2 *India: Proportion of Urban and Rural Households Reporting Emigrants Abroad in Major States, 2007–08*

State	*Percentage of households with emigrants abroad in*	
	Urban areas	*Rural areas*
Andhra Pradesh	13.2	6.0
Arunachal Pradesh	1.18	0.1
Assam	2.7	0.1
Bihar	1.8	2.4
Chhattisgarh	1.0	0.3
Goa	51.8	18.8
Gujarat	10.4	1.8
Haryana	3.1	2.1
Himachal Pradesh	6.3	1.6
Jammu & Kashmir	3.4	1.1
Jharkhand	9.4	0.4
Karnataka	13.6	1.2
Kerala	35.4	34.5
Madhya Pradesh	2.4	0.2
Odisha	4.3	0.4
Punjab	15.3	25.3
Rajasthan	6.5	3.6
Tamil Nadu	14.7	12.3
Uttarakhand	8.5	0.2
Uttar Pradesh	3.3	2.5
West Bengal	2.6	1.0
India	9.3	4.9

Source: NSSO Report Migration in India: 2007–08, 2010.

Map 7.2

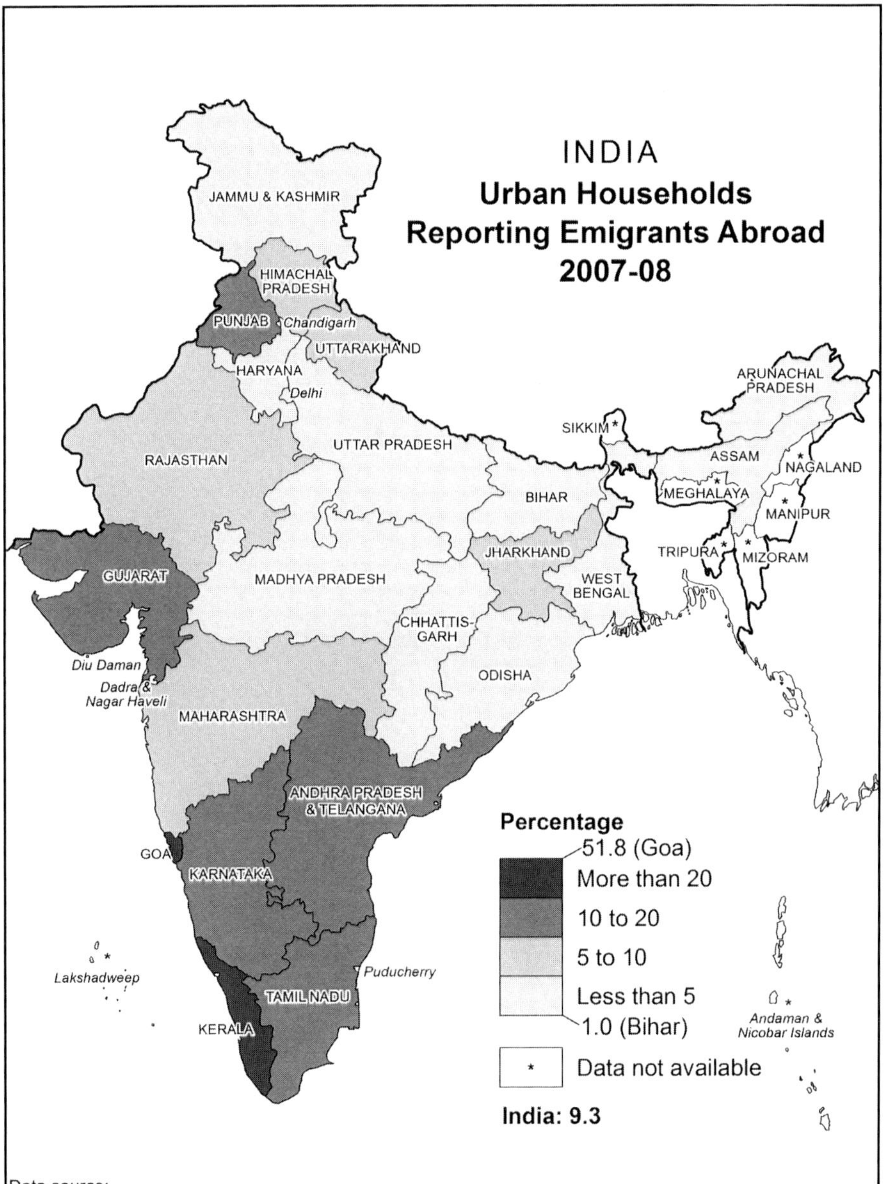

Data source:
National Sample Survey Organisation.

Every second urban household in Goa, one in every three in Kerala and one in every seven in Punjab and Tamil Nadu have at least one member abroad; for Bihar the ratio is just one in every one hundred.

Map 7.3

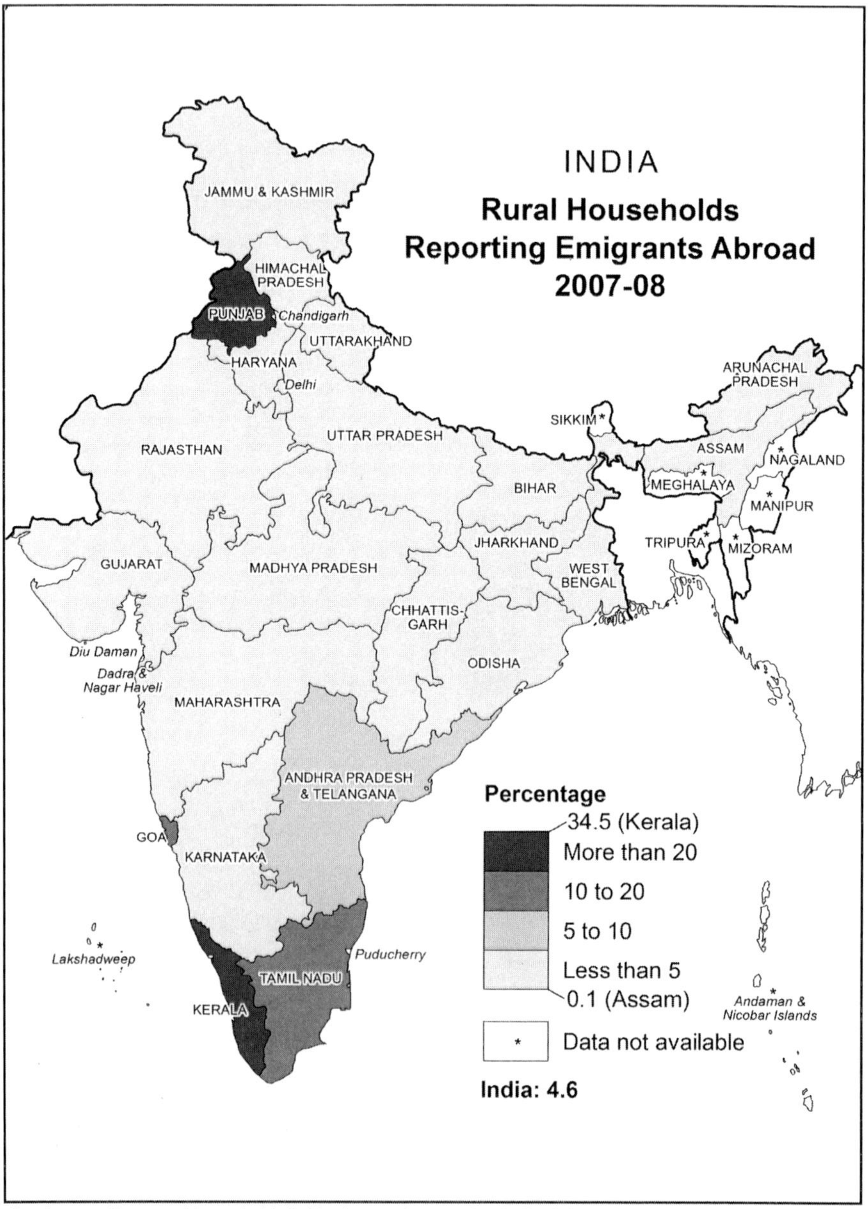

One in every three rural households in Kerala, one in every four in Punjab, and one in every five in Goa has at least one member abroad.
Source: National Sample Survey Organisation.

Putting things together, the incidence of emigration from urban areas is two times of that from rural areas (Table 7.2). Emigration is on large scale from both urban and rural areas of Kerala and Goa. Rural emigration is more pronounced than the urban in Punjab. The reverse is the case of Gujarat where emigration from urban areas is more frequent than from rural areas. Same is true of other coastal states of Tamil Nadu, Andhra Pradesh and Karnataka (Map 7.3).

The most striking feature of Indian diaspora is its diversity by region. That is how we define the Malayali diaspora or Gujarati diaspora or Punjabi diaspora. They hail from different states of India. Emigration studies by states are in plenty. Meanwhile research exercises focusing on specific tracts of massive emigration within these states are scanty. It will be worthwhile to identify such regions, explore their peculiarities, and place them in the context of their state. This will help in discerning the parameters of their vitality.

Table 7.3 *India: Vibrant Emigration Sub-Regions*

Sr. No.	*Name of sub-region*
1	All metropolitan cities, in particular the national and state capitals
2	Goa
3	Northern Kerala or Malabar
4	Central Gujarat Plain
5	Kutch
6	Tamil Nadu Coastal Region
7	Godavari-Krishna Delta
8	Bist Doab of Punjab

A bird's-eye view of such sub-regions or tracts in India would suggest that the national capital and all the state capitals, more particularly the large metropolitan ones, such as Delhi, Mumbai, Kolkata, Chennai, Bengaluru, Hyderabad and Pune are scenes of significant emigration today. Among the sub-regions, northern segment of Kerala, Central Gujarat Plain, Kutch, Godavari-Krishna delta, the *Bist doab* of Punjab and coastal region of Tamil Nadu emerge as prominent. Goa territory as a whole is vibrant with the process of emigration. The entire coastal belt is a virtual emigration field (Table 7.3). This is said by way of generalization and not to detract from the significance of emigration from several other parts of mainland India (Map 7.4).

Vitality Dimension of Diaspora

The idea of diaspora is subject to a variety of perspectives. One way is to view it as an ingredient of globalization in which dynamic interconnections get built between the source and destination countries of migrants. Another way is to consider such mobility as a process of energy exchange in terms of labour, money, ideas and culture between the homelands and hostlands of

Map 7.4

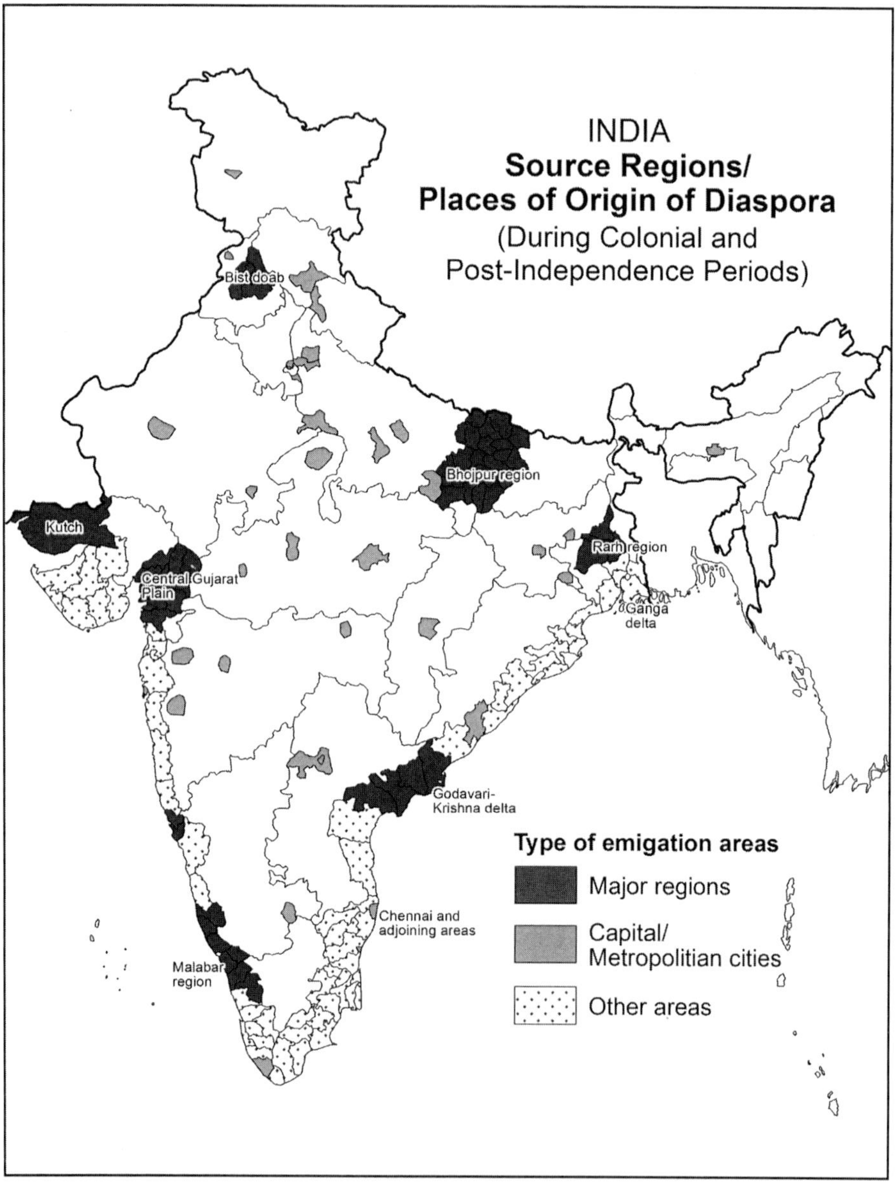

The entire coastal belt, the state capital/metropolitan cities, and Punjab are the noteworthy areas of emigration today; Bhojpur and Rarh regions in prominence during the colonial period are no longer significant.

the people concerned. Still another way is to value this as an expression of the vitality of the regions from where the diaspora originates.

Herein the dynamics of emigration calls for a comparison with that of outmigration. While outmigration is impelled more by a thrust of push factors, emigration is stimulated more by attraction of pull factors. While the former is uprooting often under compulsion of economic conditions, the later is a search for greener pastures by those who are inclined to take great risk, have requisite qualities to meet the challenges of a distant, unknown setting, and also possess adequate financial resources to invest in such a venture. *A Survey of Emigration from India,* conducted from July 2004 to February 2005 at the behest of Government of India, confirms that emigration is far more frequent among the better off socio-economic households in both urban and rural areas. It is no surprise that the pace of emigration has become faster during the current phase of rapid economic growth.

The *Migration and Development Brief,* prepared by the World Bank, informs that globally 232 million international emigrants in 2013 sent $ 414 billion back home. In this inventory, Indians were at the top with $ 71 billion, followed by China at $ 60 billion and Philippines at $ 26 billion. The figure for Pakistan and Bangladesh stood at $ 15 billion each. Such remittances accounted for about 3 per cent of India's Gross Domestic Product. On per capita basis, this works out as nearly $ 60 or around ₹ 4,000, with far greater gains accruing to areas which are scene of sizeable emigration, such as Kerala, Goa and Punjab.

This inflow of money is a critical factor in changing the geography of local areas and strengthening their overall vitality. It takes many forms, such as financial support to family for domestic purposes, purchase of land, construction of house or buying of modern gadgets; donations to religious and non-governmental organizations; setting up of educational and health institutions; and investment in real estate, business or bank accounts (Kapur, 2010). Equally important to consider are the social remittances in the form of transfer of knowledge, ideas, technical know-how, professional collaborations and dissemination of political or religious ideologies (Upadhya and Rutten, 2011). Emigrants, on the one hand, influence the national economy through remittances, philanthropy and investment; on the other hand, they transform the economy, society, polity and culture of local areas. They also spread 'Indianness' in terms of language, religion, festivals, cuisine and political ideas to various parts of the world. Diaspora has implications for both homelands and hostlands, depending upon their size, personal attributes and mental make-up. They are a source of vitality not only for their destination avenues but also for their source regions.

References

Carens, Joseph H. 2014. *The Ethics of Immigration.* Oxford: Oxford University Press.

Davis, Kingsley. 1951. *Population of India and Pakistan.* New York: Vail-Ballou Press.

Government of India. 2015. *Annual Report: 2014–15.* New Delhi: Ministry of Overseas Indian Affairs.

Indian Council of World Affairs. 2001. *Report of the High Level Committee on Indian Diaspora.* New Delhi.

Jain, Prakash C. 2003. Indian Diaspora: An Overview. *Think India.* Vol. 6, No. 1, pp. 8–17.

Jayaram, N. 2004. *The Indian Diaspora: Dynamics of Migration.* New Delhi: Sage Publications.

Judge, Paramjit S. 2011. Diversity Within the Punjabi Diaspora. In N. Jayaram (ed.), *Diversities in the Indian Diaspora.* New Delhi: Oxford University Press.

Kapur, Devesh. 2010. *Diaspora, Development and Democracy: The Domestic Impact of International Migration from India.* New Delhi: Oxford University Press.

Kelegama, Saman. 2011. *Migration, Remittances and Development in South Asia.* New Delhi: Sage Publications.

Nanda, Ashwani Kumar and Jacques Veron. 2015. *Dynamics of International Out-Migration from Punjab.* Paris: INED and Chandigarh: CRRID.

Panagariya, Arvind. 2013. Migration: From Poverty to Prosperity. In N.K. Singh and Nicholas Stern (eds), *The New Bihar.* Noida: HarperCollins Publishers.

Pande, Amba. 2013. Conceptualising Indian Diaspora. *Economic and Political Weekly.* Vol. 48, No. 49, pp. 59–65.

Richards, Alexandra. 2016. *Mauritius.* Waterstones: Bradt Travel Guides.

Shukla, Sandhya. 2003. *India Abroad.* Hyderabad: Orient Longman.

Tinker, Hugh. 1977. *The Banyan Tree: Overseas Emigrants from India, Pakistan and Bangladesh.* Oxford: Oxford University Press.

Upadhya, Carol and Mario Rutten. 2011. Migration Transnational Flows and Development in India: A Regional Perspective. *Economic and Political Weekly.* Vol. 47, No. 19, pp. 54–62.

World Bank. 2013. *Migration and Development Brief.* New York.

8

India in the *National Geographic* (1947–2015)

Founded in 1888 as a magazine of 98 pages wrapped in a brown cover, the *National Geographic* celebrated 125 years of its publication in 2013. It had reached a worldwide circulation of 8.3 million by 2011. Commanding the world's largest readership, it represents the best in geography, may be in the entire gamut of knowledge, through lucid texts, impactful maps, and above all engaging colour photographs. By that token, it is the greatest educational magazine of the world, holding a uniquely objective publishing mirror, and is read with avid interest by people all over the world (Garrett, 1988a).

There are several things that make this journal front ranking for millions of readers across the globe. First, the best asset of the magazine is its beautiful photographs, elegant maps and neat diagrams which infuse life into the text. Second, its lucid and conversational literary style makes a stimulating read. Third, there is a human touch in every article which stirs imagination and sustains interest. Finally, the magazine strictly adheres to the principles of accuracy, fairness and balance.

National Geographic defines its mission as celebration of the world through incessant exploration of the unknown and graphics of storytelling. This is how it enriches our knowledge of the earth, sea and sky. An elaborate description of the way *National Geographic* influences the worldview of the people in the United States is provided by Lutz and Collins (1993). For the twenty-first century, it has set in addition the watchwords of 'above and beyond' (National Geographic Society, 2013). The goal is to inspire people to take care of the planet's diversity of places, people and non-human life, *beyond* acquiring knowledge of it.

Being a monthly magazine, *National Geographic* brings out 12 issues in a year. By that reckoning, it has appeared for about 800 times on the commercial news-stands, library shelves and domestic tables since India became independent in 1947. Each issue generally carries two area focused articles, giving a rough estimate of around 1600 since then.

their path. In several rural markets all over, sellers use solar panels to attract customers.

Switzer (1971) underlines that the history's first precious diamonds came from the medieval city of Golconda. Ward (1979) adjudges Koh-i-noor as the world's most luminous diamond. Royalty of India as also that of England, France and Russia was hugely captivated by its sparkling beauty.

On the basis of such articles published in *National Geographic,* one can say that the vitality of India can be referred to spectacles and objects like Indus Valley civilization, the monsoons, Great Indian Desert, solar energy, spices and diamonds. These offer a great variety. More of this comes to the fore in articles that the magazine carries specifically on India.

India as One Unit

Seven articles in the category treat India as one entity. These cover political events, development of rail and road transport and population issues. A note is taken of both traditional and modern India. The effort is to capture the existential parameters of the country.

National Geographic made it special to celebrate the landmark event of the 50th anniversary of India's Independence in 1997. On this occasion, Ward (1997a) revisits India, the country of his childhood. For him India marks strong contrasts of grand wealth and abysmal poverty. He compares the pace of its development to an elephant's march, slow but moving. On an admiring note, he credits India for having sustained democracy, having achieved food sufficiency through the Green Resolution, having promoted a free media, and having created a burgeoning middle class.

Even in the wake of the disastrous Chinese invasion in 1962, Scofield (1963) had a positive word for India. He observed that in a situation of such a crisis, the whole country stood more united than ever. Meanwhile he discovers several contrasts on a reality check of India: It is atomic physicists at Bombay and Naga tribesmen in Assam; ruby decked maharajas in palaces and ragged street sweepers on roads; and Oxford trained philosophers in libraries and unlettered farmers in the field.

India runs primarily on its railways (Theroux, 1984). Dusty and monumental, India's trains often seem as ancient as the country itself. These are indispensable fact of Indian life. As one of the greatest contributions of the colonial rule, these are now one of the largest systems in the world. These carry a powerful aura around. A similar sentiment is echoed by Satow (1984), applauding India for maturing with pride and competence, benefitting from this legacy bequeathed by the British.

From rail to road, Arden (1990) quotes Rudyard Kipling most effectively. Borrowing the latter's words he eulogizes the Grand Trunk Road: Such as a river of life as nowhere exists in the world; the backbone of all Hind. You don't take the Great Trunk Road; it takes you.

Now a new 5846 kilometre superhighway, known as the Golden Quadrilateral, is strengthening the bond between four mega cities of India: Delhi,

Mumbai, Chennai and Kolkata. In the nature of a technologically advanced conveyor belt, this is bringing old and new India together on the way (Belt, 2008). On several counts, it is a visiting card of India.

But India has to cope with several serious problems among which unrelenting population growth is one (Rai, 1988). Most of its populace remains on an edge under conditions of uncertainty and anxiety. This is a nation of both an urban industrial society and an impoverished majority living a traditional life in villages.

A variety of ingredients of India's vitality come to surface in the foregoing portrayals. The prominent among these include democracy, free media and rising middle class. The magazine, in addition, applauds the strengths and virtues of a number of India's states and regions.

States and Regions

National Geographic has covered almost the entire length and breadth of the country – from the 'idyllic vale of Kashmir' in the north to the 'jewel of Malabar', Kerala in the south; from the feudal 'splendour of Rajasthan' in the west to the 'tiny Himalayan garden in the clouds, Sikkim', in the east. *National Geographic* fostered a fascination for Sikkim even before it became a part of India in 1975. Known for its beauty, Sikkim is described as enchanting land of charming people (Doig, 1963). Gangtok, its seat of power, is like a storybook capital of a gentle kingdom (Scofield, 1970).

Kashmir has been a favourite haunt of *National Geographic*. Its tangled history of glory and calamity, tolerance and oppression is least discernable to a fresh traveller savouring delights of Kashmir (Cameron, 1958). One has to delve deep to reach its soul (Wentzel, 1948a). The Kashmir of today, torn by military and strife, was revisited by Simons (1999). He believes that, through Kashmir, India wants to demonstrate that an Islamic population can co-live with the Hindu majority. Nationalists in Pakistan insist that the country will remain incomplete without inclusion of this Muslim majority area. Kashmir on both sides remains an armed camp. Most critical aspect of Kashmir is its strategic location, being in the nature of a gateway to both China and Afghanistan.

Within the state of Jammu & Kashmir, Ladakh has historically been an independent monarchy for more than a thousand years. It lay on the caravan crossroads connecting Tibet, Kashmir and Turkistan (Abercrombie, 1978). Here is a land, resembling little Tibet, where people have happiness and contentment (Bhavnani, 1951). Described as the last Shangri-la – 'dwelling place of gods' – it is now experiencing the penetration of the twentieth century. Even the remote Hanley valley in Ladakh attracts the attention of Lange (2004). It is a seventeenth century gompa or Buddhist monastery on the ancient trade route which connected Tibet and Ladakh. This sacred place is steeped in the ideals of humanity, fraternity and compassion.

From the cold desert of Ladakh to one of the hottest deserts of the world, the Thar transfers us to a harsh land of sun and sand, wind and rock

(Singh, 1977). Within this setting, Wentzel (1948b) discovered the incomparable pageantry, pomp and splendor of palaces and courts. Any part of the world offers a variety; it all depends on what you want to see.

Over to Kerala, 'India's Corner of Paradise', as Miller (1988) eulogizes it. Competitive in daily life, the people of this state lead in education, health and some say ambition as well. Shortly after the state was formed in 1956, it voted the communist party into power through ballet, first time ever in the world history.

As expected, the mighty Himalayas were ever a source of attraction and several articles focusing on this macro-region of India appeared in *National Geographic*. A journey through the Himalayas was always a high adventure (Weir, 1952). The highest and most inhospitable peak of the Mt. Everest, known as Chomulaungama (the golden mother of the earth) was conquered by Edmund Hillary and Serpa Tenzing Norgay in May 1953. Hunt and Hillary (1954) came out with a detailed account of their expedition under the title 'Triumph on Everest'. Even though Mt. Everest finds its location in Nepal, the expeditions were undertaken via India. This loftiest peak was the nature's final stronghold after explorers had reached the North and South poles. Under its continuing spell, Hillary (1955) undertook another expedition and explored the Himalayas around this highest point on our planet and mapped large areas of this unknown territory. Interest in Mt. Everest resurfaced in the 1980s in the form of articles by Washburn (1988) and Garrett (1988b).

Ward (2002) takes a note of the India's Western Ghats which are emerging as a biodiversity hotspot. It is a threatened natural habitat rich in species of plants that live nowhere else. Some 160,000 kms^2 of undisturbed forest here has been reduced to 13,000 kms^2. Slopes near Munnar were overlayed by gardens and groves of eucalyptus trees. Lower down evergreen forests were lost to tea and coffee as well as cashew and cardamom plantations. Massive hydroelectric and irrigation projects took an additional toll. The ancient Sanskrit name 'Sahyadri', meaning 'benevolent maintain' needs to be honoured through conservation.

National Geographic has equally been interested in taking a note of development projects aimed at harnessing the potential of local territories. A.D. Chapelle and G.D. Chapelle (1956) highlight the success of Community Development Programme in Bastar district, now in Chhattisgarh state. Rosenberg (2008) narrates the story of a Comprehensive Rural Health Project in Samkhed, Maharashtra, where village health workers were trained to take care of a local problem, leading to a significant drop in infant mortality rate. The Hirakund dam raised on the Mahanadi in Odisha amounted to moving a mountain and putting it across the river (McDowell, 1970). Corbett (2009) celebrates a success story pertaining to a Watershed Development Project in Satchiwadi and Darewadi villages of Maharashtra. The idea behind such projects is simple: Where the rain runs, make it walk; where it walks, make it crawl. This is the essence of water management for transforming the areas of subsistence agriculture into commercial farms.

In the spirit of a situational analysis, Loyd (2015) provides a picture of catastrophic mismanagement resulting in spread of Maoism in the north-eastern part of Indian peninsula. This 'Red Belt', as it is called, elongates from the forested tracts of Andhra Pradesh to those of West Bengal. Chhattisgarh and Jharkhand constitute the cockpit of this Naxal insurgency against the government. These states are rich in minerals, especially coal, but are also high on the score of poverty. Naxalites get their recruits from the tribals whose land had been acquired and got displaced in the process. They raise their funds through mineral wealth and extortion. A kind of symbiosis exists between mining industry and Maoism. Naxalite belt always begins where the road ends. At the end of the road, one enters into a zone of parallel authority of communism, armed cadres, extortion of even government development funds, peoples' court and jungle of punishment. This Naxalite sanctuary is spread over 35,000 kms^2.

Evidently *National Geographic* has tried to explore both vitality and vulnerability of different regions of India. Large parts of India shine in glory. There are venues of darkness as well. This is the geographic reality of this great country. The fact that India has resolutely challenged its vulnerability is an evidence of its vitality.

Super-Metros

Of the four largest metropolitan cities of India, *National Geographic* covered three, New Delhi, Bombay (Mumbai) and Calcutta (Kolkata). Madras (Chennai) is yet to receive its due attention. The distinct identity, specific culture and daily life of each of the cities covered are captured in captivating words and engrossing photographs.

Soon after India gained Independence, *National Geographic* came out with an article on the nation's capital city, New Delhi, the seat of power (Talbot, 1947). The British withdrawal was grand and graceful in nature. A conference table, rather than a battlefield, marked the succession. Hodgson (1985) describes New Delhi as a mirror to India. A blend of traditional and modern, the city at large epitomizes the nation's problems as well as potential. Its life is vibrant beyond limits. Ward (1997a), who visited the country in the wake of 50th anniversary of India's Independence, highlights a contrast between the vibrancy of the city and sluggishness of the Indian villages at large.

Scofield (1981) confers on Bombay the title of 'glamour queen of Indian cities'. The unchecked prosperity and not poverty threatens its very survival. Almost anyone can find work in Bombay but not a decent place to live. Drenched by monsoon floods and drowned by problems of drinking water, traffic snarls and above all housing, the people still remain optimistic. No wonder McCarry (1995) calls Bombay as the 'India's capital of hope'. He does not miss the communal riots in this city, otherwise rated as most integrated on religious, linguistic and regional lines. Such an integration is most visible in its Dharavi slum. Jacobson (2007) calls this teeming locality of a million as 'Mumbai's shadow city'. As a huge mosaic of people hailing from different parts of the country, it is the most assorted slum in India's most diverse city.

Calcutta by contrast is ascribed most distressing words; a dreadful greenhouse, scary, a dying city (White, 1973). It suffers from inadequate housing, insufficient drinking water, poor drainage and bad sewerage but is being milked by millions as best they can. Among the great cities of the world, it is the only one which still has a large fleet of hand pulled rickshaws (Trillin, 2008).This man-yoked vehicle is the symbol of India's colonial past; a hallmark of exploitation but also a handy way of going around by the poor in service of the better off. On the other side of the coin, Calcutta is a commercial and cultural hub of India, vibrant with money matters and intellectual debate.

Despite their crushing problems, the super metros remain magnet for millions seeking work, fortune and excitement. These also mark a comparison on the scoreboard of relative vitality. Calcutta is a city of yesterday, Bombay of today and Delhi of tomorrow. The story of Madras is yet to be constructed and told.

History and Events

India is not without funny narratives in its history. Abercrombie (1991) focuses on the journey of Ibn Batuta, the 'Prince of Travellers', who visited India during the Sultanate period of the fourteenth century. Batuta provides a thrilling description of the ruler of his days, Mohammad bin Tughlak, in whose court he spent seven years. This ruler was, in his words, generous and brutal at the same time, most unpredictable and full of idiosyncrasies. He was addicted to both giving gifts and shedding blood. His gate was never without some poor getting enriched or some other being executed.

Edwards (1985) had evinced an interest in the medieval period of Indian history. The Mughals are credited for raising India as a paradise on the earth. They enriched its face and destiny. Things changed subsequently after the fall of their empire. During wars Mughal palaces were damaged, forts disfigured, and precious stones disappeared from inlays. Aesthetically laid out gardens met a similar fate of indifference. The Mughal legacy, however, did not vanish. It remains an aura, a state of mind, a tongue, a taste.

Notably, in its coverage, *National Geographic* bypassed the ancient and colonial periods of Indian history. Meanwhile its attention to a variety of natural hazards, political events and cultural celebrations was remarkable. Any social happening was duly recorded.

Kingdom (1952) provides a vivid account of the Assam-Tibet earthquake of 1951 which caused extensive rock strewn destruction in the east. It measured 8.6 on Richter scale. Another devastating event, now contrived by man in 1962, was the mountain top war in remote Ladakh in the west (Garrett, 1963). This battle was fought at Chushul, India's highest airfield at an altitude of 4,360 metres. At that time, China had simultaneously attacked India's North East Frontier Agency, now Arunachal Pradesh.

On a different note, Silverstone (1965) offers a graphic picture of a royal wedding. It was a four-day marriage celebration of Princess Rukmani Kumari of Jaisalmer with Prince Raghbir Singh of Rajpipla. The moment was splendid, full of pomp and power, but also representing the sunset glory of *maharajas* (princes). By comparison the wedding of the crown Prince of Sikkim, Polden Thoundup Namgyal, with an American beauty, Hope Coke, was on a different note. It was a wedding of two worlds, the East and the West (Battaglia, 1963). A tribute to oriental nostalgia, it was performed in traditional Sikkimese style, where an American girl became the 'consort of deities.'

An event of a somewhat different nature was the visit of President Eisenhower to India in 1959 for strengthening of Indo-US ties (Grosvenor, 1960). Not only the Indian Parliament but also millions of people welcomed him. The crowd that had gathered was the largest ever witnessed in Delhi. A special interest was generated also by the visit in 1963 of Mary French, Chairperson of the Young Women's Christian Association (Rochefeller, 1963). In the same spirit, Putman (1985) gives the details of the festival of India in the United States. This was a display of an ancient culture geared to become a modern economy. Exhibits included not only a display of the traditional folk products but also of the state-of-the-art scientific equipment.

Thus, events of contrasting nature found a place on the pages of *National Geographic*, devastating ones like earthquakes and wars and festive ones like weddings and celebrity visits. Everything that happens in India is on a massive scale. Such vitality leaves a powerful impact ever.

People

India is marked by a remarkable diversity of people, their cultures and customs. One special category is of nomadic kind. Lancaster (2010) identified 500 nomadic groups in India, with a total of about 50 million persons. They include snake charmers, animal doctors, basket makers, salt traders, fortune tellers, acrobats, jugglers, conjurers, and so on. They do not have an affixed address; hence remain deprived of the welfare benefits, such as subsidized food, kerosene oil and free medical aid, dispensed by the government.

In manifest anguish, O'Neil (2003) testifies that one out of every six Indians is branded impure from the very moment of birth. Traditionally called as *shudras*, they lie at the bottom of the caste system and are treated as untouchable. He adds that Manu is engraved in the mind of every Hindu. The caste system devised by him believes that people are born unequal.

Naga tribes, who inhabit the forest covered hills on Assam-Burma borderland, remained isolated for long from rest of the world (Ripley, 1955). They lived in a remote natural setting. Their habitat is distinguished by most varied flora and fauna.

By comparison, the Rabaris are a semi-nomadic pastoralist tribe who move across the border of Rajasthan and Gujarat in search of green pastures

(Davidson, 1993). They continue with their centuries old lifestyle, rituals and practices. The shrinking size of grasslands, as a result of regular extension of cultivable area by the farming communities, has emerged as a livelihood issue for this pastoral community.

Among the various martial and farming communities, the Sikhs hold a place of pride. Frazer (1972) finds them most energetic. They lead their life with greater gusto and enterprise than most Indians. They have every reason to glorify their history and religion.

On the cultural plane, Wentzel (1953) finds a flavour of antiquity in the shrines of Andhra Pradesh, in the precious heritage of Ajanta and Ellora caves, and in the Hindu pilgrimage centre of Kailash Parbat. In Ajanta complex, which is now a UNESCO World Heritage Site, Indian artists portrayed their gods as a vision of perfection (O'Neil, 2008). The cave temples were raised during the reign of Harishena in fifth century AD, and carry the images of Buddha, Bodhisattvas (a Buddhist deity who represents infinite compassion), jataka stories, princes, elephants, horses and lotus flowers, among others. These paintings follow the rules laid down in Chitrasutra, the oldest known treatise on paintings in Sanskrit. Evidently, India's art is both mirror and window to life, inspiring a higher level of consciousness.

A reverse of this coin is represented by Bollywood, the icon of modern India (Mehta, 2005). India is the largest producer of films which draws no less than 3.6 billion visits by the cine-goers in a year. Indian movies are equally popular in several other parts of the world, including in particular the Middle East, Central Asia, East Africa, South Africa, the United Kingdom and the United States. Though these movies stay banned in Pakistan since 1965 but everyone accesses them in pirated discs. Bollywood films present the impossible as possible. These affirm that true love conquers all. They demonstrate that history is defeated by sentiment.

Jacobson (1977) takes a note of the traditional custom of *purdah* (veil) which still persists in some parts of India, as also in Muslim countries in general. This is seen as something obnoxious in the western world but is valued as facilitating a smooth functioning of family life in rural India. The custom is said to be providing security to women and also defining their duties as a faithful member of a patriarchal society. Another persistent custom of child marriage is analysed by Gorney (2011). He observes that in defiance of the national laws, forced early marriage thrives in many parts of India. Since such a wedding is in violation of law, it is solemnized in secrecy at late night, as typical of Rajasthan.

The diversity of people, richness of cultural heritage and abundance of Bollywood emerge among the ingredients of India's vitality. There is a mix of a lot good and some bad. Complexity is ingrained in the DNA of India.

Religion

National Geographic carried a strong fascination for portraying varying dimensions of different religions in the country. These included their respective philosophic parameters, holy sites, pilgrimage practices and joyous festivals. The sanctity of rivers has been in special focus.

There is no better way to know the world's people else than through an understanding of their religion, which essentially is the man's quest for purpose of life. Smith (1971) reviewed the book, *Great Religions of the World*, published by *National Geographic*. The author traces the story of five major religions – Hinduism, Buddhism, Judaism, Islam and Christianity – all of which have millions of adherents. These religions share many similar ethical concepts. Over centuries they have shaped nations and individuals, political systems and societal codes, and ways of thinking and daily lives of people.

The Buddhism, with 379 million adherents, is the world's fifth largest religion (Garfinkel, 2005). It is attracting new western followers drawn by ideals of pacificism, selflessness and social action. In 2004, more than 25 million Americans reported that the Buddhist teachings had a strong influence on their spiritual leanings and life decisions. Evidently Buddhism is moving out of monastery and entering into the living room.

A pilgrimage to the holy cave of Amarnath, located in the Kashmir Himalayas, was undertaken by Rand (1956). It lies at an altitude of 3,660 metres and is devoted to Shiva, a Hindu deity worshipped widely. Amarnath literally means 'immortal lord' and its *linga*, a white pillar of snow, is meant to signify man's spiritual search for abiding bliss.

National Geographic extends a tribute to the holiest of the Hindu places, Banaras, situated on the banks of Ganga. The whole splendid façade of the city gets washed in the daylight with a golden hue of incredible purity and one can easily understand why the Hindus call it by the ancient name of Kashi, the luminous city. Despite the dirt around and decay in the life of many Indians, an extraordinary faith attracts multitudes of pilgrims to this sacred place every day (Rau, 1986).

Two major Hindu fairs, Maha Kumbh and Mysore Dushera, have been of immense excitement to *National Geographic*. Maha Kumbh is the largest religious gathering on earth every 12 years when millions of Hindus of all castes, classes, doctrines and sects come together in and around Allahabad. Gathering at the confluence of Ganga and Yamuna rivers, where underneath flows the mythical river of enlightenment, Sarasvati, worshippers wash their sins and pray to escape the cycle of endless reincarnation (Heiderer, 1990). Spinney (2014) narrates his experience of Maha Kumbh Mela of February 2013. It drew an estimated 70 million people. The cornerstone of such an event has been the 'shared identity'. This generates positive emotions contributing to mental and physical health. This *mela* or fair, on such a grand scale, makes a success because of the excellent arrangements made by the government and psycho-religious cooperation rendered by the people.

The Mysore Dushera is one of the oldest and most colourful festivals (Boucharge, 1958). It is celebrated to mark the victory of goddess Durga over the demon king, Mahishasura. Symbolically it represents the triumph of the good over evil.

Two major rivers, Ganga and Brahmputra, were also visited by *National Geographic*. Putman (1971) extols Mother Ganga as the 'river of faith'. The river is a vibrant part of the daily life of the Hindus. A few drops of its water on a person's tongue at the moment of death ensures salvation. Though fouled by sewage and garbage, Ganga provides its people with domestic water, field irrigation and pious blessings. Anyone who bathes in its holy water, having the source in Shiva's plait, gets endowed with virtue and spiritual strength (Schreider and Schreider, 1960).

The long journey of the other great river, the Brahmputra, is traced by Dyk (1988). From the Hindu God, Brahma, the river derives its name and literally it means 'son of Brahma'. Mt. Kailash, the centre of universe for the Hindus, Buddhists and Jains, is the holy origin of this river. Like a Hindu deity, the river has many reincarnations and nomenclatures, changing its name from Tsangpo in Tibet, to Brahmaputra in India, and further to Meghna in Bangladesh.

The vitality of India has strong roots in religion in the form of devout pilgrimages, holy cities, grand fairs and soul purifying rivers. All these generate vibrancy in a variety of places. Pilgrimages to them also render spatial inter-connectivity to different parts of India.

Wildlife

National Geographic devoted as many as 12 articles to wildlife in India. Elephant, tiger, lion and cobra received extensive detail. The loss of wildlife habitat has also been voiced as a major concern.

Elephant has been a favourite topic for the magazine. Chaturvedi (1957) informs their greater frequency in the southern and eastern states of Kerala, Karnataka, Odisha, West Bengal and Assam in India. He describes them as four-footed jungle bulldozer, and as a great help in varied settings. The princely rulers in the past used them for royal processions. During the wars, they were deployed as rams to batter the gates of besieged forts. In difficult areas, they were turned into mobile bridge to ford streams. Miller (1969) adds that machines cannot replace elephants as lumberjacks not only because of the latter's gentle gait but also due to their inclination to do any assignment competently. The Elephant Festival celebrated in Jaipur is a tribute to this animal. India's royalty glitters from the back of an elephant at such occasions (Shea, 2013). Also the fact that god Ganesha is elephant headed cannot be ignored. This bestows holiness on the elephant. Chadwick (1991) takes a note of the overwhelming loss of habitat from which the elephant is suffering. The fundamental issue with elephants is that they require a lot of room to roam around and humans are squeezing their space. Ultimately people, not poachers or guns, are the serious threat to the survival of elephant.

The tiger is a recent favourite of *National Geographic*. India is home to some half of the world's nearly four thousand tigers (Alexander, 2011). Ranthambore National Park houses Panthera tigress, one of the most ferocious carnivores on the planet. Her roar can be heard at a distance of two kms. Nichols (1997) photographs the majestic Sita, the Bengal tigress, who bred more litters than anyone else. This boosted the tiger population. Earlier Reed (1961) had paid a tribute by addressing her as an enchantress, the Queen of India. It also took Breeden (1984) no less than 10 years to track this greatest carnivore throughout India to come up with his article under the title 'Tiger, Lord of Indian Jungle'. He felt the privilege of having been so close to an animal that is not only formidable but also extremely rare.

Lions exude vitality (Klum, 2001a). They are a symbol of royalty and majesty. India has about 300 of them, confined to the Gir sanctuary in Gujarat. Extinction stalks them since a disease or a natural disaster may take their sudden toll. The plan to move some of them to the Kuno sanctuary in Madhya Pradesh is a sensible proposition.

Miller's (1970) deep interest in cobra – India's hooded snake, Nulla Pamba in Tamil – is evident from his elaborate informative account of this reptile. Klum (2001b) informs us that the king cobra requires dense undergrowth as its habitat which is typical of mangrove swamps or forests along the streams. The cobra has great religious significance for the Hindus, primarily as a symbol of fertility. He is not the vicious killer as imagined by the uninformed. He is worthy of both reverence and fear.

With 100 tigers, 2000 one horned rhinos and 1800 wild buffaloes, Kaziranga Park is India's Wildlife Kingdom (Chadwick, 2010). Spread along both sides of Brahmaputra river, it covers an area of 860 kms^2. It got the National Park status in 1974 and was designated as World Habitat Site in 1985. This was in due recognition of its contribution to conservation of ecosystem.

An extensive loss of wildlife habitat is now a major concern (Ward, 1992). The dwindling number of tiger population is a matter of worry, in particular (Ward, 1997b). The land hunger of rapidly growing poverty stricken farmers is threatening the future of India's unique natural heritage. Both humans and animals vie for space as farms and cities are encroaching upon habitat of wildlife. The human tide continues to sweep over the great forest that covered an estimated 40 per cent of the country at the beginning of the twentieth century. It had got reduced to half of this spread by the close of this century.

Discovering Vitality in Literature

National Geographic has been successful in capturing the spirit of India by projecting the ethnic, laying bare the indigenous and enlivening the traditional. The thematic variety of the articles is astounding: regions, states, cities, culture, religion, critical events, wildlife to mention some. The greatest interest has been expended on select regions and places, followed by religion. Religion is noted for an overreaching eye as rarely any article, including on metropolitan cities like Bombay (Mumbai), New Delhi and Calcutta (Kolkata), misses this chorus.

Vitality of India gets reflected in ways more than many. The mention could begin with the Indus Valley Civilization, the monsoons and the culture of diamonds. A vibrant democracy, free media and rising middle class are other parameters as representative of India's vitality. The vitality has also been reflected in the exquisite beauty of the landscape of states like Jammu & Kashmir, Sikkim and Kerala. Super-metro cities of New Delhi, Bombay and Kolkata are presented as most expressive of the nation's vitality as of today while the heritage sites, royal palaces and traditional fairs can be construed as its representatives of the yore. A delicious ingredient of India's vitality is Bollywood, the widely popular film industry. The wildlife, such as elephant, tiger, lion and cobra, has its role in rendering vibrancy to the rhythm of India's biological life. More than anything else the abiding vitality of India has its roots in religion, in the form of devout pilgrimages, holy cities, grand fairs and ever purifying rivers.

Such is the India story of the *National Geographic*. It is in the form of vignettes of the country's vitality. There are expressions of its vulnerability too.

References

Abercrombie, T.J. 1978. Ladakh: The Last Shangri-la. *National Geographic*. Vol. 153, No. 3, March, pp. 332–358.

——. 1991. Ibn Batuta: Prince of Travellers. *National Geographic*. Vol. 180, No. 6, March, pp. 332–358.

Alexander, C. 2011. Cry for the Tiger. *National Geographic*. Vol. 220, No. 6, December, pp. 62–91.

Arden, H. 1990. Searching for India: Along the Grand Trunk Road. *National Geographic*. Vol. 177, No. 5, May, pp. 118–138.

Battaglia, L.E. 1963. Wedding of the Two Worlds. *National Geographic*. Vol. 121, No. 5, November, pp. 708–728.

Belt, D. 2008. Fast Lane to the Future. *National Geographic*. Vol. 214, No. 4, April, pp. 72–99.

Bhavnani, E. 1951. A Journey of the 'Little Tibet'. *National Geographic*. Vol. 99, No. 5, May, pp. 603–634.

Boucharge, L. 1958. Mysore Celebrates the Death of a Demon. *National Geographic*. Vol. 113, No. 5, May, pp. 706–711.

Breeden, S. 1984. Tiger! Lord of Indian Jungle. *National Geographic*. Vol. 166, No. 5, December, pp. 748–773.

Bumstead, N. 1955. Around the World in Eighty Days. *National Geographic*. Vol. 100, No. 6, December, pp. 705–750.

Cameron, N. 1958. The Emperor's Private Garden: Kashmir. *National Geographic*. Vol. 114, No. 5, November, pp. 606–647.

Chadwick, D.H. 1991. Elephants: Out of Time, Out of Space. *National Geographic*. Vol. 179, No. 5, May, pp. 2–49.

——. 2010. A Grassland Kingdom: India's Kaziranga Park. *National Geographic*. Vol. 218, No. 2, August, pp. 98–117.

Chapelle, A.D. and G.D. Chapelle. 1956. New Life for India's Villagers. *National Geographic*. Vol. 109, No. 5, April, pp. 572–588.

Chaturvedi, M.D. 1957. The Elephant and I. *National Geographic*. Vol. 112, No. 4, October, pp. 489–507.

Corbett, S. 2009. A Harvest of Water: Harvesting Monsoon Rains. *National Geographic*. Vol. 216, No. 5, May, pp. 110–127.

Davidson, R. 1993. Wandering with India's Rabari. *National Geographic*. Vol. 184, No. 3, September, pp. 64–93.

Doig, D. 1963. Sikkim, Tiny Himalayan Kingdom in the Clouds. *National Geographic*. Vol. 123, No. 3, March, pp. 398–430.

Dyk, J.V. 1988. Long Journey of the Brahmaputra. *National Geographic*. Vol. 174, No. 5, November, pp. 672–711.

Edwards, M. 1985. Paradise on Earth: When the Moguls Ruled India. *National Geographic*. Vol. 167, No. 4, April, pp. 463–493.

——. 2000. Indus Civilization. *National Geographic*. Vol. 197, No. 6, April, pp. 108–131.

Eller, E.M. 1954. Troubled Waters East of Suez. *National Geographic*. Vol. 105, No. 4, April, pp. 483–522.

Frazer, J.E. 1972. India's Energetic Sikhs. *National Geographic*. Vol. 142, No. 4, October, pp. 528–541.

Garfinkel, P. 2005. Buddha Rising: Out of the Monastery into the Living Room. *National Geographic*. Vol. 208, No. 6, December, pp. 88–109.

Garrett, W.E. 1963. Mountain War in Remote Ladakh. *National Geographic*. Vol. 123, No. 5, May, pp. 664–687.

——. (ed.). 1988a. Within the Yellow Border. *National Geographic*. Vol. 174, No. 3, September, pp. 270–286.

——. 1988b. Exploring Cradle Earth. *National Geographic*. Vol. 174, No. 5, November, pp. 612–623.

Gore, R. 1979. The Desert: An Age Old Challenge Grows. *National Geographic*. Vol. 156, No. 5, November, pp. 586–639.

Gorney, C. 2011. Too Young to Wed: The Secret World of the Child Brides. *National Geographic*. Vol. 219, No. 6, June, pp. 78–95.

Grosvenor, G.M. 1960. When the President Goes Abroad. *National Geographic*. Vol. 117, No. 5, May, pp. 588–649.

Hayden, M.E. 2015. Power to the People. *National Geographic*. Vol. 228, No. 5, November, pp. 74–85.

Heiderer, T. 1990. India's Maha Kumb Mela Draws Millions: Sacred Space, Sacred Time. *National Geographic*. Vol. 177, No. 5, May, pp. 106–117.

Hillary, E. 1955. Beyond Everest. *National Geographic*. Vol. 108, No. 5, November, pp. 579–610.

Hodgson, B. 1985. Mirror of India: New Delhi. *National Geographic*. Vol. 167, No. 4, April, pp. 506–533.

Hunt, J. and E. Hillary. 1954. Triumph on Everest. *National Geographic*. Vol. 106, No. 1, July, pp. 1–45.

Jacobson, D.W. 1977. Purdah: Life Behind the Veil. *National Geographic*. Vol. 152, No. 2, August, pp. 270–286.

Jacobson, M. 2007. Dharavi: Mumbai's Shadow City. *National Geographic*. Vol. 211, No. 5, May, pp. 68–93.

Jones, S.E. 1949. Spices: The Essence of Geography. *National Geographic*. Vol. 95, No. 4, April, pp. 401–420.

Kingdom, W.F. 1952. Caught in the Assam-Tibet Earthquake. *National Geographic*. Vol. 101, No. 3, March, pp. 403–416.

Klum, M. 2001a. Asia's Last Lions. *National Geographic*. Vol. 199, No. 6, June, pp. 46–61.

——. 2001b. King Cobra. *National Geographic*. Vol. 200, No. 5, November, pp. 100–113.

Lancaster, J. 2010. India's Nomads. *National Geographic*. Vol. 217, No. 2, February, pp. 102–121.

Lange, K.E. 2004. The Sacred Community of India's Forbidden Hanle Valley in Their Own World. *National Geographic*. Vol. 205, No. 1, January, pp. 88–99.

Loyd, A. 2015. How Coal Fuels India's Insurgency. *National Geographic*. Vol. 227, No. 4, April, pp. 76–95.

Lutz, C.A. and J.L. Collins. 1993. *Reading National Geographic*. Chicago: University Press.

McCarry, J. 1995. Bombay. *National Geographic*. Vol. 187, No. 3, March, pp. 42–67.

McDowell, B. 1970. Orissa: Past and Promise of an Indian State. *National Geographic*. Vol. 138, No. 4, October, pp. 546–577.

——. 1981. Crosscurrents Sweep the Indian Ocean. *National Geographic*. Vol. 160, No. 4, October, pp. 422–457.

McMillan, P. 1995. The Vimy Flies Again. *National Geographic*. Vol. 187, No. 5, May, pp. 2–43.

Mehta, S. 2005. Bollywood. *National Geographic*. Vol. 207, No. 2, February, pp. 52–69.

Miller, H. 1969. Wild Elephant Roundup in India. *National Geographic*. Vol. 135, No. 3, March, pp. 372–430.

——. 1970. The Cobra: India's Good Snake. *National Geographic*. Vol. 138, No. 3, September, pp. 393–409.

Miller, P. 1988. Kerala: Jewel of the Malabar Coast. *National Geographic*. Vol. 173, No. 5, May, pp. 592–617.

National Geographic Society. 2013. 125 Years. *National Geographic*. Vol. 224, No. 4, October, pp. 422–457.

Nichols, M. 1997. Sita: Life of a Wild Tigress. *National Geographic*. Vol. 192, No. 6, December, pp. 36–47.

O' Neil, T. 2003. Untouchable. *National Geographic*. Vol. 203, No. 6, June, pp. 2–31.

——. 2008. Faces of the Divine: India's Ancient Art. *National Geographic*. Vol. 213, No. 1, January, pp. 122–139.

Putman, J.J. 1971. The Ganges: River of Faith. *National Geographic*. Vol. 140, No. 4, October, pp. 445–482.

——. 1985. Focus on India: Festival Across U.S. Celebrates a Diverse Culture. *National Geographic*. Vol. 167, No. 4, April, pp. 460–461.

Rai, R. 1988. India: Life on the Edge. In P.R. Ehrlich and A.H. Ehrlich (eds), Population, Plenty and Poverty. *National Geographic*. Vol. 174, No. 6, December, pp. 914–945.

Rand, C. 1956. Himalayan Pilgrimage. *National Geographic*. Vol. 110, No. 4, October, pp. 520–535.

Rau, S.R. 1986. Banaras: India's City of Light. *National Geographic*. Vol. 169, No. 2, February, pp. 214–251.

Reed, T.H. 1961. Enchanters! Rare White Tigress Comes to Washington. *National Geographic*. Vol. 119, No. 5, May, pp. 628–642.

Ripley, D. 1955. Roaming India's Naga Hills. *National Geographic*. Vol. 107, No. 2, February, pp. 247–226.

Rochefeller, M.F. 1963. YWCA: International Success Story. *National Geographic*. Vol. 124, No. 6, December, pp. 904–933.

Rosenberg, T. 2008. Village Health Workers. *National Geographic*. Vol. 174, No. 6, December, pp. 914–945.

Satow, M. 1984. India's Railway Life Line. *National Geographic*. Vol. 165, No. 6, June, pp. 744–750.

Schreider, H. and F. Schreider. 1960. From the Hair of Siva. *National Geographic*. Vol. 118, No. 4, October, pp. 445–503.

Scofield, J. 1963. India: Subcontinent in Crisis. *National Geographic*. Vol. 123, No. 5, May, pp. 599–566.

——. 1970. Gangtok: Cloud Wreathed Himalayan Capital. *National Geographic*. Vol. 138, No. 5, November, pp. 698–714.

——. 1981. Bombay: The Other India. *National Geographic*. Vol. 160, No. 1, July, pp. 104–129.

Shea, R.H. 2013. Parade of the Painted Elephants. *National Geographic*. Vol. 224, No. 4, October, pp. 127–133.

Simons, L.M. 1999. Kashmir Trapped in Conflict. *National Geographic*. Vol. 196, No. 3, September, pp. 2–29.

Singh, R. 1977. The Pageant of Rajasthan. *National Geographic*. Vol. 151, No. 2, February, pp. 219–243.

Silverstone, M. 1965. Royal Wedding at Jaisalmer. *National Geographic*. Vol. 127, No. 1, January, pp. 66–79.

Smith, H. 1971. Great Religions of the World. *National Geographic*. Vol. 140, No. 4, October, pp. 587–590.

Spinney, L. 2014. Karma of the Crowd. *National Geographic*. Vol. 225, No. 2, November, pp. 120–135.

Suplee, C. 1998. Unlocking the Climate Puzzle. *National Geographic*. Vol. 193, No. 5, May, pp. 38–71.

Switzer, G.S. 1971. Questing for Gems. *National Geographic*. Vol. 140, No. 6, December, pp. 835–864.

Talbot, P. 1947. Delhi: Capital of New Dominion. *National Geographic*. Vol. 92, No. 5, November, pp. 597–630.

Theroux, P. 1984. By Rail Across Indian Subcontinent. *National Geographic*. Vol. 165, No. 6, June, pp. 696–743.

Trillin, C. 2008. Last Days of the Rickshaw. *National Geographic*. Vol. 213, No. 4, April, pp. 92–105.

Vesiland, P.J. 1984. Monsoons and South Asia and its People. *National Geographic*. Vol. 166, No. 6, December, pp. 712–747.

Ward, F. 1979. Diamond: The Incredible Crystal. *National Geographic*. Vol. 155, No. 1, January, pp. 85–113.

Ward, G.C. 1992. India's Wildlife Dilemma. *National Geographic*. Vol. 181, No. 5, May, pp. 2–29.

——. 1997a. India: Fifty Years of Independence. *National Geographic*. Vol. 191, No. 5, May, pp. 2–57.

——. 1997b. Making Room for Wild Tigers. *National Geographic*. Vol. 192, No. 6, December, pp. 2–3.

——. 2002. India's Western Ghat. *National Geographic*. Vol. 201, No. 1, January, pp. 90–109.

Washburn, B. 1988. Mapping Mount Everest. *National Geographic*. Vol. 174, No. 5, November, pp. 653–659.

Weir, T. 1952. High Adventures in the Himalayas. *National Geographic*. Vol. 102, No. 2, August, pp. 193–234.

Wentzel, V. 1953. India's Sculptured Temple Caves. *National Geographic*. Vol. 103, No. 5, May, pp. 665–678.

——. 1948a. The Idyllic Vale of Kashmir. *National Geographic*. Vol. 103, No. 5, May, pp. 665–678.

——. 1948b. Feudal Splendor Lingers in Rajputana. *National Geographic*. Vol. 94, No. 4, October, pp. 411–458.

White, P.T. 1973. Calcutta: The World's Most Maligned Metropolis. *National Geographic*. Vol. 143, No. 4, April, pp. 534–563.

——. 1994. Rice, the Essential Harvest. *National Geographic*. Vol. 185, No. 5, May, pp. 48–79.

9

Synthesizing Regional Vitality

The idea of India as one-world-many carries an appeal wherein each region has a distinct identity and makes a specific contribution to the country's vitality. Region for this purpose has been taken as coterminous with a state/union territory. States in India are vital organs of the national system.

The most striking dimension of India's vitality is its sustained integrity since its emergence as an independent entity in 1947. The national policy ever since has been quite a success story in nation-building. The Constitution of India acknowledged the federal nature of Indian polity but found a unitary bias as necessary in its formulation. It emphasizes the indestructible character of the union. This empowered the nation-state with the necessary sovereignty and authority to deal with any secessionist movement.

In addition to a political design of federalism, secularism as a social policy was adopted to deal with the question of ethnicity. An economic policy of planned development was simultaneously put in practice to stimulate growth, reduce regional disparities and involve people in the process of national development. The education policy was geared toward reinforcing all such sensibilities toward a spirit of Indianness.

The evolved spatial framework of states and union territories enhanced their dependence upon each other when development became a cherished goal. There was a realization on the part of the constituents that they were better off as a component of the union rather than as separate entities. The situation got a further fillip from the protectionist economic policy that independent India followed for decades. Various states looked towards each other rather than to other countries for sharing their surplus or meeting the deficit. Economic federalism matured along with political federalism. The ingrained style not only persisted but gained a momentum after the adoption of globalization policy in early 1990s. This was a response to the demands and upshots of the economic vibrancy.

The singular credit for sustaining India unified goes to its democratic polity. The nation-state has withstood the onslaught of very difficult situations of widespread discontent, violent protests and even insurgency. Indian democracy convincingly demonstrated its strength and virtue in reconciling conflicting interests and fusing diverse perspectives. Effective policies of both conflict resolution and territorial reorganization were harnessed to meet the popular demands. India is not only surviving but also thriving as a democracy. The vitality of India is manifest in its capacity to constantly nourish and expand the democratic space.

Today the very idea of India is taking a fascinating turn. The nation-state is getting transformed into a state-nation. An upsurge of healthy *stateism* is visible on the political landscape as a mark of economic maturity. Traditional ethnic identities are getting transformed into state identities. The issue of ethnic identity having been resolved, the pride of belonging to a particular state is deepening. Every state is moving with its specific agenda and brandishing dynamism. Maharashtra would like to be described as a great state, Rajasthan a land of royalty, West Bengal a radical arena, Telangana a global Information Technology destination, and Sikkim a rising star. Self-definitions on such lines by every state are meant to uphold identity and invigorate vitality.

The different states are in competition with each other on development trajectory. Some of them have acquired brand distinctions. That is how we talk about Gujarat model of development, or for that matter of Kerala, Tamil Nadu, Punjab, Himachal Pradesh, or even of Bihar. Before economic reforms, they vied with each other for location of public sector industry; now they are in race for attracting private sector investment. In an era of globalization, foreign capital is a catch prize. The vitality and dynamism of different states are in surge at varying pace though. Quantitative differences among various states may be gradually getting reduced, their increasing qualitative differences have emerged as a more serious concern.

The vitality of a state is concomitant with the quality of its governance. A peaceful law and order situation, stable policy regime, and healthy functioning of the system are the hallmarks of quality governance. The propensity of private sector to invest is a summary expression of all such conditions in a liberal context like that of India. The operational dynamics of investment by this sector is contingent upon the capacity of governance to create and ensure a milieu which is promotive of individual and collective effort. Notwithstanding the essential contribution made by the public sector, it is the private sector which has been pivotal to development of various states.

A regional pattern can be discerned in the quality of governance. The states in the West and South India are on a comparatively high score on this count. The same is the case of the union territories. The states in the middle belt are noted for a recent improvement in this regard. The small ethnic states in the North-East and the hill-states in the North-West India are in race for putting their administrative culture in proper order. The record of North Indian states leaves much to be desired.

Too large a population size of a state, such as in the case of Uttar Pradesh, Bihar and West Bengal, is a constraint to efficient administration, and too small, such as in the case of Sikkim, Mizoram or Meghalaya, makes the administration rather expensive. The impact of the population size of a state on its governance quality is, however, not consistent. Among the better administered ones are the large states like Maharashtra, medium states like Kerala, and small states like Goa. The coastal states excel over the mainland ones on governance quality exposed as these are to external modernity influences to a greater degree.

Economic dynamism is a high spot of a symbiotic relationship with the quality of governance. The spatial contours of 'economic dynamism' of India are evident enough. The four South Indian states, along with the three West Indian ones, constitute together an extensive zone of dynamic economy. Indications are that they are doing well not only in terms of economic growth but also in governance and social welfare. A coastal location is to their advantage.

North Indian states, on the other hand, suffer from acute resource/population imbalance and problems of their social structure are complex. The politico-administrative culture is also not beyond question. Adversely affected is economic dynamism. The middle belt states are acquiring comparatively a higher degree of economic buoyancy. Notable is the fact that new states, such as Uttarakhand, Chhattisgarh and Jharkhand, carved out in the name of backwardness are better placed than their parent states. Now the utilization of their rich natural resources is under their own purview.

In the case of hill states in both North-West and North-East India, peace is the key to economic dynamism of any state. The peaceful states and their politically disturbed neighbouring ones in these two regions present a contrast to each other in economic dynamism. Consider Himachal Pradesh and Kashmir in the first case; Mizoram and Manipur in the second. Peace goes with good governance and that determines its economic vigour. Also one cannot miss the vibrant economic dynamism of the national capital region, which covers the national capital territory and parts of its neighbouring states.

Testimony to above observations is the data pertaining to statewise addition to Net State Domestic Product of India during the period from 1980–81 to 2011–12. Over one-fourth of this addition was contributed by only two West Indian states of Gujarat and Maharashtra. If the four states of South India are also pooled in, this contribution works out as nearly three-fifths of the total. On the other extreme, the aggregate contribution made by two North Indian states of Uttar Pradesh and Bihar and two East India states of West Bengal and Assam does not approach even one-fifth of the total. An overriding fact remains that every state made a positive contribution, albeit in varying magnitude, and has its own pie in the cake.

In tandem with economic dynamism, the rise of middle class is another manifestation of India's vitality. Almost one-third of India's population meets this description. This approximates the proportion of urban population and carries a numerical strength of around 400 million. The number is larger than the total population of the United States and not far from that of continental Europe. Goa and Punjab are the two states where majority of population belongs to the middle class. The former is coastal and latter inland. Both are marked by high per capita income and urbanization level; both have a long tradition of emigration to the developed world; and both are marked by a total fertility rate of two or less. Virtually all the union territories are also distinguished by middle class demographics.

A number of hill states like Himachal Pradesh, Uttarakhand, Jammu & Kashmir and Sikkim are to be noted for a comparatively high proportion of middle class population despite the fact that these are at a low level of urbanization. The income level here is significantly higher than that of an average Indian state. This is attributed to their status as 'special category states' which entitles them to liberal devolution of funds from the central government not only for development projects but also for meeting the salaries of the relatively large number of government employees vis-à-vis population. Considerable additional income accrues to these states through tourism, sale of horticultural products and royalty on hydroelectricity. Such a play of governance and economy has been vital to expansion here of the middle class.

One cannot miss the fact that in Bihar barely one person out of every six falls in the category of middle class. The situation is no better in Odisha, Jharkhand and Chhattisgarh. Madhya Pradesh, Assam and Uttar Pradesh are also to go long miles before they raise a sizeable size of middle class. In all these states, the society has a thin upper crust of well-off, educated, urban class sited on a vast mass of the poor, predominantly agricultural, rural masses. None the less, the rise of middle class is a pan-India phenomenon.

In evolutionary terms the formation and growth of middle class during the colonial and post-colonial periods till the adoption of new economic policy in early 1990s is to be attributed largely to the public sector. In the post–1990 phase the role of private sector has become more pivotal. The rise of middle class at present hinges more upon private sector in the relatively developed states of India and upon the public sector in the less developed as well as special category hill states. On the whole, the role of private sector has become more pivotal. Importance given to English at the school level finds a strong association with expansion of middle class. As a symbol of modernization, it is a reliable route to a job in the organized sector, admission in a professional institute, and entry into the technology world. In many ways, it is a hallmark of middle class.

Notwithstanding the homogenizing role of the middle class, India remains a land of religious, linguistic and regional diversity. For coping with a situation of bewildering social complexity, internal cultural diversity and historical political fragmentation, the country had to muster a policy skill for management of multiculturalism. It has by and large been a case of success.

This was made possible by adopting a Constitution which enshrined democracy and secularism, and also by designing spatial strategies which responded to and met regional aspirations. Ethnicity and development were made to move hand in hand with each other.

A scrutiny of religious diversity vis-à-vis development equation reveals that most of the homogeneous states, namely Odisha, Chhattisgarh, Madhya Pradesh and Nagaland, are at a low or relatively low level of development. On the other hand, the states with significant heterogeneity of religious communities, namely Kerala, Goa, Maharashtra and Sikkim are distinguished by high level of development. Among the minorities, Christians find a positive association with development. A dual pattern is observed in respect of the Muslims. If they mark a greater concentration in urban areas, this tends to be pro-development, as in Gujarat, and if they are largely in rural areas, this gets associated with low level of development, as in Bihar. A strong positive impact of the Sikhs on the development process cannot be missed.

Ironically the linguistic diversity of different states vis-à-vis their respective development level does not display any consistent relationship. Both Kerala and Rajasthan are linguistically homogeneous but differ widely in development. This is a departure from the pattern of religious diversity. The inflow of people from outside the state introduces a domicile-based variety. This may be called as regional diversity. Virtually all the states noted for regional diversity, such as Maharashtra, Punjab and Haryana in addition to Goa and Sikkim, are at a high level of development. Multiculturalism is embedded in the DNA of the country and is positive to both democracy and development. In total terms, multicultural contexts are more supportive of vitality.

The diversity of India's population is very much represented also in its 25 million strong diaspora. Indiaspora is the third dimension of our country, the other two being India (urban) and Bharat (rural). To them we owe the global spread of Indianness and also the nourishment of vitality back home.

No less than 184 countries are home to Indian diaspora in varying numbers. These offer diverse contexts. It has been rightly observed that Indian diaspora is in a multicultural democratic ambience when in the United States but lives under an authoritarian regime in Singapore. They are an integral part of the Caribbean society but face exclusion in Gulf countries. They bear with pluralism context of Fiji Islands but enjoy a majority status in Mauritius. They find themselves as more acceptable and settled in democratic countries. Contrast this with very friendly socialist countries which ironically were destination of only a few. The vitality of Indian diaspora is reflected in their capacity to adapt to the specific ecology, ideology and technology of their hostlands.

Even a bird's-eye view of places and subregions of sizeable emigration in India would suggest that all the state capitals, more particularly the large metropolitan ones, such as Delhi, Mumbai, Kolkata, Chennai, Bengaluru and Hyderabad, are scenes of significant emigration today. Among the subregions, Malabar tract of Kerala, Central Gujarat Plain, Godavari-Krishna delta, the Bist doab of Punjab and coastal region of Tamil Nadu emerge as prominent. Goa as a whole is animated with the process of emigration. The entire coastal belt is a virtual emigration board. Economic dynamism and pre-eminence of middle class is common to all these areas.

All in all, the quality of governance, economic dynamism and rise of middle class emerge as the three salient expressions of the vitality of different states. A research exercise using the technique of summation of standardized scores was carried out to arrive at the vitality score of various states on these parameters. This placed Goa at the top and Bihar at the bottom in terms of overall vitality with composite scores of 4.7 and 1.7 respectively (Table 9.1).

Table 9.1 *India: Vitality Scores* of Different States, 2011*

Rank	*State***	*Standardised score on****			*Composite vitality score*
		Quality of governance	*Economic dynamism*	*Middle class*	
1	Goa	1.04	1.88	1.83	4.74
2	Sikkim	1.04	1.60	1.37	4.01
3	Punjab	1.09	1.00	1.65	3.75
4	Tamil Nadu	1.12	1.36	1.26	3.74
5	Haryana	0.98	1.24	1.42	3.65
6	Himachal Pradesh	1.10	1.11	1.43	3.64
7	Maharashtra	1.09	1.29	1.23	3.62
8	Uttarakhand	0.98	1.23	1.38	3.59
9	Gujarat	1.09	1.26	1.18	3.53
10	Kerala	1.16	1.24	1.10	3.50
11	Mizoram	1.11	1.04	1.30	3.46
12	Andhra Pradesh and Telangana	1.02	1.21	1.09	3.32
13	Karnataka	1.12	1.06	1.08	3.26
14	Tripura	0.93	1.14	0.90	2.96
15	Arunachal Pradesh	1.00	0.87	0.97	2.84
16	Jammu & Kashmir	1.00	0.76	1.06	2.81
17	West Bengal	1.03	0.96	0.80	2.79
18	Nagaland	0.94	1.01	0.82	2.77
19	Rajasthan	0.97	0.94	0.73	2.64
20	Meghalaya	0.99	1.00	0.58	2.57
21	Manipur	1.02	0.51	0.98	2.51
22	Uttar Pradesh	0.94	0.61	0.68	2.23
23	Madhya Pradesh	0.92	0.68	0.63	2.23
24	Chhattisgarh	0.96	0.63	0.52	2.11
25	Assam	0.91	0.53	0.65	2.10
26	Odisha	0.90	0.69	0.46	2.05
27	Jharkhand	0.79	0.62	0.50	1.92
28	Bihar	0.76	0.52	0.40	1.67

* Based on processing of data in Table 3.2 for quality of governance, Tables 4.2, 4.4 and 4.6 for economic dynamism, and Table 5.4 for middle class in the main text.

** States are listed in descending order of their composite score.

***Standardized score on a given parameter is the specific value of the state divided by the mean of values of all states.

Map 9.1

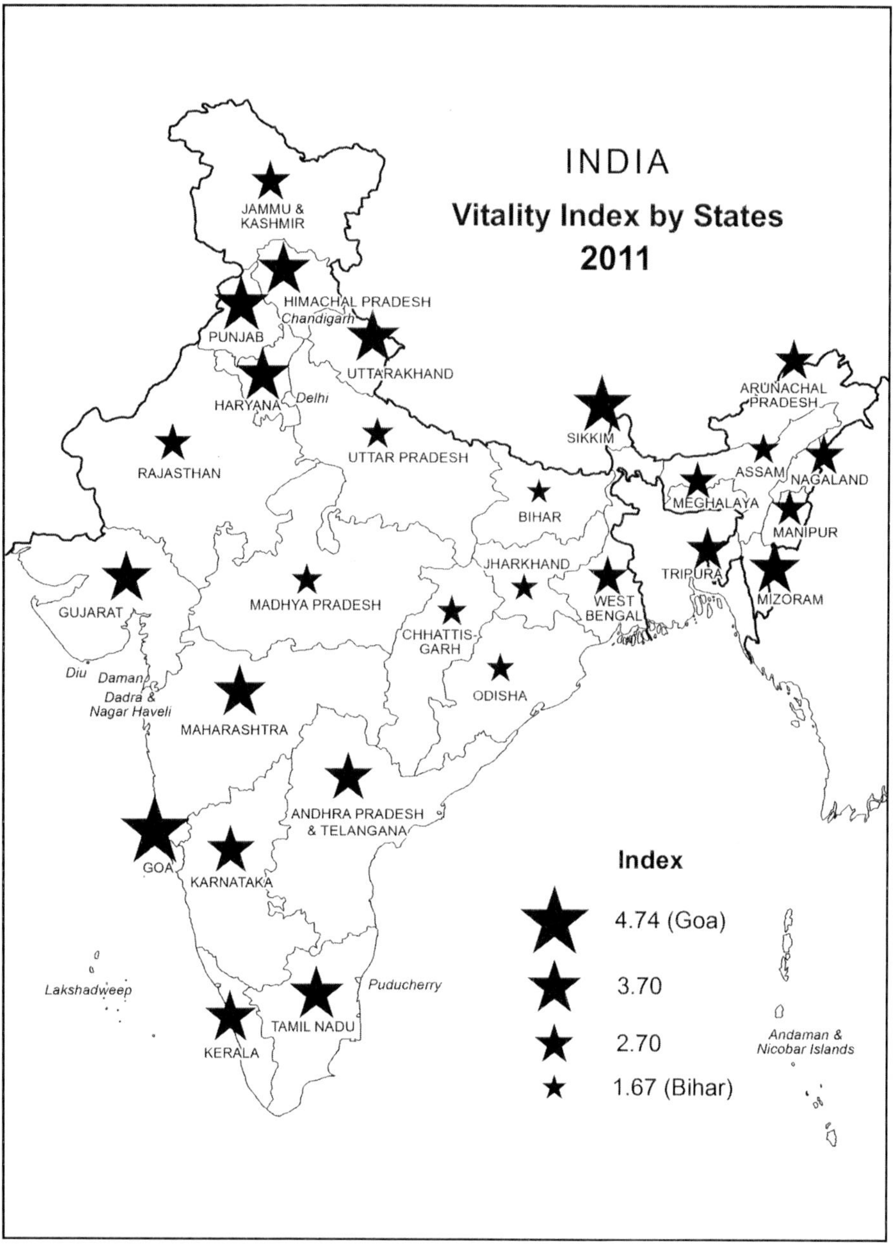
INDIA
Vitality Index by States
2011
JAMMU & KASHMIR
HIMACHAL PRADESH
Chandigarh
PUNJAB
UTTARAKHAND
HARYANA
Delhi
RAJASTHAN
UTTAR PRADESH
SIKKIM
ARUNACHAL PRADESH
ASSAM
NAGALAND
MEGHALAYA
MANIPUR
BIHAR
JHARKHAND
TRIPURA
MIZORAM
WEST BENGAL
GUJARAT
MADHYA PRADESH
CHHATTIS-GARH
ODISHA
Diu
Daman
Dadra & Nagar Haveli
MAHARASHTRA
ANDHRA PRADESH & TELANGANA
GOA
KARNATAKA
Lakshadweep
Puducherry
TAMIL NADU
KERALA
Andaman & Nicobar Islands
Index
4.74 (Goa)
3.70
2.70
1.67 (Bihar)

Sikkim is at the second rank, followed by Punjab. The coastal states of Tamil Nadu and Kerala in the south and Maharashtra and Gujarat in the west also occupy relatively high positions. Haryana, Himachal Pradesh and Uttarakhand in the North-West bear a similar description. The rest of Indian states are low to modest vitality cases in comparative terms. Evidently regional vitality in India is spreading in adherence to the law of contiguity. More vital states form clusters and so do the less vital ones. The western half is more vibrant than the eastern half in both South and North India. Geography is proving destiny in creating such a spatial patterning (Map 9.1).

Going by a computation of a correlation matrix, the rise of middle class comes out as the strongest among the three parameters, followed by economic dynamism and quality of governance in that order. It is the middle class which defines and projects the vitality of a state. This is the one which voices the identity and concerns of a state. They are the vitality.

A search for the mother factor capable of explaining the differential vitality of various states is to continue. The 'quality of political culture' seems to be emerging as a candidate of overriding importance. Essentially a link between people and government, political culture is a collectivity of the behaviour of the politicians in power, style of functioning of the administration, and electoral preference of the people at large. Upright politicians, efficient administration and discerning populace are a recipe for a healthy political culture. Within a common framework of democratic development, the vitality of various states in India differs primarily in line with quality of their political culture.

In its own turn, political culture is linked to societal awareness and salience in respect of matters of state. All this is subject to factors like urbanization, education, income and modernization. Hence, the faultlines on the vitality map of India today are between the coastal regions and the interior, within the interior between the green revolution areas and others, and at the local level between the metropolis and the hinterland.

The frequency with which India finds a place in world literature is recognition of its eminence. A great interest is evinced in its civilizational history, development experience and political ethos by the British, German, French and American scholars. A glimpse of this is discernible from the references listed for each essay of this book. Of equal value are the articles on different aspects of India carried from time to time by the *National Geographic*, a magazine of the largest circulation in the world. The vitality of India found a variety of expressions. It was discovered in the exquisite beauty of its landscape, the pervasive hold of religion, and no less in stable democracy, free media and rising middle class.

The vitality of India is saga of civilizational unity in history and an example of sustained democracy after Independence. India's model is neither of 'melting pot' as of the United States, nor a 'salad bowl' as of Canada, nor a 'mosaic' as of Belgium, nor a 'conglomerate' as of Malaysia, nor a 'consociation arrangement' as of power sharing on ethnic basis in Lebanon.

Its model is of 'Rigveda tree', with thousands of branches emerging out of a common trunk. This sacred tree, unlike the banyan one, allowed a lot of undergrowth to flourish. The fresh vigour of India's different regions or the states is enriching the vitality of the nation. Notable is the fact that while vitality of India is often projected through its past, its regional vitality or vitality of different states is a modern discourse. Roots of all this are deep. Listen to the regional and local songs which extol the exceptionalism and beauty of each part of the country. You will discover the vitality of each region as embedded in the heart of its natives.

India and its various regions bear vitality and have always re-emerged and reinvented themselves in several surprising ways to maintain wholeness and equilibrium. Adaptability has always been a hallmark of the people of India. Equally admirable is their capacity to cohere concentric rings of their spatial identity at local, regional and national levels. This is particularly evident in their response to issues pertinent to different scales at the time of elections. One thing, however, stands sure that many strengths, some known and many unknown, will nourish and endure the vitality of India.

Index